PIERRE CHAREAU

© Drawing by Jean Lurçat. Couch MP 169.
M-shaped low stool #1.

PIERRE CHAREAU

Architect and craftsman
1883–1950

Marc Vellay

Kenneth Frampton

with 377 illustrations, 28 in colour

Thames and Hudson

Translated from the French by Bridget Strevens Romer

First published in Great Britain in 1985
by Thames and Hudson Ltd, London

This edition © 1985 Thames and Hudson, Ltd, London
and Rizzoli International Publications, Inc., New York

© 1984 Editions du Regard, Paris

Printed and bound in Switzerland

CONTENTS

For J.D.

ANNIE,
You can share this letter with Jean.
I'd like to tell you all about the work, that's my firm intention, and, as I continue,
I'm held back by a kind of modest reticence that paralyzes me completely.
On the one hand, I'm working out the pipes, drainage, and heating system, such
an essential but thankless task, while on the other, I grow quite excited and fancy
I'm being of use.
Out of all this there's one thing I'm certain of, I'm certain of love, and this certainty
in itself is worth living for.
Tell me I've battled like a lion for your house.
Your house I'll cherish closest to my heart.*

PIERRE CHAREAU
June 13, 1932.

* tr. note: The original French expression is untranslatable: "Pour votre maison, je garde les premiers battements de mon coeur."

Pierre Chareau, photo: Laure Albin-Guillot.

EDITOR'S NOTE

Descriptions of items presented as photographic captions are based on a system laid out in the following order: MB 152

This is the reference appearing on the original photographic document that was bound into an album for consultation by visitors to La Boutique.

It consists of two letters followed by one to four figures. Certain letter codes are self-explanatory. E as the first letter indicates an "ensemble," while M ("meuble") refers to a single item of furniture. Thus EB is an "ensemble de bureau," or office ensemble; EN an "ensemble de nursery"; MA are single "armoires" or wardrobes; MB are "bureaux" or desks; MT are "tabourets" or stools. Some codes are unclear, as for example, PD or EZ, which seems to correspond to the metal furniture ensembles of the Semaine à Paris period.

While the numbers following the letter code are not in chronological order, a sequence of numbers does indicate that the photographs are of a single installation. Thus the different installations that Chareau made can be reconstructed. It should be noted that the same photographic document appearing in several albums is generally given the same code.

FOREWORD

Architect, designer, interior decorator, furniture maker,* inventor, or innovator? Pierre Chareau is hard to categorize. Thirty years have passed since his death and there has been no exhaustive study of all the aspects of his work. He is, along with Djo-Bourgeois, Charlotte Alix, and Guévrékian, still largely unknown. So should he perhaps be classified, like some lesser known Cubist, as a "minor master"? Surely not. Pierre Chareau defies all efforts to pin him down. He was, in some way, an outsider. No work of his, not even the Maison de Verre, is of a scale to compare with buildings by the better known amongst his contemporaries. His output hardly matches that of Le Corbusier or of his friend Mallet-Stevens. What he did share with these two major figures in the Modern Movement was a wide range of interests. The field of work he covered, from unique pieces of cabinetwork to mass-produced tubular steel furniture, from boat fittings to film sets, was quite as extensive. And while his architectural production as such was more limited—there are only five houses to his name—he looked more closely into certain aspects of it, such as lighting, had a more daring approach (as the Maison de Verre amply demonstrates), and paid more attention to understanding the needs of the inhabitants, among other things.

The Grand-Hôtel at Tours was demolished, the LTT offices no longer exist, and all that remains of the clubhouse at Beauvallon and the "Vent d'Aval" villa is the bare framework. As for the studio-house designed for the painter Robert Motherwell in the United States, it has been altered beyond recognition. What then does remain of the work of a man who, with Francis Jourdain, was considered to be one of the most distinguished precursors of the Modern Movement? The most exceptional example of his work that is still intact is the Maison de Verre in Paris, the architecture and furnishings of which form a perfectly united whole. There are also rare items of furniture treasured by their owners or bought for high sums by private collectors or archive collections.

The term *archive* is something of an exaggeration when used, as it is, to refer to a few gouaches of projects and three or four design sketches for pieces of furniture. However, as luck would have it, several hundred photographic documents have been preserved. In general, this material is coded by letters and numbers, but they have no labels or descriptions. As for the original architectural plans, working drawings of furniture, notebooks, and letters to clients, almost nothing has survived their author's peregrinations. What does remain is dispersed. The New York Museum of Modern Art has a few documents, as does the

* The French word for a furniture maker or designer, *meublier*, has fallen into disuse. Critics contemporary with Chareau made a further distinction between designers of individual items of furniture and designers of sets, suites, or "ensembles" of furniture, *ensembliers*. In his review of the Exposition Internationale des Arts Décoratifs et Industriels Modernes (*L'Amour de L'Art*, no. 8, August 1925), Waldemar George refers to *meubliers*. Guillaume Janneau, on the same occasion, defined *ensemblier* as "the fancy name for the upholsterer" (*Art et Décoration*, May 1925).

[1] *Un Inventeur, l'Architecte Pierre Chareau*, Paris, 1954.

Musée des Arts Décoratifs in Paris (a gift from René Herbst who had conserved them after using them for his book),[1] and the descendants of the Dalsace family own the rest. Up to the writing of this book, all these documents were largely unknown.

Since the only, and essentially incomplete monograph devoted to Pierre Chareau is out of print, it was felt that there was a place for a new and fuller examination of his work. The pages that follow cannot hope to provide the reader with a complete descriptive catalogue of Chareau's furniture production. Most of the examples of the work in question were produced in small numbers. There are less than ten in museum collections. The remainder of what has not been destroyed is still in private collections. Since no sales or order books have been found, the only trace we have of the furniture is in publications of the period, salesroom catalogues, and accounts from those of his contemporaries who are alive today. Such sources must still be checked and double-checked.

It is the results of such an examination that this book records. In line with other books on artists that merit wider reputations, it aims not only to define the characteristics of Chareau's art, but also to provide the reader with a reliable guide to his work.

First and foremost, the reader will find a portrait of the artist based on contemporary accounts and drawing also on comments by his friends and patrons. Chapter II examines the underlying duality in Chareau, his mastery of situations in which, for example, furniture could be seen to conflict with the architectural setting. With the context of and the approach to his work defined, what remains of Chareau's production is examined in light of the positions he held during two debates within the Modern Movement. The first of these debates, dealing with the individual artifact and standardization, is looked at in Chapters III and IV, and the second, concerning the use of metal, is the basis of Chapter V. Chapter VI concentrates on Chareau's own particular creative obsessions.

Chapter VII, by Kenneth Frampton, deals with the work of Chareau as an architect "comme bricoleur"—that is, as an eclectic.

At the end of this book, the reader will find a list of Chareau's submissions to the various salons and exhibitions, with the comments they gave rise to in the press of the time, as well as a bibliography and index.

Bust of Pierre Chareau, by Chana Orloff

I

A PORTRAIT

A portrait of an artist might seem relatively easy to paint. Once a likeness has been caught, many people are satisfied, and rightly so, with a few indications of his life to help them understand a fuller analysis of his work. While it is best that there are no close ties with the sitter, the portrait painter or the writer should not be restrained by a fear of losing his objectivity.

A few guidelines will then suffice, before accounts by the artist's contemporaries complete the picture. Pierre Paul Constant Chareau was born in Bordeaux on August 3, 1883. His father, Adolphe Benjamin, was aided by his wife, Esther (née Carvallo), in his work as a trader.

What is striking in photographs of Chareau is the bright but also extremely gentle look in his eyes. It is a look that is both lively and steadfast, strangely tender and yet restless. His eyes are clear, under well-marked eyebrows, and his nose is strong and prominent. His mouth is at once childlike and sensual, the upper lip curving upward and determined, the lower lip distinct and relaxed. He was small but of a commanding presence. There is a photograph where he is dwarfed by Ernö Goldfinger at his side, and yet his impeccable style is all the more apparent.

Ernö Goldfinger and Pierre Chareau at the Weissenhof in 1928.

LETTERS TOWARDS A PORTRAIT

Nathalie Dombre, who wrote the two following letters, was a close friend of the artist. Russian by birth, she lived in Belgium from 1927 to 1938. In that year, she moved to Paris and married a fellow Russian, the architectural student André de Heering. Soon after, she worked as secretary to Jean Lurçat, then living in the Villa Seurat. Not long before the outbreak of war, she worked for Jeanne Bucher, who introduced her to the world of painting. Around the same period, André de Heering worked as a journeyman draftsman for Chareau, becoming, as time wore on, his pupil and his spiritual son (see Dollie Chareau's letter below). War separated husband from wife and friends. The Chareaus left for Marseille and Pierre was the first to sail for New York. Nathalie Dombre went back to join the Forces Françaises Libres in London where she was secretary to Emmanuel d'Astier de la Vigerie. André de Heering joined the troops fighting for Free France. In March 1943, he was killed in French Equatorial Africa.

U.A.M. banquet at the Clair Obscur, Impasse Lebouis (fourteenth arrondissement), on February 4, 1932. *Left to right:* (back row) M. Bastard, Mme René Herbst, M. J. Van Melle, Mme Goska, M. Salomon, Mme Martel, M. Pierre Chareau, Mme Mallet-Stevens, M. Raymond Templier, Mme Salomon, M. René Herbst; (near side) Mme Bastard, M. Martel, Mme Pierre Chareau (back turned), Mme Hélène Henry, M. Mallet-Stevens, Mme J. Martel.

Letter to M. X., journalist, 1973

I'm going to try and tell you about Pierre Chareau. It will not be easy; it's not that he's become a distant figure to me, no, just that he belongs to another time, another world, a time gone by when society did not have such a complete hold on the individual.

The first encounter with Pierre Chareau was painfully intimidating; you felt you were being watched, you didn't dare speak since words had a more pronounced, deeper, and even shattering effect upon him. You could feel that instantly, and were paralyzed by the fear of causing him pain.

Even the most friendly, the most intimate conversations with Pierre Chareau were trials out of which you emerged quite exhausted.... There was no doubt he had a way of getting beyond words, beyond thought even, to what was most central in a human being. It was at once exhausting and enriching. There are people I know who found this intolerable.

... You either loved him or were exasperated by him. He could even fill you with love and exasperation at the same time. This was especially true among men, and he had few men friends. There were women he loved passionately or had long-lasting friendships with. What was exasperating was his hypersensitiveness coming from a nature so highly strung that it was almost catching. Contact with him made you more receptive, more lucid as you plumbed new depths.

His perfectionism—in his work, where he was absolutely uncompromising, and in his speech, marked by the relentless search for the perfect phrase, the precise definition—gave you the impression of someone who was hesitant, indecisive, reluctant to come forward, almost as if he lacked virility. This was far from the truth; he was quite capable of making a decision when he had to, and his hesitancy had its origin in his farsightedness, and in his ability to consider a problem in its entirety, weighing up all the pros and cons.

As has often been said, he was ahead of his time, not only in his work but in the wider context of his life. Whether it was foreknowledge, presentiment, or great perspicacity, the fact remains that he foresaw events, lived and suffered them before everyone else. The Spanish Civil War opened his eyes to the impending triumph of Hitler, and when war was declared in 1939, he saw clearly that France would be defeated and the Jews suffer persecution. The creeping spectre of bureaucracy alarmed him, as did ever-increasing negligence and offhandedness.

I think that all this upset him, physically upset him. Hypocrisy, triteness, meanness, and vulgarity were for him what wrong notes are to a music lover. They wounded him.

He was a vulnerable person.

Enough has been said of the importance he gave to the individual in his work. Francis Jourdain, Herbst, and Bijvoët have shown this better than I could hope to. His aim was to free man as much as he could from material shackles and outworn conventions. He wanted him to feel at ease and in harmony with himself and his environment. Harmony was his favorite word and the sheer variety of his output is the result of a desire that the work should harmonize in each case with the individual. He could only work in close liaison with his clients and collaborators and they had to have full confidence in him. Perhaps this is why he worked so little in France, where he never received the consideration he deserved and is, or has been until quite recently, little known.

Letter to the author, December 1980

I never knew Chareau's grand parties with Paul Poiret and the Parisian society of the twenties, a period long past, when Pierre was known as a designer and was kept busy, the period before the slump.

What about Pierre Chareau himself?

Well, it's easy enough to say he was an exceptional person, but this doesn't really mean anything. It's quite another thing to try and explain to you in what ways he was exceptional and give you an outline of the man, but I'll have a go.

Chareau was alert.

Alert to people, to their needs, their aspirations, to what made them tick; he would watch the way they reacted, and listen to the way they spoke and laughed. Alert and demanding, he hated discord, would blanch when they lied to him and wince at incomprehension.

He was alert to the times, to the world in progress, to new tendencies in thought and dress, to discoveries in the arts, to the movements of people, classes, and society. The social aspect of things was of prime importance to him, and here, architecture had a major role to play. That now fashionable word *lifestyle* was, in his terms, expressed by the proportions of rooms, by modernizing a kitchen to make housework easier, by doing away with garden fences and useless partitions, by giving new status to humble objects and areas previously hidden from view, by letting light in through glass walls, by designing folding tables for more space, by opening up staircases, eliminating stair risers, and by finding countless other ways of making life easier, letting the air in, feeling less hemmed in.

Today all these devices are not only accepted but common currency, yet in the thirties they startled and shocked people. I recall a lady who could not bring herself to go up the stairs in the Maison de Verre as there was neither a rail nor stair risers. All of Chareau's inventions served some purpose, arose out of a need discerned in the close observation of people's movements and the lengths they went to. Innovation was not the aim but perfection.

Yes, Pierre was an alert, attentive person.

He was also demanding. He made demands on himself, his work, his colleagues, and all those admitted into his circle, making no allowances for any irregular behavior, and taking exception to any sign of posturing or deviousness. With him you had to be on your guard. He commanded absolute integrity and sincerity.

Pierre was also a very vibrant personality. I can still see him standing squarely on his short legs, his white shock of hair tossed back, his blue eyes focusing on some invisible object, set on an idea in the making, quivering with the urge to give it a perfect form, or again, lost in some dream before his drawing board, wanting to give it shape, make it real.

Every competition he entered meant a relentless struggle with himself, rather than with other competitors. It required an immense effort of thought and concentration to attain perfection. Never really content or satisfied, he would often go back to square one after spending weeks perfecting an idea, to the despair of all working with him. He was incapable, physically incapable of submitting a project, however worthy, if he had some intimation of a better solution to the problem. This is why competition projects cost him so much and why collaborators were few and far between. You had to believe in his genius.

He was alert and demanding, but above all highly sensitive. He was sensitive to men and ideas, to the beauty of cityscapes, to natural light, to the events, challenges, and dangers that beset the world. His sensitivity bordered on presentiment. When war was declared in 1939, he foresaw the full sequence of events that were to follow—the defeat, the occupation, the persecutions. I saw him cry in despair, and remember having been stupid enough to criticize his lack of self-control. Yet in May–June 1940, when disaster was upon us, he was much calmer than most, telling everyone, "But we knew it was going to happen, we've known it since last September, it was inevitable. . . . "

Like all sensitive people, Pierre Chareau was highly vulnerable and had no way of defending himself against mean behavior and intrigues that he simply could not account for. Easily wounded and perhaps, in that sense, weak, he was no fighter or orator and was happier in close conversation with someone than in a gathering. He never played the professional game. He needed someone to promote him, as he hated publicity.

Without Doctor and Madame Dalsace to put their entire trust in him, Chareau's name would have been forgotten.

Letters from Dollie Chareau to René Herbst

The two letters that follow come from exchanges between Dollie, Pierre Chareau's wife, and the architect René Herbst (1891–1983), founder of the Union des Artistes Modernes and great friend of the Chareaus. Two years after Chareau's death, Herbst asked Dollie for certain details of his life, for a monograph to be published by the Union, with the help of his friends, in honor of the architect of the Maison de Verre.

The somewhat abrupt style of these letters is due to Dollie Chareau's English upbringing. Written in French, there are various grammatical faults and inaccuracies, but there has been no attempt to reproduce these in the English translation. As first hand accounts, they are an indispensable contribution to our knowledge of her husband.

New York, October 25 (1952 or 1953)

When I first met Pierre (he was sixteen years old), he was gifted at music, painting, and drawing alike. At twenty-one, he had adapted the music for the "Damoiselle Elue," written for piano, violin, and quartets, to be sung in four-part harmony, so that he could stage it in a series of *tableaux vivants*, the back-cloth for which he designed himself. It was a show of rare quality that was performed in our little apartment not long after our wedding. Annie Dalsace, still a child at the time, was there. The apartment at 101 Rue Nollet had great charm. Pierre made various pieces of furniture for his office, a desk and a small bookcase.

Pierre's first loves were the Impressionists and his painting continued to be influenced by them. I only have one painting by him now of our first country house.

Later he was attracted to the Cubists and their architectural sense of structure. It was at that time, 1913–1914, and then on his return from the army in 1919, that we bought those "horrible" paintings, as my bourgeois friends used to call them: Juan Gris, Braque, Picasso, La Fresnaye, Miró, Masson, Pascin. Also during this period, Jean Lurçat painted a very poetic mural for us, which we later had installed in my Louveciennes sitting room. Subsequently, we had a very fine Mondrian, the only picture in Pierre's office in Louveciennes, Torres Garcia, Max Ernst, Max Jacob, Arp, Bauchant, Campigli, Brignoni, Chagall, Charles Lapique, Reichel, Vieira da Silva (the last present Pierre gave me before the war was a Vieira da Silva which I have here now). Then Robert Motherwell, a young Hungarian painter, and others. Pierre admired and believed in the art of Nicolas de Staël who had two fine drawings sent to us here, and the same was true for that of Charles Lapique. I also have a picture of Charles's which has been in our possession for over twenty years.

Pierre loved sculpture too. In 1919, at Jacques Lipchitz's request, he bought the great caryatid by Modigliani, which was in our garden over twenty years, on a plinth designed by Jacques. It is now in the Museum of Modern Art, New York. There's a curious story behind this. In 1939, on the occasion of the World's Fair, a request was made for it. We made the loan. Then the war came and the statue stayed here. We had a great deal of difficulty recovering it. It was thanks to an American, Mr. Catesly Jones, a lawyer and a great art lover, that we were able to prove that we were the Chareaus from Paris who had made the loan. I had to sell it, along with the Mondrian.

We had seven small statues by Lipchitz. I've kept two; one is here, and the

Pierre Chareau in his Paris apartment, 54 Rue Nollet (circa 1927). On the walls are sections of fabric designed by Hélène Henry, hung on wrought-iron frameworks. Pictures include the works of Braque, Picasso, Juan Gris, and La Fresnaye. Sculpture is by J. Lipchitz.

other is, as you know, in the Museum of Modern Art. Pierre was also fond of Laurens and Brancusi, but didn't own any examples of their work.

And what about our life in Paris?

After the war, following his first exhibition in 1919, where he presented the office and bedroom for the Dalsaces, Pierre was kept very busy. It was then that he asked me to work under him, a good deal of work, but a good deal of pleasure too, from time to time.

We were both great music and ballet lovers. I remember seeing *Petrouchka* three times in one week, and Pierre, who'd heard *Pelléas* at least fourteen times, went back twice to see it here, with Maggie Teyte, whom we'd seen so many years before in France.

When we gave a party (and I loved giving them), we would often invite dancers who would perform on our garden lawn or in the hall. This is how we met Djemil Anik, who became a good friend, Uday Shankar, and others.

Pierre's friends?

He wasn't easy to get to know. He had a great affection for Charles Lapique. Max Jacob, a neighbor of ours who lived opposite at the Hôtel Nollet, was fond of Pierre and the feeling was mutual. Pierre and Jacques Lipchitz visited him at the monastery in 1940. Jacques and Pierre were very close. But I think he preferred female company. He adored Annie who was always so understanding and supportive. But this I must emphasize: Pierre's work as an architect was due to none other than the marvelous man who was Annie's father, a man endowed with a real understanding of beauty. He demonstrated his belief in Pierre by commissioning from him the clubhouse at Beauvallon.

New York, around 1942. First row, fourth from the left, Pierre Chareau.

Later, in the hard years after 1932 (when those "horrible" paintings saved us from ruin), Pierre had a group of young architects around him to help him with the donkey work. We had to keep our studio to a minimum. Sometimes they'd work all night and I'd keep music playing and give them strong coffee. André de Heering, a young Russian architect, became a spiritual son to us, and with him his young wife, who joined us on our last trip in August 1939. He was killed in the war.

We used to meet Darius Milhaud, whom Pierre greatly admired, and Poulenc, too, from time to time, but strangely enough, the people we were closest to were our clients. And principal among them were often my old pupils. Madeleine Fleg, wife of the poet Edmond Fleg, was one of my Paris pupils. Pierre did a beautiful installation for them. I can still see a drawing by Lurçat, of a corner of the bathroom and an armchair covered in Lurçat's tapestry, made for the Flegs.

New York, October 28

...I didn't mention the group of people around you (these were the U.A.M. founders). You know more than I do about Pierre's dealings with them. I knew of his great admiration for Franz Jourdain, thanks to whom he didn't exhibit his work before he was ready, and also for Francis* and Mallet-Stevens. Pierre was rarely very forthcoming and it was principally in our shared enthusiasm for certain things that I could be at all certain of his responses.

---

* *tr. note*: Francis Jourdain, the son of Franz Jourdain, who was president of the Salon d'Automne and architect of the La Samaritaine stores in Paris.

PREMIERE EXPOSITION
DE L'UNION DES ARTISTES
M O D E R N E S

MUSÉE DES ARTS
DÉCORATIFS
PAVILLON DE MARSAN
II JUIN - 14 JUILLET 1930

Cover of the catalog to the first U.A.M. exhibition.

PREFACE BY FRANCIS JOURDAIN TO
UN INVENTEUR, L'ARCHITECTE PIERRE CHAREAU

There are certain words which anyone who seeks clarity and respects nuances in meaning will be doubtful about using. Some words have changed with continued use; others have such a wide application that they can give rise to confusion. This is why I hesitate to say that Pierre Chareau was "precious" in some way.

The most common definition of *preciosity* is the "affectation of refinement or distinction" and this is in no way applicable to Chareau. But the dictionary also defines *precious* as "choice, fine, refined, or nice," as something or someone who is "excessively delicate." And its first meaning—particularly relevant here—should not be forgotten, serving to indicate something or someone of "great value."

Pierre Chareau's work continues to be of great value. As for affectation, only someone who had given his work the most cursory glance could impute that to him. No one but a fool could fail to seize upon what was original and fundamental to Pierre Chareau, what was innate and therefore utterly unaffected in him. Of course, he could be shocking, but he did not set out to be so. His was a rare spirit, and he had a taste for rare things. But again these terms should be defined. Chareau did not go in for that distorted and eccentric love of rarity in itself. He never made the mistake of confusing rarity with beauty, believing all that was rare was beautiful and that all beauty was by definition rare. Chareau enjoyed discovering beauty in the commonplace, but he also knew how to extract it and give it a precious setting, as it were. He could make a jewel out of a pebble.

I am absolutely convinced that the poet's role is not, as is all too often said, to take us into another world, but quite the opposite—to captivate us with the charm or to move us with the grandeur of all that we look at day after day and do not actually see, to give form to our most confused and most immediate desires, to satisfy our unconscious, often inexpressible needs. It is because Chareau also believed this, because he joined me in thinking that the true poet's function is to prospect and uncover, to reveal, that I feel I am justified in seeing my friend as a poet, in claiming that as a poet we may call him an inventor, and that it was indeed because he was a poet that he was an inventor. Refusing to see any solution to a problem as definitive and impossible to improve upon, the inventor had something of the rebel about him. At least, he would never give up or give in, or cease to criticize. He was a nonconformist in the fullest sense.

This was Pierre Chareau and yet scandals and aggressive stances were not to his liking. In private, in fact, he was a tolerant man, by which I mean that he would not dismiss an opponent to his plans as an out-and-out fool. As the demands of his own conscience and inquisitiveness made him continually throw everything into question, he cared as little about criticism as he did about praise, and he went his own way with no thought as to the reactions he might provoke.

Occasionally he found himself in a quandary, but he always confronted it. Chareau did not adopt any kind of system; while he wisely accepted the consequences of a nature such as his, he was not necessarily at peace with himself. Sensitive sometimes to a fault, he was not obsessive, yet he was, in a sense, tormented by his love of exploration. It is surely wrong to classify him as an interior decorator. . . . To limit him to such a narrow field would be absurd, even. Neither was he a lover of mere ornament. He set his sights far higher. Since there is no easy continuity between an object and the room in which it is placed, between that room and the house and the house and the town, since between the similarly created object and town, there is a difference of degree but not of nature, Chareau worked in every capacity as an architect. He applied his inventiveness not to decorating the home but to rethinking it, to organizing it in terms of both the material and spiritual needs of the person who lived there. His originality grew out of his long meditation on these two factors, the physical and spiritual needs. He started from the beginning every time, without preconceptions, guided by his sure taste and thinking—the taste and thinking of a modern man.

It is fashionable these days to smile at the adjective I have just used. As if art has ever been anything other than modern! As if the main quality of an architect

Pierre Chareau in East Hampton after World War II.

30

were not to know how to use his intelligence to adapt contemporary resources to the problem in hand; and to be knowledgeable about the product, the resources available, the circumstances which brought them about, the aesthetic which gave rise to them and the social impact they had!

Chareau was modern. He was unaffectedly modern. He did not create problems for himself by dwelling on the past, or on what was to come. He faced the problems of his own time, regretting only that he could not know what the future would bring, although he had some sense of it and was proud of the open-minded interest that could sometimes give him a foretaste of it, given that it was better to look ahead than to look back.

The only true tradition lies in boldness, in daring. Chareau was daring. And he was modern, more even because of his endless searching, his unquenchable thirst for discovery, than because of what he discovered, fine though it was. While the ingenuity behind those discoveries is striking, the mind that produced them is even more significant. Chareau's art is singularly representative. Chareau opened up new vistas. As a man of his time, he was also a precursor.

Chareau was daring. And so he did not deny the past. There is a French saying: "Flowing to the sea, the river remains faithful to its source."

FRANCIS JOURDAIN

FRIENDS AND PATRONS

It may seem quite irrelevant to complete the picture of an artist by looking at his clients. Most would say, and not without reason, that the former exercises his art quite independently of the latter. It is the patron who approaches the artist, not the other way round. The art buyer and dealer help the artist to live and work, but in general are not expected to have anything other than a secondary influence on his work. However, the moment such work entails the production of studies, maquettes or working models, the payment of assistants and high costs, this artist-client relationship changes. The customer's demands carry more weight, even if he is acting through some kind of commercial intermediary. Yet he is still set apart as "the client" wherever he is and however kind he may be. Each keeps to his own ground, and the purchase or commission is nothing but the transfer of a finished work or project from the life of one into the surroundings of the other.

But such truisms do not apply to Chareau. And if the picture of him must be completed with a description of his clients, it is principally because they were his friends first and foremost, and in this respect they merit inclusion. It is rare for creativity and finance to be linked in such a harmonious way. The Renaissance represented a similar union. But the system of patronage has not always given free reign to the Prince's artist. There is no word that covers the far rarer connection between friendship and passion, creative freedom and finance. Such a word should be coined for Chareau's case alone. It is embodied in one building, the Maison de Verre in the heart of Paris. The Bernheim-Dalsace family were patrons, but they did not confine themselves to financing Pierre Chareau. They did a good job as bankers. But they were also his closest friends, sharing with the artist his parties and holidays, his enthusiasms and moments of despair. Such daily association helped Chareau to know, in all their complexity, the overt and implicit needs of his clients, and their way of life. As for them, close friendship and familiarity with his way of thinking entitled them to be more exacting of him, and helped them find more suitable ways to formulate their plans for building improvements. The life of artist and clients often overlapped. Chareau's production matched the needs as they arose in the privacy of his clients' lives. In 1920, with the birth of the Dalsaces' first child, a girl, he designed a bedroom, a nursery changing table, chairs, and storage space. Soon after, he worked on a nursery for Hélène Bernheim. In 1923, he made use of his experience and exhibited The Children's Corner ("Le Coin des enfants") at the Salon des Artistes Décorateurs.

It has to be said that Chareau was architect–furniture designer to a limited circle that would have been called the "Bernheim-Dalsace salon" in eighteenth-century France.

At its origin were two women, brought together by an accident of education: Annie Dalsace and Louise Dyte.

Annie Dalsace, née Bernheim, on a couch by Pierre Chareau, at Villeflix, Noisy-
le-Grand, around 1920. A pupil of Chareau's wife, Dollie, she was a staunch
supporter of his work and was at the start of the project for the Maison de Verre.

René Herbst and Aline Vellay-Dalsace in the Maison de Verre, during a general meeting of the association of friends of the Maison de Verre, 1978.

There was nothing in particular to push Anna Bernheim, the future Annie Dalsace, to a liking for things modern, unless it was her impeccable taste and her great sensitivity. Her father Edmond and uncle Emile, sons of a horse dealer in Bar-le-Duc, had left for Paris before the turn of the century, and had made their fortunes as property dealers. In common with most girls of her generation and background Anna was educated at home, and took additional lessons at the Cours Dieterlen. Her mother gave her complete freedom to choose the decoration she wanted for their family apartment in the Rue d'Anjou, and as early as her teens she took charge of all dealings with the decorator-upholsterer. The style was eighteenth-century English, the materials of first quality, and there was no hint of modernity. The death of her brother Pierre in the Argonne in April 1915 left her an only child, focus for all the hopes and generous warmth of her parents. Now all the conditions were met; good taste and the means to pay for it. She preferred a painting by Picasso she had seen in a gallery to the jewel her father offered her for her birthday.

As for Louise Dyte, she was born in London in 1880. In 1904, she married Pierre Chareau. She, Dollie, was the breadwinner during the war years, giving English lessons, and in 1905, she had a new pupil, Anna. A friendship soon formed. Sixteen years her senior, Dollie introduced Anna to modern art. In 1918, Anna married Jean Dalsace. Born in Epinal and from a long line of high-ranking civil servants (traditionally associated with the Jewish communities of eastern France), Jean intended to take up a liberal profession. Alongside the law studies his family insisted upon, he attended classes at the faculty of medecine.

For twenty years, up until Pierre Chareau's departure for the United States, the two couples were inseparable. Even after, they maintained regular contact until the artist's death in 1950 and that of his wife in 1967.

Newly installed at 195 Boulevard Saint-Germain at the end of 1918, the Dalsaces asked Chareau to re-decorate their apartment. He drew up the plans on his last leave, just after the armistice. Once out of the army, he exhibited the two rooms as "A young doctor's consulting-room and bedroom," at the Salon d'Automne of 1919. At Villeflix, the Bernheims' country house, he worked with Jean Lurçat, who had been at school with Jean Dalsace in Epinal. Together they created the furnishings. Pierre designed the furniture and Jean the tapestry cartoons. Jean's wife, Marthe, executed the latter in needlepoint and sewed them onto the framework. And thus the armchairs, couches, screens, and cushions were made.

The circle of friends—and patrons—grew rapidly. While Emile or Edmond Bernheim would take an occasional financial risk commissioning furniture or a house from the artist, Annie wielded her influence over more distant relatives, persuading them of Chareau's genius.

Her great aunt Hélène Bernheim, her cousin Georgette Lévy, Edmond Fleg, her uncle by marriage, Robert Dalsace, the family in the wider sense, Teplansky, Hélène Bernheim's brother, but also friends like Daniel Dreyfus and the Grumbachs all commissioned items of furniture or interior design from Chareau.

It would, however, be unfair and wrong to limit the circle of enthusiasts and clients to Bernheim family connections alone. The Chareaus had a circle of their own at 101 and later at 54 Rue Nollet, where they did a lot of entertaining. Guests included Poiret, Radiguet, Max Jacob, Vieira da Silva, Marcel l'Herbier, Charles Lapique, Jacques Lipchitz, Djemil Anik, Jeanne Bucher, and Hélène Henry. Chareau did private work for them as well as commissions. At Mallet-Stevens's request, he designed a hanging bed and a bedroom for the Noailles' villa at Hyères. Robert Mallet-Stevens was a friend and colleague, and at his own home there were a desk and a chair in wood and metal designed by Chareau in 1927. The designer of a number of fabrics used by Chareau, Hélène Henry commissioned from him a large desk with sloping sides. Other items designed by Chareau adorned the home of her and her husband, Van Melle, such as a low pillar table

Doctor and Madame Dalsace in the "Petit Salon Bleu" of the Maison de Verre.

for the telephone. Pingusson acquired, perhaps soon after it was made, another sloping-sided desk mounted on folding metal stands. And Marcel l'Herbier kept the furniture from the sets of his films *L'Inhumaine* and *Le Vertige* for his own subsequent use.

Chareau also had private clients like Thérèse Bonney, Lise Deharme, and Madame Reifenberg, who asked him to decorate her apartment in the Rue Mallet-Stevens, M.R.M.B., Roger Gompel, Octave Homberg, Marcel Kapferer, and M. Simon,* who greatly admired him and asked him to redesign his Mulhouse home.

The same was as true of architecture as it was of interior design. In 1926, Emile Bernheim commissioned his first building from Chareau, the Beauvallon clubhouse. Two years later, Anna's father, Edmond, financed the plans for the Rue Saint-Guillaume, and it was also he who laid out the specifications for the "Vent d'Aval" villa, designed for the use of three generations of the family, near Beauvallon. In 1928, his cousin, Paul Bernheim, Hélène's husband, financed improvements to the Grand-Hôtel at Tours.

There were others who put their trust in Chareau. The dancer Djemil Anik, and later, in the United States, Germaine Monteux, Nancy Laughlin, and Robert Motherwell all commissioned work from him.

Chareau's clientele was not large, but some of the commissions were, like the series of furniture for the Grand Hôtel at Tours. Such large assemblies have rarely been kept together, or have been destroyed with time. And today, within the small circle of collectors interested in Chareau, if there are only a few high-quality examples to be found on the market, it is undoubtedly because they were exceptionally well made† and were well cared for by their first owners. Belonging most often to unified and harmonious ensembles, such furniture represented a lifetime's investment to the owners and the idea of parting with it would never have crossed their minds. Symbolic of a certain world and the expression of a choice, it has grown old with its owners.

As for prices, they may be seen, quite simply, as a kind of posthumous homage paid to someone who lived modestly and, in 1933, sold his painting collection to keep out of the hands of creditors.

Robert Motherwell (1950).

---

* An art lover and collector, M. Simon had work done by Jacques-Emile Ruhlmann as well as by Chareau. A photograph shows the two of them with him.
† The Prinz atelier did most of the cabinetwork. Dalbet made most of the metal and metal and wood furniture.

Still from *Le Vertige*, a film by Marcel l'Herbier, 1925. Architecture by Robert Mallet-Stevens, sets by Cavalcanti, Chareau, and Léger, carpets and picture by Lurçat.

Le Vertige. Table MB 130, chair MF 310.

Le Vertige. The carpet, designed by Jean Lurçat, appeared in the "Study-library of a French embassy" shown at the Exposition Internationale des Arts Décoratifs et Industriels Modernes, Paris, 1925.

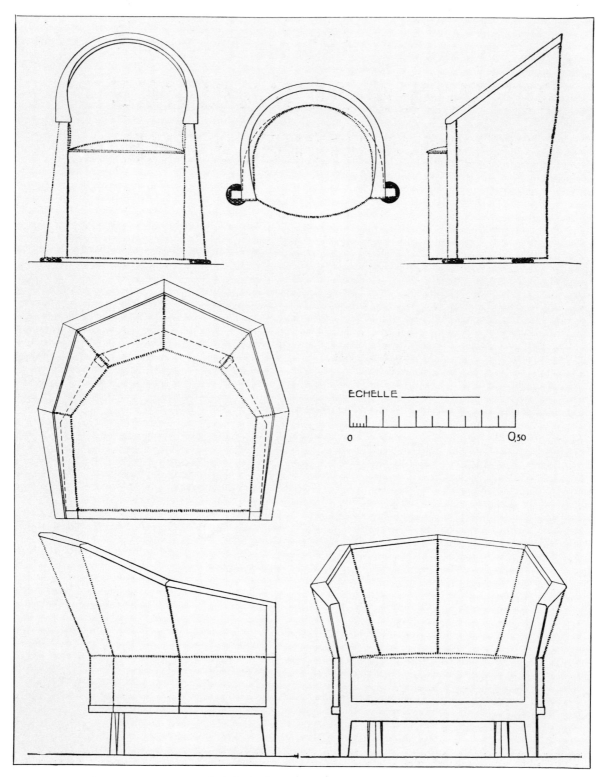

ECHELLE

0   0,50

Armchairs by Pierre Chareau, 1924.

II
BETWEEN FURNITURE AND ARCHITECTURE

Unnumbered. Salon d'Automne 1923. The unfolding fan partition looks ahead to the "Study-library of a French embassy" of 1925. Furniture in amourette and palisander. Composite lamp 33, table MB 97, lamp 32, known as the "La Petite Religieuse."

THE CONTEXT

The importance of Pierre Chareau's contribution to furniture design cannot be appreciated without defining the period in which his new concepts were to make themselves felt. When he began work, just over a year before the outbreak of World War I, the decorative arts were undergoing a revolution. Magazine articles of the time bear witness to this, and despite their period slant they can give us a closer understanding of the context in which Pierre Chareau emerged and started upon a professional life.

What exactly was happening when Pierre Chareau entered the scene? Christian Zervos gives us an initial answer.[1] Looking for the origins of the Modern Movement, he traces the development of the art of furniture design. To start with, he suggests that the tradition of French decorative art to which the modern revival of interest was linked was all but lost under the Empire. He saw the last traces of it in the later examples of the Restoration style. The product of "probity and a respect for natural forms," the Louis-Philippe style survived until around 1860, when Empress Eugénie's passion for Marie Antoinette finally won the day. This was a step backward and the "Louis XVI-Impératrice" style triumphed. This victory, Zervos continues, saw the beginning of half a century dominated by the "vieux-neuf."

In another equally significant article[2], Raymond Cogniat looks more closely at social and psychological conditions. He considers the love of antiques or period furniture as "another expression of the desire to reclaim from the past what people had been denied; in acquiring such possessions they felt they were on a level with those who were more privileged. To be on a par with the favored of former times, they had to have the illusion of living like them, in the same kind of environment, in other words, in the midst of similar furniture.... To live surrounded by new and original furniture would not have given them the illusion of at last possessing what had been denied them."

1. Christian Zervos, "Les tendances actuelles de l'art décoratif. I. Le mobilier d'hier et d'aujourd'hui," La Revue de l'Art Ancien et Moderne, January-May 1925, pp. 68–75.

2. Raymond Cogniat, "L'art décoratif en 1932: point de vue sur l'art appliqué," L'Amour de l'Art, no. 10, December 1933.

THE SOURCES OF THE REVIVAL

Most writers agree that the prescription for change and renewal is to be found in the work, writings, and lectures of Viollet-le-Duc. It does indeed seem to be the case that the movement for innovation in architecture, as well as in design, arose after certain prejudices died out in the wake of the rediscovery of Gothic art and its architectural principles.

But the first tentative movement away from the "vieux-neuf" soon led to excesses, in a search for originality at any price. Furniture designers who often had a fine-arts background, turned every article into a vehicle for self-expression and virtuosity. Form and function became two different things. Ornament took precedence over construction. Artists were carried away in their mania for decoration. Often inspired by natural forms, the decoration of furniture dictated the shape and function it would have. The "decorative spirit" ruled. Grasset, Gaillard, Charpentier, and Majorelle broke away from tradition, but bound furniture to design.

There were a few who resisted this temptation, and most of these were architects. The straight lines, perfect balance, and clear-cut angles of their furniture reflected their training and their respect for architectural rules. Sauvage, Plumet, and Selmersheim were typical of this tendency. But their work "often lacked life, grace, and sensibility."[3]

3. Zervos, *op. cit.*, p. 70.

The real break came only later, after the turn of the century. For Zervos, it arose out of the observation of machines, the intrinsic beauty of which greatly impressed certain designers. The radically different materials now employed gave rise to new forms and new ventures. As these were designed for the economics of machine production with profit as its objective, a strict, rational, economic logic lay behind them. They reflected the spirit of the age. Already Baltard had constructed the Paris "Halles" and Eiffel built the Garabit viaduct.

Other features of the time included the idea of sobriety and the subordination of ornament to composition. Artists and designers translated this into their own areas of interest. Influenced by the first examples of industrial production, furniture designers, or at least the most modern of them, did not forget the utilitarian aspect of the articles they made. And it was around this time that the Munich furniture designers exhibited their work in Paris.

THE FAILED REVOLUTION OF 1910–1913

In an article in 1924, Henry Clouzot examined the origins and ramifications of contemporary design. "And to begin with," he asked, "is art as it is now the result of what we called modern twenty years ago? We are by no means sure. Who is left in the ranks of decorators, out of all who were, in 1900, proponents of the naturalistic style of Nancy? Gaillard seems to have abandoned furniture designing, Guimard is retreating, Lambert exhibits only rarely, Prouvé and Carabin teach, Iribe is in America, Landry is dead, and Majorelle has changed. A few laggards make timid sacrifices to floral decoration.... The modern style [Art Nouveau] is dying, the modern style is dead. No floral tributes please. That fickle guide led decorative art to a dead end which it would still be in today if, around 1913, Vera, Sue, Mare, Groult, and others had not given their colleagues a good lesson in boldness and discipline, dragging them back to a tradition that had been forgotten or betrayed. Let us not forget, however, that without the example of Gallé, say, or Guimard, we would still be admiring pastiches of the past, and we must not be too hard on a period when, without our knowing it, the living art that now reigns was gradually emerging. You have to destroy before you can rebuild."[4]

4. Henry Clouzot, "En marge de l'art appliqué moderne," *L'Amour de l'Art*, no. 4, April 1924, pp. 105–125.

The analysis is to the point, paying homage to past glories, but above all to the innovators who, before World War I, very nearly succeeded in pulling decorative art out of the mire it had got itself into. Clouzot, however, gives no details of the source or contents of this attempt.

In 1924, while there were those who found it hard to admit to German influences at work, others were quick to mention them: "Three generations have brought the fruits of their labor to the exhibition: the generation of 1900, the exponents of which, like Majorelle or the Selmersheims, have developed to varying degrees; the generation that emerged around 1907, which was, in 1910, particularly influenced by the exhibition of Munich work; and finally the postwar generation which for the most part follows the lines laid out by Auguste Perret or Mallet-Stevens, and in furniture design by M. Pierre Chareau."[5]

Louis Vauxcelles makes it even more explicit in his virulent summary of the history and contribution of the Salon committee: "It invited the Munich furniture designers [to Paris], which of course prompted the accusation of selling out to Germany." But, he hastened to add, "This German exhibition was ... one of the best ever held at the Grand Palais, as it stirred up our sleepy manufacturers of applied art and stimulated the Faubourg Saint-Antoine."[6]*

5. "Les ensembles mobiliers à l'exposition des arts décoratifs," La Revue de l'Art Ancien et Moderne, Vol. XLVIII, June-December 1924, p. 224.

6. Louis Vauxcelles, Preface to the Salon d'Automne catalogue, 1927, p. 109.

A CHANGING ORDER

This much needed shot in the arm led to nothing. The 1910–1913 revolution did not take place because of the war. The decisive break with the old order came only after the armistice.

Around 1918–1919 the debate on the nature and substance of modernity resumed, and now the stakes were clearer and the terms better defined. At the Exposition des Arts Décoratifs et Industriels Modernes, Waldemar George opened fire with a review of the ambiguities inherent in the word *modern*: "Certain journalists, among them M. Prévost, seem to believe that the term *modern* is synonymous with 'new' and 'original.' A whole generation of critics, writers, and artists not only in France but elsewhere, have the firm idea that current forms must replace traditional forms. And thus all the efforts of this generation have been confined to the quest for new forms. The exhibition is manifest proof of this."[7]

The critic's words are harsh but not far from the truth. In 1925, a half-way point was reached, a style between two styles. That forms were simplified and lines more austere was clear for all to see, but the development was not over yet. Statements from the better designers were still veiled by the effects of Cubism. Nineteen twenty-five was a step along the way that led from line to volume and function.

7. Waldemar George, "L'Exposition des Arts Décoratifs et Industriels de 1925, Les tendances générales," L'Amour de l'Art, no. 8, August 1925, pp. 288–289.

* The Faubourg Saint-Antoine was the traditional center of the Paris cabinet-making trade.

In order to survive, the ornamentation of furniture that had been in vogue around 1900 developed a Cubist look to it. "Architects, furniture designers, decorators are uniformly applying the principles of composition that Pablo Picasso, Georges Braque, and Juan Gris have brought in.... In a word, progress in the current production of the decorative arts as a whole is being made under the auspices of Cubism."[8] And Marie Dormoy adds, "Cubism, to which we are indebted for a complete change, has itself become a formula, and a less appetizing one than many others."*

8. George, *ibid.*

9. Marie Dormoy, "Les intérieurs à l'Exposition Internationale des Arts Décoratifs," *L'Amour de l'Art*, no. 8, August 1925, p. 312.

MODERNITY

Although it was held at a time of contradictory currents, the 1925 Exhibition was an outlet for the innovators. It is worth stressing, however, that even among the "moderns" there were different minds at work. In an analysis that is still surprisingly relevant today, Zervos examined five different approaches:

"To begin with, there are those artists who, following P. Vera's example, submit their feelings to a strict discipline (Sue, Mare, the Compagnie des Arts Français, and André Groult). For them, the initial outlines of an object may spring from the imagination, but its construction is determined by geometrical figures, which, for the most part, derive from Renaissance sources, particularly from the writings of Serlio. These artists emphasize the respect due to tradition. For something new, they are going back to the last of the French styles dating from the end of the Restoration and the beginning of Louis-Philippe's reign, the first style to display all the qualities we now require from our furniture: adaptability, practicality, and comfort. They are trying, and with good reason, to carry on the work that was left unfinished and forgotten in the midst of the craze for the 'vieux-neuf.'†

"At the opposite end of this discipline should be placed an artist (Ruhlmann) with a highly fanciful imagination whose preoccupation with rhythm, and search for what may be called musical forms, whose use of the laws of proportion and mastery of contrast and variegation override all principles and canons. Like the

---

* On the same subject as Marie Dormoy, Roger Brielle writes, "With varying degrees of resemblance within one family, the ensembles exhibited nevertheless reveal profound differences of sensibility" (*Art et Décoration*, 1933, "Le 4ème Salon de l'UAM," p. 232). Gaston Varenne wonders, "When is an artist modern? When he gives true expression to the needs of his time, when what he creates is closest to the thoughts or feelings of a whole generation. Now what differences there are among the names grouped under the same heading! Included in this group are artists who are very moderate, classic even, I'd call them, who'll be labeled reactionaries one day, as well as adventurers who thrust forward in a somewhat haphazard way, in no particular order, caring little whether the public is following them or not, anticipating the future at the risk of being totally mistaken" (*L'Amour de l'Art*, 1930, "L'UAM," p. 367).

† *tr. note*: Literally, "old-new," referring to the taste for copies and imitations of Louis XV and XVI furniture.

artists mentioned, Ruhlmann holds that an original style is simply the addition of new elements to past forms and consequently that efforts to pick a style out of the blue as it were, should be abandoned. But instead of re-creating the last of the French styles, Ruhlmann allows his vivid imagination to wander over each and every period and style.

"Francis Jourdain represents the tendency that seeks freedom from the domination of tradition, to abstract from the past as far as possible. Despite his valiant and commendable efforts, it is impossible to say that he has done what he set out to do. Excellent as his work is, in terms of massing, purity and simplicity of line, and in matching modern requirements, no new forms are suggested. The furniture is simplified in the extreme, down to the elements of carpentry. Where his talent really shows itself is in the art of subordinating each article to the general effect of an ensemble, which he succeeds in doing very well.

"More complex is the art of Pierre Chareau, who could be seen to be in the avant-garde of the modern design movement. In the wake of Francis Jourdain, Chareau is trying to extricate himself from the influence of a tradition that he holds in deep respect. His furniture is composed of straight lines occasionally accentuated by gentle curves. Chareau's conception of objects is quite clearly architectural. It is this that inspired him to follow the architectural principle of making every element of his furniture correspond to a well-defined intention. The construction and the fine disposition of Chareau's furniture seem designed to draw our attention to its durability, to a desire that it should be more than merely ephemeral, as well as to its appropriateness, to the harmonious movement of its lines. Volumes are the expression of opposing and balancing forces. Sturdy supports respond to the force of gravity that is the very nature of a solid object. For him, furniture is all about construction and so its supports are like the substructure of a building. His furniture does not merely meet the ground, it weighs down upon it on sockets that recall architectural foundations."[10]

10. Zervos, *op. cit.*, pp. 73–74.

It is a masterly analysis. There is little to add with the benefit of hindsight. To complete the picture, Zervos concludes his survey with an artist whose finesse, strength, and sensibility were close to Pierre Chareau's: "Miss Eileen Gray has been blessed with an extraordinary personality. Her work shows much originality and it is well thought out despite the impression of an aggressive newness. Her interiors are, however, intended to be evocative, and this is where the problem lies. Aestheticism and literature have a disastrous effect on art. Thankfully the artist's development is to include more light, and there is a more architectural vision of objects and interiors. Even now, her screens, lacquer-work, carpets, and light fittings are evidence of her potential."[11]

11. Zervos, *ibid.*

FROM LINE TO VOLUME

In 1925, all the ingredients for a revolution were reunited. Raymond Cogniat added something more, when, seven years later, he drew up a history of styles, starting from the end of the nineteenth century:

"1860–1890, obsession with detail, skillful arrangements, the upholsterer's task. Judicious draping, curtains and wall hangings make up for the impersonality of the furniture. Triumph of the upholsterer.

"1900 did not see the end of the vogue for upholstery. Not only did it not disappear, but it was accepted and made use of, promoted even, because of the fashion for the sinuous line.

"By 1920, there was still no sign of a break. This was what linked it to 1900. 1920 was more than a vogue for upholstery. We could say it was the couturier's style which triumphed.

"1930, on the other hand, is dominated by architecture, and this seems to us to be infinitely more understandable.

"We find that there are fewer differences between 1900 and 1920 than between 1920 and 1930. . . . For life was much the same in 1920 as it was in 1900. As yet, there was no real awareness of a new state of things, of a new kind of life. 1920, like 1900, was preoccupied with line; 1930 is preoccupied with volume. In its search for a greater simplicity of line, 1920 was guiding us, however, towards the primacy of matter, the beauty of matter itself. . . . This taste took us some time to acquire, led to the suppression of decoration, to fine, bare surfaces which could bring out the inherent value of materials more than the most lavish of decorations. And when all that remains of furnishings are the materials appreciated for their own sake as great expanses of bare surfaces, volumes are rendered in all their expressive power by the very nature of things, and we must acknowledge their paramount importance."[12]

12. Cogniat, *op. cit.*, p. 331.

It is, therefore, hardly surprising that in 1932 Cogniat considered that the major revolution in furniture design came about with the introduction of metal.

PIERRE CHAREAU, A PERSONAL CHRONOLOGY

The two major articles by Zervos and Cogniat enable us to situate Pierre Chareau's work and its progress.

At the time of the "failed revolution of 1913," he was almost thirty. When war put an end to his tracing job at Waring and Gillow, an English firm based in Paris, his designs still bore the imprint of the preceding period, although they were marked by exceptional creative energy. Ahead of his contemporaries, he stripped form of its models, and limited ornamentation as much as he could. Three stylistic sources seem to have been at work. The Restoration style is still apparent in the first bergère chairs. There are also traces of influences from England, resulting from his own cultural awareness, or, as seems more likely, from his time at Waring and Gillow's. But the clearest, the guiding influences came from the east. Certain chairs and tables from the period from 1913 to 1919 recall Hoffmann and Loos. Viennese inspiration is undeniable. Perhaps it was Francis Jourdain, himself very close to the Viennese and Munich schools, who introduced Chareau to their new forms. At any event, he saw them and learned from them, as his furniture clearly shows. His designs are austere and could be seen to be somewhat cumbersome. Since Chareau provides no explanation for this, we are set wondering whether this relative lack of grace comes from an architect's reaction against the elaborateness of Art Nouveau, or whether it betrays a certain weakness in his furniture design. Throughout his work, in fact, Chareau does seem to be very preoccupied with solidity. Unafraid of bulk as such, he would strengthen the structural supports of his wood furniture whenever possible.* Cubism also left its mark, particularly on light fittings, with Chareau treating a lampshade as if it were a piece of sculpture.

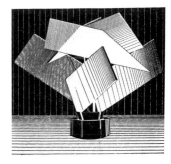

LP 166

When in 1925 he designed the "Study-library of a French embassy," and the dining room of the Indochinese pavilion for the Exposition Internationale des Arts Décoratifs et Industriels Modernes, he was almost forty. People saw him, along with Francis Jourdain, as one of the leaders of modernity, and he was one of the most universally acclaimed furniture designers. His experience was a formidable weapon to add to his open outlook and sensibility.

Louis-Charles Watelin, who was by no means a great fan of his, had to admit that "in the realm of the unexpected, we find Pierre Chareau forever in search of volumes that will correspond to a new sensibility. He is a bold and stimulating man. While I am not with him in all his attempts, the most recent of which seem to me to be questionable, although he can be very persuasive, I recognize that he is opening a number of doors for his colleagues to go through, albeit at their peril. This artist can do little else than to ensure that an idea that preys on him will be expressed in an impassioned style and brought to fruition at whatever cost."[13]

In 1933, the same year that Raymond Cogniat completed his article, Chareau finished work on the Maison de Verre. He was turning fifty. Six years previously he had exhibited his first wood and metal furniture. He had abandoned the Salon des Artistes Décorateurs to exhibit with the Artistes Modernes, where he joined Francis Jourdain, born in 1879, as a senior member. A veteran of the modern revolution, he remained on the sidelines, coming up with his own personal solutions that were at times innovative, like the metal school furniture, at times backward-looking, like his use of wrought-iron work, and at times totally unprecedented, as in the duralumin cupboards in the bathroom of the Maison de Verre.

He was thus, with Francis Jourdain, the youngest of the forerunners in 1913, and the oldest of the moderns in 1930. His position at a turning point of history must have had some bearing on his marginality. Young enough to be part of a revolution, he was probably too "old" to believe in militant action, too pragmatic to draw up a manifesto.

[13]Louis-Charles Watelin, "Les possibilités de notre art décoratif en 1925," *L'Art et les Artistes,* no. 40.

*Sometimes the legs are held firmly in place by wide stretchers. Often seats are solid and encased in a tub support which has skirting down to floor level.

EB 194, oval table MB 97, low table with wings MB 130, standard lamp 31,
known as "La Religieuse" ("The Nun"), couch MP 169, lamp LP 166.

Josef Hoffmann, 1905. Entrance hall of the country house of Jacob and Josef Kohn.

Josef Hoffmann, armchair, 1906.

MF 11   Josef Hoffmann, chair, 1901.

Pierre Chareau, apartment, circa 1923.

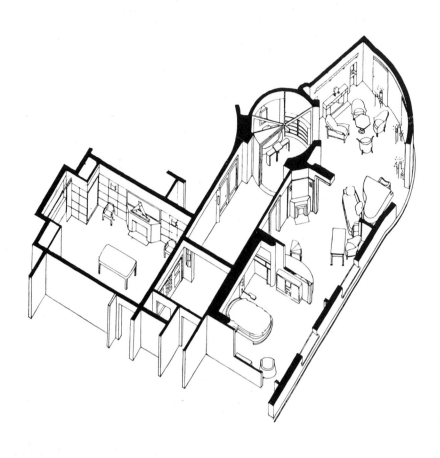

Plan of an apartment executed in 1924. The
project was shared between Francis Jourdain
and Pierre Chareau. (See photographs pp. 186–
187 of entrance hall and small lounge.)

From *Les Arts de la Maison*, Winter 1924.

Unnumbered. Dining room of the Indochinese Pavilion, Exposition Internationale des Arts Décoratifs et Industriels Modernes, Paris, 1925. Chair MF 275, buffet MD 237, table 8, composite lamp LP 270.

Dans ce salon de Coromandel on voit apparaître un principe qui va devenir essentiel à la technique de Pierre Chareau : celui de la mobilité du décor intérieur. Dans ce salon, où la rigueur architecturale semble s'assouplir aux jeux d'une plus libre fantaisie, et dont les parois roulantes peuvent, soit enclore complètement un espace ovale, soit s'ouvrir sur des espaces triangulaires, qui laissent apercevoir, d'un côté, un bureau et, de l'autre, une bibliothèque. Mais la mobilité prend ici un caractère plus subtil encore : le plafond, en forme d'anneau, s'abaisse en gradin jusqu'au coffre de la cheminée, tandis qu'en face il s'élève, au-dessus de la porte que surmonte un large bandeau ; et les lignes de ce plafond, qui semblent elles-mêmes en mouvement, imposent au regard inconscient, un mouvement fécond en plaisir esthétique.

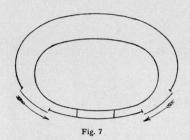

Fig. 7

La mobilité est plus généralisée dans l'appartement dont il avait tracé le plan pour le Salon des Artistes Décorateurs. L'idée dont Pierre Chareau était parti est celle-ci : nous avons, dans nos appartements modernes, un espace libre et rigide, celui de la galerie sur laquelle viennent s'ouvrir les diverses pièces également immuables : il conviendrait de disposer cet espace de telle sorte qu'il puisse agrandir à volonté telle ou telle partie fixe de l'appartement. Dans le plan de Pierre Chareau, la galerie n'est plus qu'un espace circulaire, et que peuvent enclore ou non des portes qui s'enroulent autour des piliers ou se replient avec des plafonds : grâce à cette disposition, le bureau, la chambre à coucher, la salle à manger, s'agrandiront tour à tour ou séparément et, selon l'heure ou le besoin, les pièces se commanderont ou ne se commanderont pas entre elles.

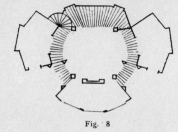

Fig. 8

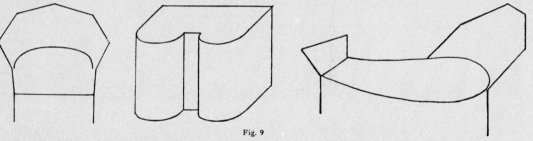

Fig. 9

Ces trois meubles que l'artiste a dépouillés de tout ornement et auxquels il ne semble vouloir laisser que ce qui est strictement nécessaire à l'usage qu'on fera d'eux, reçoivent du seul mouvement qu'ils appellent ou contiennent ce on ne sait quoi qui transpose l'utile en valeur de beauté.

From *Les Arts de la Maison*, Winter 1924.

III

ARCHITECTURE, INTERIOR DESIGN, AND ENSEMBLES

Voici une chambre rectangulaire et d'une parfaite banalité, destinée à devenir le cabinet d'étude d'un jeune médecin. Ni la porte, ni la cheminée, ni la fenêtre ne sont dans l'axe ; de plus, la fenêtre est beaucoup trop grande pour la pièce ; la corniche à gorge, la cimaise à moulure ont également des proportions empruntées à l'architecture monumentale des temps passés, tandis que les panneaux recouverts de papier peint ont été arbitrairement réduits, pour obéir à la nécessité de diviser en cinq étages la hauteur de l'immeuble. Ne pouvant rien changer à la fenêtre sans toucher à la façade de la maison, Pierre Chareau va la considérer uniquement comme une source de lumière autour de laquelle les parois devront jouer harmonieusement. En mettant de chaque côté de la cheminée une armoire à livres, dont la destination de la pièce justifie la présence, il replace la fenêtre dans l'axe ; et pour faire avancer légèrement la cheminée sur cette nouvelle paroi, il lui ajoute des masses qui serviront également de bibliothèques. — L'espace qui reste, du côté de la porte, après la deuxième armoire à livres, va former une alcôve où le canapé indispensable trouvera tout naturellement sa place. Pour que cette alcôve soit intime, on en surbaissera le plafond, et pour établir un rapport satisfaisant entre l'éclairage de cette alcôve et celui du cabinet de travail proprement dit, on coupera largement les angles du plafond, dans la partie la plus importante de la pièce. C'est aussi pour permettre une agréable distribution de la lumière que les plafonds et les parois (dont la corniche et la cimaise a été supprimée) sont uniformément peints de la même couleur grise ; mais dans l'alcôve, les parois paraîtraient disproportionnées si l'on n'en divisait pas la surface ; c'est pourquoi le décorateur les a compartimentées en cet endroit au moyen de lattes de bois, mais sans en modifier la couleur. Le résultat obtenu par Chareau est des plus satisfaisants.

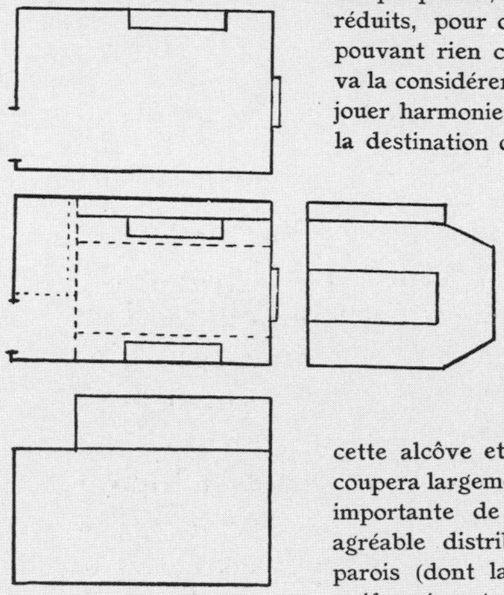

Fig. 5

Voici deux chambres que sépare une étroite salle de bains (dont la fenêtre est plus petite que celles des chambres). On veut faire d'une de ces chambres un vaste cabinet de toilette, et agrandir l'autre en abattant la cloison qui la sépare de la salle de bains. Mais, dans cette chambre nouvelle, les fenêtres vont se trouver inégales. Pour justifier cette inégalité, Pierre Chareau est amené à créer dans la pièce deux volumes inégaux, l'un, principal, auquel les dimensions de la grande fenêtre sont appropriées, et l'autre secondaire, en rapport avec les dimensions réduites de la fenêtre plus petite ; il réalise ce programme au moyen d'un double pilastre, qui motive, au-dessus de l'espace secondaire, un aspect différent du plafond ; et pour que cet espace secondaire ait bien sa vie propre et nettement circonscrite, il fait légèrement avancer, dans l'espace principal, la paroi contre laquelle le lit viendra se placer.

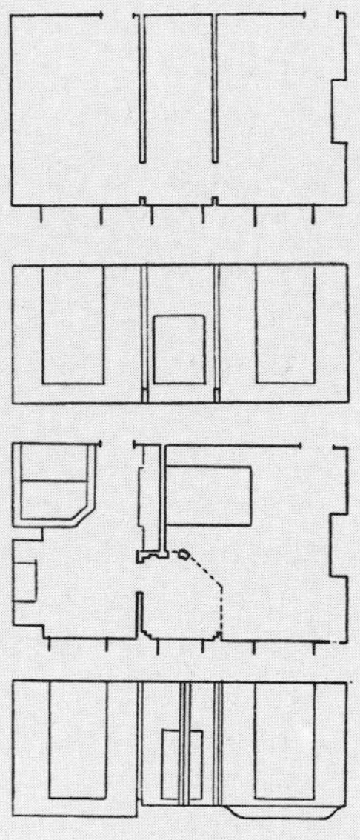

Fig. 6

From *Les Arts de la Maison*, Winter 1924.

Pierre Chareau worked, then, in a period characterized by a decline in the ornamentation of furniture and a renewed respect for architectural rules, in the construction of it. However, experiments in modern architecture as such were not very much in evidence immediately after the war. Behind the times when compared with the fine arts which had broken with tradition, furniture design was, in many ways, far in advance of domestic architecture. And so, to begin with, Chareau had above all to devote his attention to crossing the great divide between the old style apartments and his modern designs.

ARCHITECTURE VERSUS FURNITURE

Edmond Fleg, well qualified to talk of Pierre Chareau given his connection to the Bernheim family, described his approach thus: "In order to bring about the aesthetic transformation he regarded as imperative, Pierre Chareau felt that first and foremost he had to come to terms with and answer a basic question: with what should he begin, architecture or furniture? In other words, which most offended our conception of modernity? Was it 'period' furniture, the poor relation of the splendors of the past, or was it the interior design of our houses; bedrooms that are invariably shaped like boxes, the ubiquitous mantelpiece crowned by a ceiling-high mirror, Louis XV or Louis XVI cornices designed to provide the middle classes of today with some semblance of the palatial setting that surrounded our past kings? Pierre Chareau saw that there could be only one answer. It was the fireplaces, windows, doors, walls, and ceilings that had to be altered first; these were what overwhelmed and weighed down upon us when we entered a room. They stopped our homes from having any character of their own and no new article of furniture placed in such an outdated setting could hope to give it one.

"The first task of the designer was thus to destroy and rebuild. But when Chareau came back from the war, the construction industry was at a standstill ... he would have to be content with a compromise: he would destroy and reconstruct individual rooms or an apartment, but leave the outer building intact. His work was thus to be bound within a framework laid out by his predecessors, a plan he had constantly to circumvent."[1]

And Pierre Chareau's efforts at circumvention led to one success after another (see the plans for "A young doctor's consulting-room and bedroom" [reproduced opposite] from *Les Arts de la Maison*). He found constraints a stimulus. Gaston Varenne writes along similar lines, that "for an architect-interior decorator, who, in line with the best of traditions, builds a house and designs its interiors, it is relatively easy to harmonize the furniture with the architecture. But we can only guess at the difficulties that confront that same interior decorator when furnishing an apartment in a building he did not construct. He has to contend with the boxlike rooms, the height of the ceilings, and the lighting as well as with the

1. Edmond Fleg, "Nos décorateurs, Pierre Chareau," *Les Arts de la Maison*, Winter 1924.

cornices, paneling, and moldings against which modern furniture will look lamentable, particularly if its proportions or style contradict the all too often regrettable intentions that lie behind these fixtures.

"In such cases, Pierre Chareau will go in and grasp the bull by its horns. If he has to design a study, bedroom, and bathroom in an apartment block, he will, in accordance with his plan, alter the height of a ceiling, banish the moldings that get in the way, change the doors, and, if necessary, pull down a partition or lower a window; and with this feat of extraordinary ingenuity, he changes the whole atmosphere of the place."[2]*

This approach of Chareau's was not confined to work done immediately after the war. He made use of it in 1928 for the Grand-Hôtel at Tours, and again in 1932 for the LTT offices, Rue de la Faisanderie, Paris. Here, he used his manipulative skills to convert part of a large apartment building into administrative offices where glass and metal predominate. That same year he carried his work on interior decoration still further in Daniel Dreyfus's home, and departed even more markedly from the old setting. "The thing is," Pierre Migennes wrote,[3] "modern decoration is not just a matter of choosing carpets and paint for the walls. It is, first and foremost, about the redisposition and the arrangement of space. All the partitions in the old apartment are knocked down to obtain a single room[4] that is as large as possible. Then, into this great empty space, the rooms with all the varying functions that existed before are reinserted† in such a way as to retain all the advantages of the newly recovered large space. . . . The role of the interior decorator thus borders on that of the architect." And in this way, Pierre Chareau was able to fulfill his original vocation.‡

2. Gaston Varenne, "L'esprit moderne de Pierre Chareau," *Art et Décoration*, January-June 1923, Vol. XLIII, pp. 128–129.

3. Pierre Migennes, "Sur deux ensembles de P. Chareau," *Art et Décoration*, 1932, Vol. LXI, pp. 129–140.

4. For Chareau's obsession with single rooms, see *Un Inventeur, l'architecte Pierre Chareau*, Paris, 1954, pp. 11–12.

* The article continues: "Pierre Chareau's basic idea is that the whole question of a modern style is centered around the creation of volume in a given space. The study of this space should be the first thing to occupy the artist's attention. The space dictates the furniture, imposes its forms on it so that an overall rhythm is created, an organism in which everything is arranged not only for our comfort and well-being, but also for our aesthetic pleasure and enjoyment."

† The same tactics were used in the Maison de Verre. With the major construction work over, Chareau set to work with the ironworker Dalbet.

‡ "The profession of interior decorator thus attracted Pierre Chareau for the enormous variety of immediate problems it posed, for a man in search of something new; but in taking it up he did not abandon the ideas he had as a master-builder. It was Pierre Chareau, surely, who described himself as an 'architect-decorator.' This he does indeed remain, although he is an architect willing to submit to the limits of a social nature that are imposed on his great love of construction" (Maximilien Gauthier, "Art Décoratif, M. Pierre Chareau," *L'Art et les Artistes*, no. 45, April 1924, pp. 281–286).

ENSEMBLES AND RATIONALISM

Once, however, the conflict between the architectural setting and modern life was resolved "how could articles of furniture be given a modern dimension?"[5] Pierre Chareau had two answers to Gaston Varenne's pertinent question. Between 1919 and 1922, he was to give equal attention to the notion of ensembles and to relating furniture to its function. They were not unrelated ideas: one gave him the programme for his projects; the other provided him with solutions for the many small problems that emerged in everyday life and work.

During the twenties, the idea of an ensemble took on a special meaning. No longer was it simply a question of variations on a basic model, or of using similar ornamental elements within one setting, or even of juxtaposing pieces of furniture identical in design or material. The notion of an ensemble, in the contemporary sense, no longer applied to, say, a set of eighteenth-century English mahogany dining chairs and a table. Quite the contrary, it presupposed an attention to something more than the furniture itself; to its relationship to volume. An ensemble was a spatial response to a given activity.

From as early as 1910, critics spoke of "ensembliers." After the war, a few were quick to identify a School of 1919, which was devoted entirely to ensembles. Yet the definition still lacked a measure of clarity. In 1925, Marie Dormoy, who had consigned Chareau to the ranks of "engineer-constructors" as opposed to the "colorist-decorators," defined the ensemble in aesthetic rather than functional terms: "An ensemble is a combination of decorative elements which may have no individual importance, and which serve only to contribute to the general effect." Taking up this same distinction, Guillaume Janneau defined its terms more precisely and at last introduced into it ideas of architectural space and an overall approach: "Fifteen years ago, an ensemble consisted of a group of objects all contributing to one single effect. The evolution then underway has now reached its logical conclusion: architecture itself is being subordinated to the general effect. It has ceased to rule over the 'minor arts.' It has only its own part to play in the orchestra. Today the man in charge is not the builder, but the organizer of the ensemble in which the architectural plans, the interior decoration, lighting, hangings, and furniture are all equally important. There are two tendencies at work now which should, however, be distinguished: the colorists as represented by M. Maurice Dufrêne, and the 'engineers' as represented by M. Pierre Chareau."[6]

The endless debate between decoration, interior design, and architecture continued. Discussing some of Pierre Chareau's ensembles, Gabriel Henriot summed up the matter once again: "Whether the onlooker likes this ensemble or not, he is forced to admit that it holds together. The proportions of the rooms harmonize with those of the furniture; surfaces have been utilized after a good deal of strict reasoning; the maximum amount of light, room, and comfort has been obtained from the space available. Nothing is missing and nothing is superfluous."[7]

5. Varenne, op. cit.

6. Guillaume Janneau, "La décoration intérieure, le mobilier," Beaux Arts, no. 12, June 1925, pp. 181–196.

7. Gabriel Henriot, "Pierre Chareau," Mobilier et Décoration, no. 8, July 1928, pp. 215 ff.

All that had to be done now was to find a theoretical basis for this coherence, a principle that also fitted in with modern life. In Chareau's case, the critics confined themselves to the use of one term, *rationalism*. No one dreamed of using the word *functionalism*, as it would have detracted from the human element in his work. While functionalism is well suited to architectural work, giving a clear picture of innovations made in that field, rationalism expresses the creative approach of the furniture designer far better, and the feelings that play a part in it. Reason is in fact closely related to the use and function of a piece of furniture. A rationalist can also convey feelings that a functionalist could not give form to. Of course, rationalism is an intellectual quality, but not exclusively so.

Referring to the LTT offices Chareau designed in 1932, René Chavance writes: "The contemporary interior architect—for want of a better description—should by all accounts find a perfect chance here to apply his rational principles to every single detail of the project.... Among modern artists, M. Chareau ranks as one of the most faithful to the rational principles I mentioned above. The object of his research is determined in the first place by the requirements that must be met. To this, every aspect of his work is submitted, from the building methods, the materials used, and the architectural layout, right up to the form the furniture will take. Nevertheless, he keeps his distance from the purely theoretical discipline of some of his colleagues. There is something of the poet and the psychologist in him. Leaving nothing to chance and keeping his imagination in control, he can animate all that he does."[8]

8. René Chavance, "Bureaux industriels par Pierre Chareau," *Art et Décoration*, 1933, pp. 123–128.

In a period when interior designers and architects ruled, and opposed each other, Pierre Chareau refused to take sides. But it would be wrong to see this as some sort of noncommittal effort to keep two irons in the fire; it was rather the result of a deliberate choice, a position he took. Chareau had trained as an architect. After working as a tracer, in 1919 he decided to become a furniture designer.[9] By 1926, he had turned to architecture again. He did not see any conflict between the two dimensions, of furniture and the space in which it was located. It was all a question of volumes, and there was no reason for the approach to differ. Although of course there is a change of scale between the composition of an item of furniture and the plans of a building, the reasoning behind them need not change at all. In both interior architecture—a term then coming into use— and architecture proper, Chareau worked with the same aim in mind. Between items of furniture, as imported objects, and the building designed without furnishings, he interposed the ensemble, a balanced arrangement of volumes to be contained within another larger volume that would be redesigned to accommodate it. Out of this balanced whole came a sense of permanence, of durability: "By its very nature, an ensemble is not a showpiece. It gives us an overwhelming impression of permanence. Nothing in this arrangement, which keeps practicability and aesthetics strictly apart, is suggestive of fanciful movement. There is no place in this ordered, disciplined world for a restless spirit. The final value of each object is established right from the start and this in itself adds to the overall personality of the work."[10]

9. Gauthier, *op. cit.*

10. Léon Moussinac, *Le Meuble Français Moderne*, Paris, Hachette, p. 64.

Given this approach to space, it goes without saying that permanent fixtures*
occupied a good deal of his thoughts and output.

A permanent fixture in fact supplied the missing link between architecture and
furniture. As an immobile element of furniture, connected to the building without
being part of its structure, it guaranteed the continuity and consistency of the
furnished space. With it came guidelines or points of reference that could direct
the attention of the inhabitant or visitor away from the furniture to the walls. It
was one thing to modify space, enlarge it and alter its boundaries by pulling
down partitions—as indicated above, Chareau displayed his mastery in this field
as early as 1919—quite another, however, to create a new harmony in the interior,
to introduce new rhythms into new volumes.

Between the two poles of architecture and furniture, most of Chareau's contemporaries managed, in a more or less militant fashion, to limit their range. The
more architecturally inclined deliberately left furniture aside; others, concerned
that modernity should wield its influence over every aspect of life, applied themselves to the design of furniture, and interestingly enough, as products of architects, the articles they designed are complete in themselves, divorced from a
context, and could be placed in any surrounding. There were also the decorators
who remained attached to linear forms and fabrics and never touched structures
or volumes. Chareau does not really fit any of these categories. In his mind, line
and volume were not separate. From the start, he would not allow a modern
piece of furniture in an old apartment. But he did not stop there. He cast aside
all thoughts of adding modern furniture to a modern environment per se. The
house as a whole had to be on a modern scale, with the volumes of furniture
relating directly to the volume that contained them. In the years from 1927 to
1930, such an idea was not so strikingly new. It was common to Chareau's friends,
his colleagues from the U.A.M. But not all drew the same conclusions from it.
Djo-Bourgeois, for example, believed that unifying space and the relationship
between interiors and exteriors, along with the demands of contemporary life,
meant that movable furniture† should be done away with altogether. He happily
designed interiors with benches and tables built into the walls, like fitted
cupboards.

Chareau, however, kept to the distinction between architecture, permanent
fixtures, and movable furniture. He believed that it defined the three levels of
approach for a creator of space. With the architecture of the containing space
established, he divided it up, using built-in elements to create smaller areas and
thoroughfares. The harmony and rhythms that thus emerged were completed by

* The French term *immeuble par destination*, literally, "purpose-built fittings," was coined by the
author to cover furniture, bookcases, cupboards, etc., which are fixed or bolted down, embedded or
sealed into the building without being part of its structure.

† This covers any object or item of furniture not attached to the building, that is portable or can be
moved at will.

the movable furniture. He created the setting, setting its limits, and then placed the furniture within it. With the guiding rules laid out, he gave his client the freedom to alter the furnishings as he wished; this was the normal practice, though the freedom was sometimes illusory, since in certain cases the slightest change could destroy the harmony and effect of an ensemble. The implications of authoritarianism that this might suggest were, however, counteracted by the preliminary, and highly detailed discussion of the project with the client.

Pierre Chareau's interest in permanent fixtures is demonstrated by most of his installations. At the Dreyfus's home and the Grand-Hôtel at Tours, he made use of large metal and glass partitions that often curved round, and created rhythms by varying ceiling heights. At Hélène Bernheim's home, he fixed a wrought-iron hanging bed onto the wall and partially concealed a radiator through the use of swivel shelves. Elsewhere he would have benches built in, or devise a system of guiding rails from which doors, screens, or sliding fan walls could be suspended.

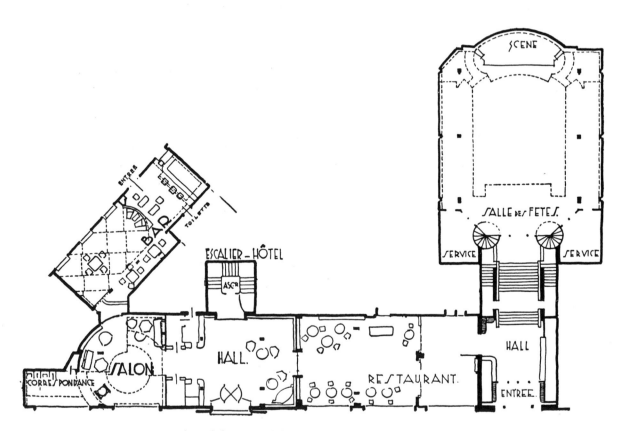

Plan of the ground floor of the Grand-Hôtel at Tours.

In the Maison de Verre, the fitted cupboards are double-sided. Access is possible from the corridor as well as from within the bedrooms. A maid can thus fill them or sort things out with no fear of disturbing her employers, who themselves can get to them from the opposite side.

Sometimes the permanent fixture takes on a sculptural look, concealing its function. A black and silver cylinder, the broom cupboard in the dining room of the Maison de Verre is aesthetically pleasing and it does not distract the visitor's attention.

This acute awareness of continuity in space is also expressed in leitmotifs that vary in scale.

In both building and furniture design, Pierre Chareau did not stop at line or even volume. He gave a great deal of thought and time to the mobility of objects, the possible alterations of volumes and transformations of space. He thus attached particular importance to doorways. Opaque or transparent, they could discourage or invite the visitor to cross their threshold. The sense of a transition could be increased if they were wide, or lessened if they were narrow. Sliding doors could close off an area, diminish it in size, lower its height by reducing the light, and redirect activity elsewhere. Open they could lighten, enlarge, and breathe life into a room. Their very position had an effect or reflected the state of mind of the user, who had the choice of communicating with the rest of the house, or shutting himself away. Similarly, but on a different scale, Chareau made frequent use in his furniture of hinged units, swiveling side tables, pull-out flaps, folding tables, surfaces that fanned open, and so on. Maneuverability meant versatility.

In every area, the thought was consistent. From the detail of an item of furniture to the overall structure of a building, there was one overriding preoccupation: volume, its nature, its aesthetic effect, and its application.

THE GRAND-HÔTEL AT TOURS
HT 647 (above) and HT 587 (below). Hotel lobby and entrance to the bar. Chair
MF 275.

66

HT 576. Lobby. Furniture in wickerwork and green leather. Oak wall paneling,
mosaic-faced pillar, pre-existing floor. Armchairs MF 310. Plant stand PF 35.

HT 649. Bar and smoking lounge. Low wall faced with mahogany blocks. The dividing panels above are an example of the designer's interest in folding-fan structures. Chairs MF 275, low chairs MF 313.

HT 583. Bar and smoking lounge (detail). "Mobile wall division between bar and smoking lounge enabling rooms to be separated when required. Walls in mahogany mosaic paneling. High bar table in sycamore and mahogany. Small bar tables, high stools, low tables, and stools in mahogany with iron bases; cubist armchairs, padded lounge chairs in green leather; green and gray rubber floor covering. Gray coffered ceiling, yellow over bar. Green curtains" (*L'Encyclopédie des Métiers d'Art*). Low chair MF 313, table MB 345, stool 3.

HT 648. Lounge. "Area of the lounge leading into the lobby, walls covered in
brown and silver mosaic design, walnut furniture upholstered in brown velvet,
brown and silver mosaic design, and brown and gold mosaic design, large rug
"Eclipse" in range of blues (these blues are taken up in an adjoining room known
as the writing room); light fittings in alabaster and iron. Another detail in the
lounge, the use of pillars containing the water pipes..." (*L'Encyclopédie des
Métiers d'Art*). Armchairs MF 732 (with floor-length skirting), MF 208, U-shaped
stool 2, ceiling lights LP 270.

HT 586. Bar.
HT 568. Dining room. "White walls, armchairs in oak, 'la ruche' strip lighting made up of alabaster plates, floor made prior to installation" (*L'Encyclopédie des Métiers d'Art*).

HT 578. Writing room. "The walls are in the blue shades of the "Eclipse" rug, walnut furniture, double-sided writing tables" (*L'Encyclopédie des Métiers d'Art*). U-shaped stool 2, armchair MF 732, lamp LP 270.

HT 571. "Lounge, adjoining the reading room. Painting in two shades of sepia,
walnut furniture upholstered in velvet, or in brown and silver or gold and brown
mosaic design, walls silver mosaic. Light fittings, double-sided wall lights.
Wallcovering reproductions of Jean Hugo's 'miroir magique.' " (*L'Encyclopédie
des Métiers d'Art*). Tulip table MB 170, armchair 37.

HT 589. Ballroom. "Rough stone ensemble, sycamore paneling inlaid within
silver polished metal, screen of wood mosaic, alabaster light fittings on walls and
section of wall in frosted glass. Inlaid wooden floor. Strip-light ceiling, spiral
staircase in walnut, iron banister, silver door, mosaic parquet floor"
(*L'Encyclopédie des Métiers d'Art*).

HT 591. Balcony of the ballroom.

HT 590. Balcony of the ballroom.

HT 651. Ballroom, general view.

HT 592. Ballroom (detail of the ground floor).

HT 587. Ballroom, entrance doors and spiral staircase leading to balcony.

ES 51 (dated 1920). Apartment belonging to Madame Fleg. Tulip table MB 170,
raised corner couch MP 526.

EB 408. Pierre Chareau's apartment, 54 Rue Nollet, Paris. Desk MB 405, nesting
table MB 106.

Above: ES 915. Apartment, circa 1928. Desk MB 405, couch in the MF 220 series.

Below: EB 757. Doctor Dalsace's study at Villeflix, Noisy-le-Grand. Desk MB 405, divan 24 in the MF 15 series.

EL 802. Apartment, circa 1928. Desk MB 405, ceiling light LP 270, chair MF 275.

Hélène Bernheim's apartment (?), circa 1930. Table 15, low M-shaped stool in
curule form, couch MP 214.

Hélène Bernheim's apartment (?), circa 1930. Small linen chest MA 374, version
with mirror.

Apartment belonging to D. and G. Dreyfus, 1932. Plant stand PF 35, bookcase MU
1030.

Apartment belonging to D. and G. Dreyfus, 1932.

ES 855 and 857. Apartment, circa 1928. Desk MB 744, armchairs MF 732, tulip table MB 170, games table MB 241a, plant stand PF 35, adjustable shelves PD 698, lamps LA 554 and LA 548.

EN 965 and 984. The Dalsace children's bedroom at Villeflix, Noisy-le-Grand,
circa 1925.

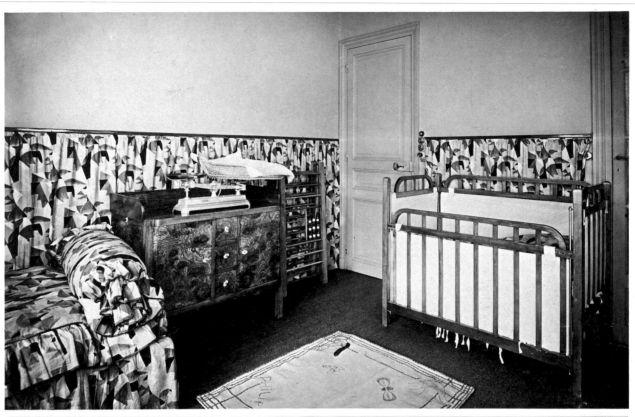

EN 740. Children's bedroom. Bed MP 23.

Couch MP 169, armchair MF 172, tulip table MB 170, strip lighting LA 321.

ES 505. The Dalsaces' apartment, Boulevard Saint-Germain, Paris, circa 1923. "La Religieuse" standard lamp 31, tapestry hanging and cushions from cartoons by Jean Lurçat.

K 265c. Apartment. Bookcase MU 1106.

EL 797. Apartment, circa 1928. Armchair MF 732, nesting table MB 106, "cosy corner."

ES 615. Apartment of M.G., circa 1925. Couch MP 169, nesting tables MB 106,
lamps LA 550.

ES 614. Apartment of M.G., circa 1925. French embassy desk MB 212, low chairs
MF 313.

ES 902. Apartment, circa 1928. Gondola chair MF 11.

ES 900. Apartment, circa 1928.

ES 828. Apartment, circa 1928. Armchair MF 232, stool 3.

EM 980. Apartment, chairs MF 275, radiator cover MT 407, MD 362, MD 407, wall-mounted table MB 440.

Above: EN 22. Armchair and occasional table, 1923.

Below: EN 12, three armchairs, 1923.

Circa 1923. The hexagonal-shaped backs with sloping panels have already been shown.

ES 66. Hélène Bernheim's lounge, known as the "Coromandel Room." Palm-tree
wood, bamboo, and coromandel screens. Circa 1925. Curved day-bed MP 167,
couch MP 174.

Hélène Bernheim's "Coromandel Room," circa 1925. Armchair MF 172, table MB 106, carpet PT 867 made by La Boutique, from a cartoon by Jean Burkhalter.

Left: ET 47. Bathroom, circa 1920. Table 10.
Right: ET 48. Bathroom, circa 1920.

ET 49. Bathroom, circa 1920. Glass marquetry, mirror.

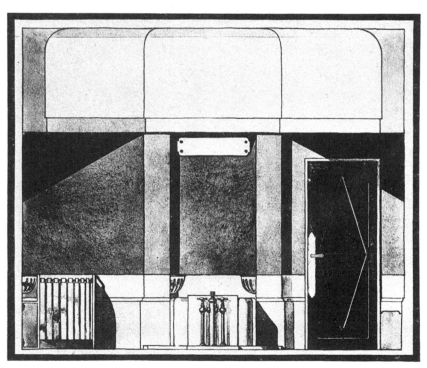

Designs for the bathroom, seen on pages 106–107.

ET 532, 508. Bathroom, circa 1925. Stool, cf. EN 508.

Bathroom, circa 1927. Dressing table MS 418, 419, bis, ter. Curved shower wall
in reinforced glass.

Bathroom, circa 1927. Chaise longue MF 980.

Bathroom, circa 1927. Low chair MF 313, dressing table MF 418, 419, bis, ter.

Floor and walls of the shower in the bathroom of the Maison de Verre. Gray
glazed mosaic tiles. 1930.

LTT Offices, Rue de la Faisanderie, Paris, 1932. Desk 11.

LTT offices, Rue de la Faisanderie, Paris. Unnumbered.

LTT offices, Rue de la Faisanderie, Paris. Unnumbered.

LTT offices, Rue de la Faisanderie, Paris. Unnumbered.

Apartment, circa 1925. Tulip table MB 170, occasional tables MB 106.

Apartment belonging to Madame G. (?). Table MB 130, lamp "La Petite
Religieuse" 32.

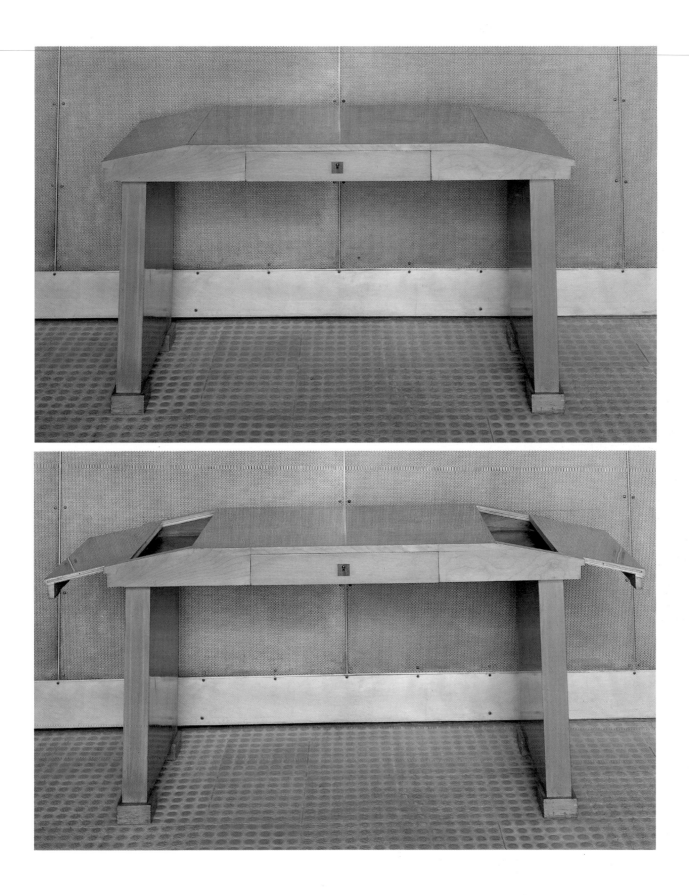

IV
THE INDIVIDUAL ARTIFACT AND STANDARDIZATION

EB 247. Entrance to the "Study-library of a French embassy." Exposition
Internationale des Arts Décoratifs et Industriels Modernes, Paris, 1925.

Characterized by the opposition between the decoration and architecture of interiors, there was also another controversy which raged during the twenties, over the costs and social application of design. Starting around 1925, it gathered momentum after 1930 when metal could be used on a larger scale. Heavily influenced by contemporary politics, the debate involved furniture designers and architects alike.

Nineteen twenty-five marked the eighth anniversary of the Russian Revolution. The influence of the Marxist approach on avant-garde intellectuals was considerable. And it was the U.S.S.R. pavilion at the Exposition Internationale des Arts Décoratifs et Industriels Modernes that attracted the attention of the more open-minded critics. Here was the modernity they wanted and could not find in many of the other exhibits. Amid the general critical disappointment, exception was made for the group of modern artists who had played a part in the project for "a French embassy."

After harsh words about the designs by Groult, Ruhlmann, and Dufrêne for a section of that embassy, Marie Dormoy wrote: "Fortunately the end of this visit made up for its beginning. Working along the same lines, from a similar starting point, three artists have come up with a fine ensemble. Chareau, Jourdain, and Mallet-Stevens worked in close collaboration and have managed to create an ensemble which we shall have little chance of seeing again. Chareau was commissioned to design the study-library. Here, at last, we find a work that is complete in itself and well arranged, designed by the artist to please himself, designed, in other words, with care and attention.

"As a member of the 'engineer-builders' rather than the 'colorist-decorators,' Chareau has designed a room with no visible walls; they are covered with shelving which in certain places is relieved by vertical planes. The wall covering is made of close-grained palm wood with a fibrous appearance to it. The room is thus in tonal gradations of a single color. In the middle of the room, two hollow posts support a cupola which reflects the light from a lamp at its center. Of use, then, only at night for artificial light, this cupola can be closed off by means of an ingenious mechanism concealed in one of the posts which controls an arrangement of palm-wood slats which fan out. The other post can also be opened out and it is designed to store valuable papers or books.

"The desk is located below the cupola; it is a perfect example of cabinetwork, designed like a piece of architecture, with sloping planes to prevent books and papers from piling up, conveying the orderliness and discipline which characterize modern life."[1]

There was, however, another question that concerned Marie Dormoy and her colleague Waldemar George. Interested as they were in the modern French school, they drew attention to its vagueness where social or political ideas were concerned. Talking of "aesthetic failure," Waldemar George considered that "the Exposition des Arts Décoratifs mark[ed] the triumph of illusion over life," and did not mince words when he concluded: "It is not the Exposition but decorative art that is antisocial, antidemocratic."[2]

Marie Dormoy went further and now linked Chareau and Ruhlmann together:

1. Marie Dormoy, "Les Intérieurs à l'Exposition Internationale des Arts Décoratifs," L'Amour de l'Art, no. 8, August 1925, pp. 312–323.

2. Waldemar George, "L'Exposition des Arts Décoratifs et Industriels de 1925: les tendances générales," L'Amour de l'Art, no. 8, August 1925, p. 285.

3. Dormoy, *op. cit.*, p. 318.

"Whatever Ruhlmann and Chareau might think, and with them, a good number of admirers, there is no question that in a period of collectivism such as our own, the original artifact will die out and give way to mass-produced furniture."[3]

This early attack was the prelude to ideas that came soon after to back up the Bauhaus experiments and, above all, the Paris exhibition of the Deutscher Werkbund in 1930. The conflict ceased to be about form, and entered the much livelier terrain of the purpose of design. Linked to this was another question of the day, centered on the industrialization and popularization of new designs.

Here, as elsewhere, Pierre Chareau left no written record of his opinions. Once again, we must look to his work for an answer. And it provides us with yet more evidence of his originality, his marginality, and the endlessly ambivalent situations he had to deal with.

A ROLE IN THE DEBATE

Deep down, Chareau was not really very interested in all the talk about popularizing design. His natural temperament and the contact he had with his clients were not likely to force him into taking a stand. He had made a choice in 1919 and sided with modernity. He knew the grounds on which it was founded; his importance was recognized, and he was even considered to be a precursor. But what happened within the Modern Movement, what followed from it, its social implications—none of this meant very much to him. Chareau tried his hand at everything. He would make use of the best of any system; he was committed to doing this and yet was no militant. He set pen to paper to make his position clearer only once, and this was prompted by his bitter reaction to the Depression. The article bore evidence of his left-wing sympathies, and is unique.[4]

4. Pierre Chareau, "La création artistique et l'imitation commerciale" in *Architecture d'Aujourd'hui*, no. 9, September 1935, pp. 68–69.

Not once did Chareau have a theory to propound. No work of his bears any sign of a wish to lead or even educate. He never drew up a manifesto. He built for the needs of his time. This in itself was a position to take, but one that was in-built, as it were, in a piece of furniture or architecture.

Chareau showed no sign of hesitation when the Artistes Modernes left the Salon des Artistes Décorateurs in 1930, and he took part in the first exhibition of the Union des Artistes Modernes (U.A.M.). Here, it was personal connections which guided him. His friends, colleagues, and oldest collaborators exhibited alongside. The option he took had a formal, aesthetic, and emotional basis to it.

When the break that led to the U.A.M. occurred, Ernest Tisserand noted: "The youngest and most committed group would not accept the conditions it had to comply with and chose to boycott it. Speaking for this congenial band of artists that were once the avant-garde of the Salon des Décorateurs, Djo-Bourgeois told me: 'I'm not in fact exhibiting at the Décorateurs. We want to form a group, Mallet-Stevens, Chareau, Francis Jourdain, Herbst, Le Corbusier, Charlotte Perriand, and others, so that we can break away from the compartmentalizing that is such a feature of the association mentioned. This couldn't be done from within. So we all decided to boycott it. There are about twenty of us with a similar outlook. Some will be delighted at the news, and the Salon will be more consistent as a result.' What Djo-Bourgeois did not mention was that the Salon committee were intimidated by the sight of artists as young, as dedicated, and as daring as Le Corbusier and Chareau, gathering around Francis Jourdain, the undisputed master of modern decorative art."

So Chareau showed his support for the Artistes Modernes by participating in their first exhibition at the Pavillon de Marsan in 1930, but he was not an active member of the group. In the catalogue he is described as a "guest." Perhaps this status indicated some divergency or doubts raised at the time. There is no real proof of this, however. His active membership in the U.A.M. was confirmed by subsequent exhibitions. Like other members of the Union, he never went back to the Salon des Artistes Décorateurs. Although once the break between the Décorateurs and the Modernes was complete, Chareau made no further commitment. In 1932, he was on the U.A.M. committee, and went as far as to advocate a general pooling of ideas,* but his attitude to the industrialization of design remained unchanged. As for manifestos, he left it to his friend René Herbst and Le Corbusier to be the spokesmen and figureheads of the movement.

* Details of this are given in the minutes of a U.A.M. committee meeting held on July 2, 1931: "Pierre Chareau asked for the aims of the U.A.M. to be defined: was it a sharing of interests or ideas? He felt it had to be a sharing of ideas, otherwise what was the point of breaking with the Artistes Décorateurs who had greater means at their disposal? Jean Fouquet suggested that if this were so, a general line should be followed so that the group's tendencies could be made clear. In his opinion, exhibitions were only one aspect of the U.A.M. This aside, was an ideal incompatible with material interests?

"Pierre Chareau thought it was. He could envisage a new approach to displaying work at exhibitions. He would like to see stands disappear. Mallet-Stevens asked for more details. Chareau suggested that everyone could be asked to contribute the money that he would have spent on an individual stand to the collective group so that a collective display could be made." This idea was followed when Chareau and Mallet-Stevens were put in charge of the 1932 U.A.M. exhibition display.

A NATURAL INCLINATION

Nineteen thirty ushered in the first decade of the reign of metal furniture. For several years already, Chareau's own explorations had led to an increasingly varied use of metal, although he did not see this as a chance to move towards mass production. He remained an aesthete.

He had held to the same elitist views ever since 1924, when he told Léon Moussinac: "It's a question of organizing space according to rhythms which come to us and are felt more strongly as each day goes past, so that our minds, and the feelings we have that arose out of, and are part of, the wondrous beauty of existence, are more fully satisfied."

In 1930, he continued to work in this direction. Two years before, he had started on the construction of the Maison de Verre. With the heavy work finished, he shut himself away with his craftsmen inside the empty shell. And here he came up with his reply to the debate over the individual artifact and industrialization. To it, he linked three questions: the relationship with clients, the relationship with craftsmen, and the use of modular units.

Chareau liked direct relationships with clients, with nothing to come between them. It is no accident that he never joined a "workshop," never worked for the Studium of the Louvre or the Bon Marché store's Boutique Pomone. There was only one exception to this; in 1925, he designed the Primavera stall for the Printemps department stores at the Exposition Internationale des Arts Décoratifs et Industriels Modernes, but it was nothing more than a temporary display. Primavera did not commercialize any of his furniture. Chareau, in fact, took care of his own affairs. He designed and made boutique no. 9 for the urban art exhibition in the 1924 Salon d'Automne, so that his skills were displayed before the public eye. In that same year, he opened La Boutique at 3 Rue du Cherche-Midi, next to the future Galerie Jeanne Bucher. Here, along with his own designs, he exhibited and displayed those of his friends (such as Rose Adler and Hélène Henry) and commercialized still more (Jean Burkhalter's carpets, for example). Since space there was limited, he resorted to a sales catalogue. Visitors could consult the large albums, bound in green leather, which contained photographs of single items of furniture or ensembles.*

Everything suggests that Chareau enjoyed talking over building or interior design projects, using such talks as a basis for the original solutions he was to come up with. He was even happier to do this when his clients were friends. For the most part, these were the friends that he would see regularly at Madame Dalsace's salon or in gatherings like the Rue Nollet circle. There could be no disputing that his friends were bourgeois! Industrialists, financiers, or professionals, his clients and patrons had sizeable incomes. And while their philosophical, religious, or political views may have differed, they had in common a love of well-

---

* These catalogues with their coded photographs are the basis of the Chareau archives together with the list of works at the end of this book.

La Boutique, 3 Rue du Cherche-Midi, Paris.

made things, of smooth, fine, or untreated surfaces, and hated lavish displays of luxury and superfluous ornamentation. The great debate thus involved his clients and friends as much as himself.

The contact Chareau had with craftsmen was also significant. Characterized by commitment, loyalty, and exigence, this relationship was one of the designer's greatest advantages. Without craftsmen, he would have been like a conductor without an orchestra. Although he was utterly incapable of running a business or even a workshop, he was able to make his ideas and preferences known, appreciated, and respected, and he knew how to use their craftsmanship and skills. When interviewed by Guillaume Janneau for *Formes nouvelles et programmes nouveaux* (Paris, 1925), he described this as follows: "The plans of a building are part of the job, the work of an architect. The interest lies in coming up with original ideas. But these should be applied freely. The initiative should be left to the builder. The architect's task should be confined to supplying a theoretical solution to a set project, leaving it to the executant to work out the measurements. This, apparently, was the way things were done in medieval times. The inventiveness of the builder should be respected and encouraged; in architecture as in furniture, the craftsman will hit upon ideas that the designer or planner would never have dreamed of. We should go back to this kind of collaboration. An architect is not a craftsman, but a mathematician and philosopher;

he's an inventor of three-dimensional arrangements, not a mason. Our more recent forebears liked to confuse these things and subordinate art to skilled craftsmanship. Art is the spirit of the work and nothing can take its place."

Chareau reveals a great deal of himself in this evaluation of his own role, and that of the craftsman, the freedom he had to have and the specific advantages of his initiative.

In this context, the part Louis Dalbet played is particularly instructive. The first record of his collaboration with Chareau dates from 1924. The Salon d'Automne catalogue reads as follows:

"*Boutique no. 9 – Pierre Chareau.*

"Collaborating: Pierre Chareau, furniture and light fittings; Burkhalter, fabrics; Survage, fabrics; Jean Lurçat, wallpaper and tapestries; Dalbet, ironwork."

This was the period when Chareau started exploring the possible uses of metal. For a while he was limited to wrought iron. He exhibited his first plant stands and the Cubist-inspired metal and alabaster light fittings.

Dalbet was then running a family ironwork business. Jean and André,* his two sons, worked alongside four other employees. Louis Dalbet trained at the Robert workshop. Around 1912, he had worked as a journeyman around France and then set up on his own. He opened a workshop at 4 bis, Rue Capron specializing in decorative wrought-iron work. Concentrating on railings, banisters, and fireguards, he also did all the ironwork for the well-known Brasserie Bofinger. From time to time, he would design items and exhibit at the Salon d'Automne. In 1917, he was awarded the Prix de Rome for a gate he designed. A year after his meeting with Chareau in 1923, their collaboration was well under way. He was Chareau's own choice and was the only ironworker to work for him from then on. He had a share in setting up La Boutique at 3 Rue du Cherche-Midi. He came up with a style that was quite different from Art Deco. In 1928, the full range of his skills was applied to the interior furnishings for the Grand-Hôtel at Tours. By the time he moved in with Chareau to work on the Maison de Verre a year later, there were numerous examples of their joint productions. The best known of these are the light fittings, and also the many variations on the metal and wood desk, with a fixed or swivel shelf, or no shelf, with or without a locker, in sycamore or walnut. Photographs of work in progress in the Maison de Verre show the benches and vises that the ironworker set up on the site of the main hallway. The permanent fixtures in the Maison de Verre, the railings, banisters, sliding doors, bathroom fittings, and wall cupboards of the third floor are essentially all Dalbet's work.

None of the worksheets or detailed plans for the building in the Rue Saint-Guillaume have survived. Were they all Chareau's work? Were they sent out to

* André Dalbet was able to check over the author's original French manuscript. His technical advice was invaluable.

Louis Dalbet (André and Françoise Dalbet photograph).

be done and if so by whom? There is no way of knowing. All that remains is a few perspective studies, some of which have been colored in, and these, it so happens, are fairly accurate. Not one of them has dimensions marked in. And this poses a question: how was it possible to produce original pieces of furniture of such complexity? André Dalbet who worked there at the time has an explanation: "You had to set to work the minute you were given an idea, some gesture, a scribbling or enthusiastic prompting." In every case, from the bow-fronted door at the foot of the main staircase, to the broom cupboard in the dining room, to the linen chest in the bathroom, hundreds of hours were spent perfecting the templates, bending the duralumin or perforated metal sheets, bolting and fixing hinges on them, and finally assembling them. Whatever Chareau, or his collaborator Bijvoët, may have specified, the responsibility for the work lay ultimately with Dalbet. It was he, for example, who had to devise the slot—and make it, he did, perfectly—that meant that a door on the landing could slide freely, in spite of the balustrade in its way.

5. Kenneth Frampton, "Maison de Verre," *Perspecta 12*, The Yale Architectural Journal, p. 78.

Kenneth Frampton spoke of the "poetry of the fittings" in the Maison de Verre.[5] These fittings were largely the work of Louis Dalbet. It is high time that he is given his rightful place in the story of the Maison de Verre. The quality of the building, its perfect state of preservation, the doors that glide as smoothly today as they ever did, are all his doing, with the quality of his soldering and finishing touches.

Dalbet's work, his ability and know-how, meant that Chareau could give more thought to the units and small ensembles.

Although Dalbet had workbenches in the Maison de Verre, he must have produced most of the items Chareau commissioned in his workshop. André Dalbet comments: "In the workshop, my father, brother, and I executed the designs on the basis of a few ideas." In the absence of more precise evidence, it is possible that only the final assembling and finishing were done on the spot. The templates, sheet-bending, hinges, and basic soldering are likely to have been done in the Rue Capron workshop. It is quite probable that the block structures at the corners of the balustrade bookshelves on the first and second floors, along with the structures that fit over the bookcases and the cupboard lockers of the dining room and second floor, were made in the workshop, then transported and soldered together in the Rue Saint-Guillaume before finally being mounted. Eight units can be counted in the first category here, and thirteen in the second. Each of them, according to type, are perfectly identical, and could be seen as a small series production. But Chareau was not content to line them up as they were. Wherever there was repetition, he broke the monotony with a joint of some kind. He also made use of the ironworkers' skills and set to work on the angle joints. He would break a unit up and rather than link two elements in a straightforward rectilinear way, he would come up with a totally new piece. A model or unit would turn into a monumental, original artifact. Chareau introduced visual rhythms in this way, which did not tire the eye.

Chareau never really knew the world of true industrial design. True, he stopped making individual items in 1932, but he did not go very far. He designed furniture for small series to be made either in wood or metal. When he had units made, he assembled them into a unique and unreproducible item on a larger scale. Clearly industrialization was not for him. His contribution lies elsewhere, in the intelligence he gave to the design of a unit and in the quality of execution. Even in his utilization of metal (which is ideal industrial material), he was still a creator of individual artifacts, working with craftsmen rather than with a factory.*

* Commissioned by Schneider and sponsored by the Office Technique pour l'Utilisation de l'Acier, he did, however, design stainless-steel units for ship cabins (1934) and made components for school furniture. We do not know whether these units were manufactured on an industrial scale.

MT 876

MT 876 (details)

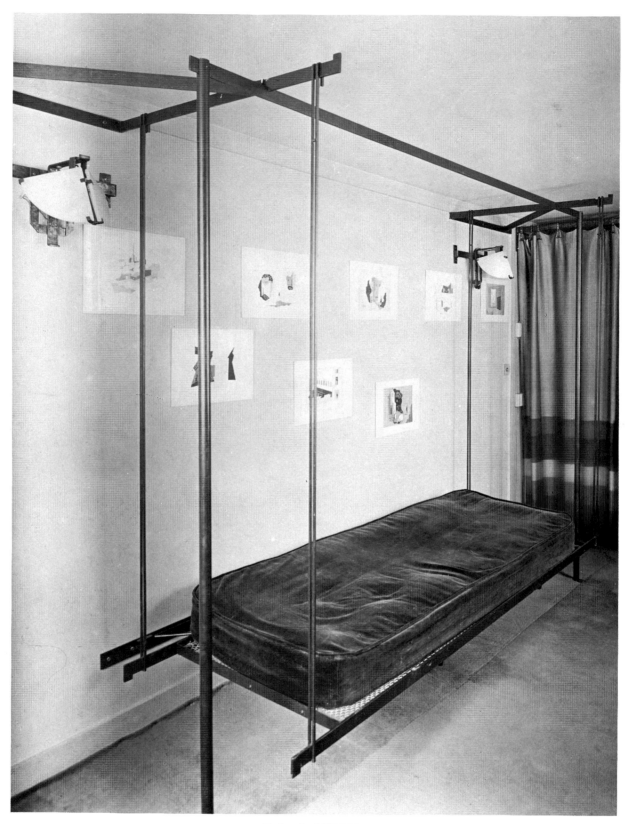

Swing bed EF 928.

V
METALWORK AND
METAL TRAINING

MB 812

"The use of metal in furniture did not arise from an aesthetic doctrine; quite the contrary, an aesthetic principle is only now emerging from what has been produced. For a long time now we have had to use metal for certain specific purposes; if the advantages it has are sufficient to make us broaden its application, then our whole environment will be utterly transformed."[1] So wrote Max Terrier in 1930. Metal had been appearing in sitting rooms and apartments for about three years already. Not that it had been totally absent beforehand, but up until then, its use had been limited to certain well-defined functions. Steel safes, painted iron garden chairs, public benches on cast-iron legs were nothing new. Metal tubing had crept into bedrooms; brass bedsteads had held pride of place there since the 1860s. But the presence of metal remained discreet, hidden away from the heart of bourgeois intimacy.

The use of iron and then steel in architecture had no repercussions on furniture. The cold materials and aesthetics of industrial design belonged to the work place, not to the home. Keen to get away from the prejudices of the past century, Ernest Tisserand commented: "We ought to have seen [it in the home] from as early as 1889 when the Eiffel Tower was built. But the nineteenth century remained stubborn to the end. And still more years passed before it became apparent that a new idea was in ferment. Even so, we cannot recall having seen one single example of all-metal furniture in 1925."[2]

Several factors led to the sudden insurgence of metal in the furniture design of the thirties. Three are widely acknowledged: the scarcity of exotic woods, new forms of domestic heating, and current tastes.

Ernest Tisserand continues: "Law is born of need. And in this case the need is twofold. First of all, exotic woods have become scarce and the need for new materials in current furniture making is becoming more and more pressing. Metal is not the only answer.... But metal has proved to be the principal material which can be used without a long prior treatment. And it has met another need, itself born out of a complete revolution in heating methods. Close proximity to radiators soon gets the better of the driest, the most supple, the best-assembled of woods." And the third factor: "Around the same time, others realized that tastes had changed with the development of industry, or to put it plainly, that a factory was no longer such a ghastly thing, and a well-designed automobile could be considered amongst the most elegant inventions."

Along with these objective factors are the characteristics of the material itself, which, in a period marked by austerity and a return to pure line, allowed for all kinds of bold experiments. "It is the most versatile 'material' we have at our disposal," Max Terrier exclaimed; "it will take any form we give it and even a very small volume has a very high resistance.

"It can satisfy an enormous variety of requirements; furniture can be made for a very specific function, which often would be impossible to make in any other way; in wood, such purpose-built furniture would not be so simple; tenon-and-mortise joints weaken an upright, but welding has no such effect.... Metallic

1. Max Terrier, "Meubles métalliques (Les Sièges)," Art et Décoration, no. 1, 1930, Vol. LVII, pp. 33–48.

2. Ernest Tisserand, "Le Meuble métallique et son avenir," L'Amour de l'Art, no. 11, November 1929, pp. 418–427.

furniture is lightweight and easy to move.... Unlike wood, it is not harmed by a slight knock or a drop of water left on its surface.... It does not require any particular care."[3]

3. Terrier, op. cit.

Given such qualities, it is not easy to understand why it should have taken so long to use metal in furniture. But it is commonly, and wrongly, assumed that the first designs for metal furniture involved such things as metal tubing for chairs. The reality of the situation was quite different. From the metal chest of the Middle Ages to the tubular chair, there were developments apart from those cited above, and a range of things to explore, from furniture accessories to construction techniques.

The increasing number of heated homes seems to have been a decisive factor in the development of techniques.

"The miscalculations of furniture makers multiplied to the point where they began to design wardrobes, bookcases, and cupboards with metal frameworks and were happy to recommend the use of wrought iron for pedestal tables and other furniture placed near radiators. It was this, more than anything else, that prompted the undying popularity of wrought-iron work."[4]

4. Tisserand, op. cit., p. 422.

But there were other effects too, and new solutions. "In order to counteract the drawbacks of wood shrinking in dry atmospheres, Ruhlmann has designed furniture consisting of metal structures over which panels of solid wood can contract or expand."[5]

5. Léon Deshairs, "Une étape vers le meuble métallique?," Art et Décoration, January-June 1927, Vol. LI, p. 104.

Pierre Chareau was part of this movement. He knew every phase of it, from wrought iron to tubing. A pioneer in the use of metal, sometimes he would stop half-way and leave his contemporaries to develop their research in specific fields (such as tubular chrome structures). Sometimes his creative mind led him into uncharted areas which he was alone in exploring, as in the case of his large duralumin ensembles. Always he displayed an unfailing ingenuity and gave free reign to his sensibility.

PIONEER RESEARCH

Chareau became interested in the possible uses of metal as early as 1923. His collaboration with Dalbet, whose technical influence was to be so great, dates from this time, as we have already seen. To start with, at Chareau's request, the ironworker was involved in making home accessories, such as plant stands, radiator shelves, and fireguards. Then work on light fittings opened up another field for exploration. The standard lamp known as "La Religieuse" ("The Nun"),* the composite and bracket lamps included in certain of the ensembles of 1923

*This passage on "La Religieuse" is taken from André Dalbet's notes: "An idea of Pierre Chareau's: a dress surmounted by a coiffe. All that remains is to convey this in sheet metal and alabaster. I cut out the horizontal base line by dipping the rolled sheet in a tub of water. This is how the line was marked in."

were made up of fabric or alabaster shades mounted on metallic structures.

Around 1926, the use of metal became more prevalent, and by the following year, it well-nigh dominated Chareau's furniture design. This was when he exhibited the series of desks with writing surfaces, lockers, or wooden shelves encased in metal floor supports. Comparing the different approaches to metal furniture making, Léon Deshairs commented, in this context: "Furthest away from every kind of tradition is the solution Pierre Chareau has come up with, in a few pieces of uncompromisingly robust furniture. Here, there is nothing to remind us of the tricks of the cabinetmaker's trade. The main wooden bodywork of the furniture is fixed in the most straightforward way possible to wrought-iron supports. A small linen cupboard, a perfectly plain rectangular chest in sycamore, is supported by a large strip of metal surrounding it on three sides, terminating at the base in inward-facing feet. Another oblong cupboard is suspended in the same way, and, hinged to another iron-framed mirror, it can open out to a more or less obtuse angle. The body of a desk in palisander rests on two supports, each consisting of four iron strips, linked at their base by another pleated strip."[6]   6. Deshairs, *op. cit.*, p. 109.

AN EARLY PREDILECTION FOR WROUGHT IRON

All through this period, Pierre Chareau employed only one technique, and that was hammer-wrought iron. He used nothing but flat sheet metal and angle bars. The strips he used for the metal and wood desks were quite thick (about 8 mm or just over ⅜ inch). He had Dalbet cut and bend them. Solderings were made only rarely, and were ground and hammered over so they were virtually invisible. Most of the pieces were screwed together. The rough quality of unpolished steel was added to by hammering;* everything was done to avoid an overly smooth monotonous surface. Decarbonized, heat-burnished, and waxed iron thus came to stand for the creative partnership between the designer and the craftsman, and the influence of the latter's technique on the designer's sensibility. Industrialization could not have been further from their minds. There was no reason why it should have been. This was the world of craftsmanship and small-scale production.

As yet, Chareau had not embarked on the production of all-metal furniture. He played with the harmonies and contrasts between materials. He joined iron to exotic woods such as sycamore, oiled mahogany, macassar ebony. He linked rigid black angle bars to supple pale wickerwork. He combined cold metal with warm leather, hard iron with comfortable fabrics. In the interior designs he carried out for the Dreyfus family and M.F., permanent fixtures (in metal for the most part) and articles of furniture in joinery or cabinetwork are featured side by side. "In both these ensembles," Pierre Migennes noted, "iron is used extremely sob-

*This technique is described by André Dalbet as follows: "It's a light irregular hammering. The hammer used can be as round as a marble or only slightly convex. It's nothing to do with decoration; it's a texturing of the metal sheet."

7. Pierre Migennes, "Sur deux ensembles de Pierre Chareau," *Art et Décoration*, Vol. LXI, 1932, p. 132.

erly, with none of that nickel-plate shine that we have got used to over the years. This and the wood create an atmosphere of warmth and intimacy, which has become increasingly hard to find in modern interior decoration."[7]

In the Maison de Verre, Chareau combined metal with glass and moved on to develop true metal joinery. At the same time, he began to look at the technique of metal tubing.

THE LARGE ENSEMBLES IN METAL AND METAL TUBING

Chareau's use of tubing started with work for the Grand-Hôtel at Tours. In the reading and correspondence room, he designed tables with H-shaped supports that were made of parkerized tubular metal. The metal was neither bent nor soldered. It was the knuckle joints that linked the tubes, ensured stability, and broke the monotony of straight lines. The writing table and high bar stools were in a sense an elegant form of mobile scaffolding. High up on their supports, the solid mahogany surfaces seem suspended in midair.

It was only when the work in the Rue Saint-Guillaume was nearing completion, around the time that the influence of the Werkbund exhibition was taking effect in French furniture design, that Pierre Chareau produced a few items of pure tubular furniture. He designed a table: a circular surface in thick glass which rests on a stand of three black tubes, soldered between two rings of tubing so that they appear to be twisted to the limits of their resistance. Another table, two fragments of a circle at different heights, stands on two bent duralumin tubes. Here, as elsewhere, Chareau allowed for black paint but not electrolysis. Chrome and nickel plating do not appear to have interested him at all, at least where movable furniture and reception rooms were concerned. When the iron or duralumin was left bare, he kept it unpolished and untreated, or at the most he blackened it. The large coat and hat racks in the Maison de Verre illustrate this. The framework, two rounded rectangles, and the base are painted black, while the hat rack and the hooks are matt, in unpolished duralumin.

In a commentary on the article by Ernest Tisserand on metal furniture, a colleague of his, F. Fosca wrote: "If we look at the illustrations accompanying the article, we find that the interior decorators have concentrated all their efforts on seats and tables, and very few have tackled large ensembles, chests of drawers, desks, and cupboards. But this is where the real problem lies, in my opinion, since heavy furniture means large, flat surfaces. How should they be treated? People have found that office furniture can be painted with satisfactory results. But this is only for want of a better alternative. Moreover, it is hard to imagine these large surfaces polished, quite apart from the difficulty of keeping them that way. When wood is mottled or veined, it has a very attractive surface quality to it. I believe it might be possible to obtain something like this stippled effect with the use of patinas, or with certain kinds of sheet-metal hammering, which the Japanese have used to great effect."[8]

8. in *L'Amour de l'Art*. See note 2.

The Dalbet workshop in the Rue Capron (André and Françoise Dalbet photograph).

This observation is particularly apposite. Chareau would have agreed entirely. He found the scale he was happiest at working on in the large metal ensembles which form the major part of the permanent fixtures in the Maison de Verre. Here he entered a territory unknown to his contemporaries. He had the courage to get fitted wall cupboards made with bow-fronted doors; he had the inventiveness to come up with the three functions of the large linen cupboard and the duralumin bathroom partitions. We are far now from the early accessories. Apart from the sanitary ware, everything in this room is made of duralumin. Depending on where they are situated, over the rubber-surfaced step onto the terrace or the terrazzo flooring towards the corridor, the wall-cupboard doors are full-length or half-length, with supports that are visible, along with their feet, which are encased in matt nickel or "old silver."

Chareau concentrated on forms, the reasons for them, their volume and color. Max Terrier made the astute observation that "in areas where metal is not essential, particularly when it is used for purely decorative purposes, the most varied metals can be utilized—copper, zinc, aluminum, duralumin, and all kinds of bronze. In this way, it is possible to obtain a range of colors from red to the palest yellow and silver white . . . . To this variety of colors may be added a variety of patinas which give a metal a shiny, matt, or very soft quality." Chareau understood this very well. To the harmony of materials allied with metal, he added a symphony of colors and tonalities.

The interest the designer had in wrought iron and in blackened metal which had no distracting reflections to it has already been referred to. Chareau changed tack in the bathroom of the Maison de Verre, but kept to his principles. He retained the natural appearance of duralumin, which he refused to polish up. Its matt quality, the absence of shine and reflection, the relationship it had with the glazed tiling pleased him. In contrast, he put up a shelf which had a glowing yellow patina, polished to give a reflection. He encased the feet of the cupboards with a metal, the pale shine of which is set against the dark gray terrazzo flooring. He selected matt nickel, copper, and brass from the color range of metals. Wishing to be consistent, he left the chrome piping of the sanitary ware uncovered. Everywhere polished surfaces were answered by matt surfaces, while warm colors softened the cold tonal register of the duralumin.

But the most admirable quality of Dalbet's metal joinery is the thought that lies behind it. The versatility of the material did not lead the designer into a dead end of pure lyricism. Form, with the new freedom it had acquired, did not override function. It was still possible, as it had been in 1923, to talk of the interior layout of a piece of furniture. Gaston Varenne had written of Pierre Chareau then: "He wants more than the exterior of an object to be 'on a modern scale,' to borrow his expression; he is concerned to match the interior layout of a piece of furniture to our needs. Creating volumes within a given space is a formula that he also applies to the inside of a cupboard, dressing table, or bookcase. To simplify life, and make it more agreeable and comfortable, he will plan a logical system for tidying objects away so that they can be found without any danger of wasting valuable time . . . ."[9]

Written about the furniture Chareau made in wood, the remark could be applied equally well to the metal joinery. For the offices of La Semaine à Paris, for example, he designed some small individual metal tables. Into them he built an electrical system that was positioned in such a way as to cast light on the paper without dazzling the person writing.*

Similarly, every detail of the wall cupboard in the bathroom of the Maison de Verre seems to correspond to some everyday requirement that had occurred to Chareau or his client: from the curtain of the medicine cabinet, the semicylindrical door that pivots round to reveal articles of a humble nature, to the hinged towel racks. And always there are a few more lyrical elements to be found, overlaying the cold, rational procedure: the rounded corners, the mirror that can be blanked off, the soap trays, and so on.

In the coldest of environments, Chareau remained true to what he was deep down, a poet.

9. Gaston Varenne, "L'Esprit moderne de Pierre Chareau," Art et Décoration, January-June 1923, Vol. XLIII, p. 134.

*Completed in 1930, the offices of La Semaine à Paris were one of the most prestigious collaborative efforts of the Modern Movement. Behind the Mallet-Stevens façade, enhanced by Barillet's stained glass and a plaque by Jan and Joël Martel, lay furniture ensembles by Chareau, Francis Jourdain, Djo-Bourgeois, Charlotte Perriand, Charlotte Alix, and Louis Sognot. André Salomon arranged the lighting. Hélène Henry and Sonia Delaunay designed the wall hangings.

Bathroom of the Maison de Verre, brass soap tray.

Maison de Verre: *Above*, slot enabling door to slide free of balustrade, made by
Dalbet (duralumin, perforated duralumin, black-painted metal).

Below, basic unit for the balustrade bookshelves of the second and third floors
(metal and perforated metal sheeting).

Maison de Verre: Main hallway. The balustrade bookshelves were assembled
from several identical units. Treated separately, the corner makes this a unique
artifact of huge proportions.

(detail)

MB 405. Desk belonging to Robert Mallet-Stevens.

Small wrought-iron table, version with three surfaces 9.

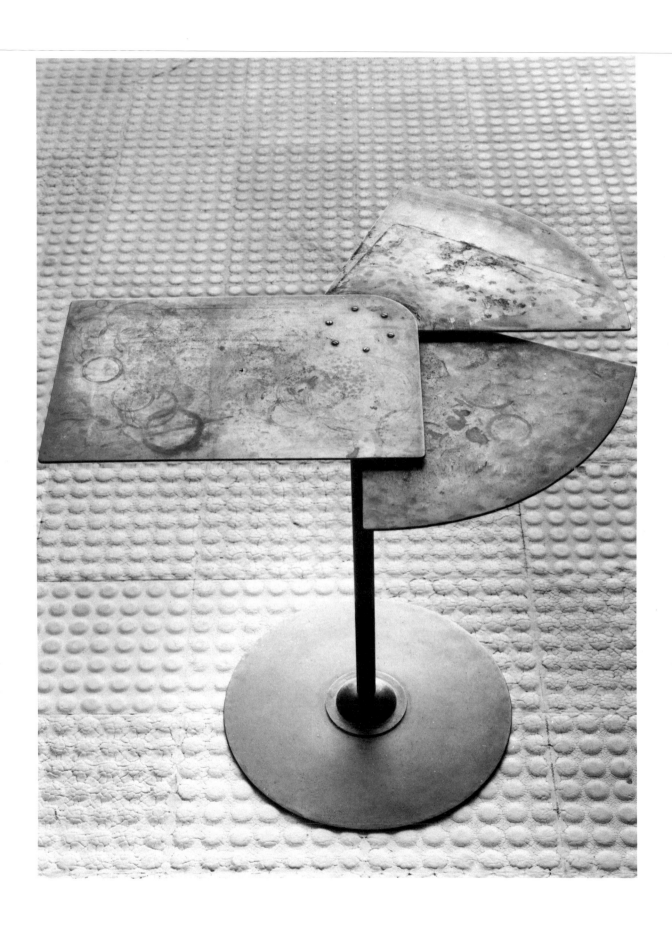

MB 744

Coat rack in the Maison de Verre 39.

Above: 14.
Below: 4.

Left: MT 1004.
Right: MT 344.

PR 291

Left: Display of furniture for the hall of La Semaine à Paris, bookcase MU 871, chair EZ 848, table EZ 849.

Right: Maison de Verre. Staircase from the doctor's consulting-room to the small study and the second floor. Black-painted metal tubing, collapsible grating steps.

174

Maison de Verre. Main staircase, with no stair risers or banister. Bolted U-shaped angle bars in duralumin. Stairs covered with natural rubber. Slate floor tiling.

Maison de Verre. Chareau's utilization of units is shown clearly here in the balustrade bookshelves of the third floor. They also serve as an additional screen between the intense light of the façade and the relatively dark corridor that leads to the bedrooms.

VI

OBSESSIONS
AND VARIATIONS
ON A THEME

MD 362, MD or MT 407.

There are certain formal propensities to be found so frequently throughout Chareau's work that we may justifiably call them obsessions. Not least among such obsessions was the preoccupation with volumes that could be moved, altered, or extended. Several architects and critics have spoken of his kinetic approach.[1] What exactly do they mean by this? Chareau was neither the first nor the only designer to see that mobility was one way of increasing the number of functions an article of furniture could have. The traditional French secrétaire à abattant with its pull-down flap serving as a writing table, and the extending table both resulted from the same kind of functional attitude to mobility. What is unique to Chareau's investigation is simply the amount of importance he gave to it. A glance at the catalogue of his designs, or photographs of his buildings or interiors will reveal an astonishing number of examples of his kinetic invention. Certain desks are equipped with lockers that can only be opened if the person at the desk is seated and pulls them out around him. Untidy drawers thus cannot be seen, valuables are hidden away. A gaming table unfolds like a handkerchief (in the eighteenth-century manner), spaces out the players around the green baize and provides them with room for their drinks, cards, and cigarettes.

Chareau seems to have been particularly fascinated by fanning or unfolding movements. We remember that as early as 1924, he devised a system for lighting the Study-library of a French embassy which was based on a fan partition. This could be opened out to reduce the light from the white cupola above it. It was, in fact, the culmination of a technique that had been put to the test in the Salon d'Automne of 1923. At the 1927 Exposition d'Art Décoratif Contemporain organized by the Union Centrale des Arts Décoratifs, he made use of the same idea above one of the first metal and wood desks he exhibited. Later in the Maison de Verre, he had two sliding partitions built out of hinged rectangular panels; when pulled out, they resemble a screen; closed, they are like a folded fan.*

But the use of elongated, linked triangular panels was not limited to interior decoration. He produced them on a smaller scale, too. In 1924, he designed a low fan or pull-out table, several versions of which still exist. Made in palm wood, solid mahogany, or mahogany exterior with palisander interior, in some versions the four separate units are linked by a bronze hinge. In others the two, three, or four units are independent and fit into each other freely, to form a nest of tables. Chareau continued this obsessive idea in his metal furniture. For La Semaine à Paris he made a small table with three wings to it, one rectangular and two quadrants, hinged onto a tubular pivot (in blackened or parkerized metal). Certain chairs of the same period have a specific function. One of them in black-painted metal has a flat back and a seat made up of three slightly curved surfaces that collapse into one when the seat is folded up.

In the same category are the palisander or mahogany shelves mounted on an axis made of thick strip metal, which fan out around the side of a radiator.

1. Guillaume Janneau refers to his "cinematographic" effects in "Le Mouvement Moderne: première exposition d'art décoratif contemporain," La Renaissance de l'Art Français, no. 4, April 1923, pp. 203–208.

*See also the partition between the bar and smoking lounge of the Grand-Hôtel at Tours (curved wooden units in metal frameworks, moving along a guiding rail).

Closer examination reveals that Chareau's work concentrated on circular motions rather than on movements to the side or up and down. All the same, there is more than one kind of circular motion.

To begin with, there is the movement of a side section of a cylinder around its own axis. Thus we have the bow-fronted door in metal and glass at the bottom of the main stairs of the Maison de Verre, which is a quarter-cylinder pivoting on an invisible axis.

There is the movement of a side section of a cylinder along one of its sides. The garden gate in the Maison de Verre, one of the bathroom cupboards, and a kitchen cupboard all illustrate this.

But there is also what could be called multiple-motion furniture, or furniture with a series of complex movements. Two examples stand out here, because of their high degree of elaboration. These are the clothes cupboard and the linen cupboard in the bathroom of the same house.

The first is in the category of cylinder sections moving around their central axis. The door turns round to reveal the clothes, but there is also a mirror behind it, which can be pulled out to replace the door. Once this is pushed back, you can pick a suit hanging from a circular structure. Three requirements of a person dressing are satisfied here; you can select an item at your ease, try it on and look at yourself, and put it back all on the spot.

The linen cupboard is even more complex. It is a real tour de force, a demonstration of virtuosity in metal joinery. When closed, the front is composed of two segments of a cylinder side by side, supported vertically on a long I-shaped mount. Pushed back to the end of two guiding rails, each compartment is immobilized. To open them, first you have to pull them towards you to the point where the rails end in circles and then swivel them round with a pull of the handles (motion 1). Once opened, two flat surfaces face you. You then push a button so that these turn again (motion 2), and disappear into the back, and the drawers then appear. In painted, perforated sheet metal mounted on rollers, these can be pulled out so that clothes can be found or put away easily (motion 3).

Another recurrent form in Chareau's work is the sloping surface or side. The best-known example with this feature prominent is the French embassy desk. Chareau felt that there should be some semblance of order on surfaces used for work. Piles of papers and files seemed to him to be unnecessary and unattractive. Recognizing that such disorder was difficult to avoid, he decided to make use of the shape of the desk itself to prevent what was, in his eyes, an offense to order and beauty. And so he tilted the outer ends of the work top. Given that no paper or note could rest on this incline, they had to be filed away if they were not to make the work surface that was available impossibly cramped. He must have considered the outcome of this reasoning as conclusive, since sloping sides can be found in several groups of furniture, in different types of furniture even. They figure in the small ladies' writing desks in sycamore, where the slopes cover pigeonholes concealed by pull-out slides, as well as in the metal-legged writing

Wardrobe in the Reifenberg apartment, MA 537–540.

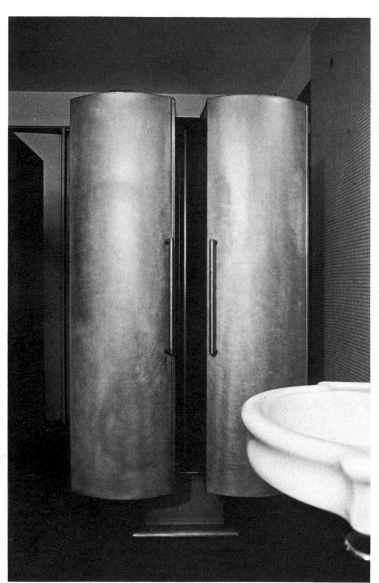

Linen cupboard in the bathroom of the Maison de Verre. Duralumin joinery. Pull-out drawers in perforated sheet metal. Nickel-plated base to stand.

tables of the Grand-Hôtel at Tours. Here the slopes are hollowed out into small coverless compartments.

VARIATIONS ON A THEME

The formal leitmotifs that are to be found throughout Chareau's work are not to be confused with variations on a single form. The architect-designer did, in fact, make use of similar linear patterns for furniture with differing functions, with all the discipline we have come to expect of him. Several large groupings that correspond to different periods of work may be distinguished here; the tulip-furniture group, the gondola chairs with hexagonal backs, the armchairs with lyre-shaped wooden legs, the wood and wrought-metal furniture, and, finally, the metal and glass furniture. This list corresponds, at least in part, to the designer's repertoire of forms.

In the tulip-furniture group, a bed, a small bookcase, a pedestal table, and a large table are to be found.

Amongst the hexagonal-backed seats, there are, of course, the gondola armchairs and two-seater sofa, but also quite a remarkable curved couch, with particularly elegant proportions and an asymmetrical line to it. It is worth noting that this range was not exclusively in exotic wood (sycamore, palisander, or ebony). Some of the large armchairs, with short or floor-length skirting, were made in black-painted cane. In the Children's Corner exhibited in the 1923 Salon des Artistes Décorateurs, there is a rocking chair with the same hexagonal back. We can attribute the broken lines and staggered triangular shapes to the interest Chareau had in Cubism.

As for the seats with lyre-shaped wooden legs, virtually every possible variation seems to have been thought of. There is a stool, a bergère chair, a gondola armchair, an armchair with a fixed back, another wider armchair with a back adjustable to two positions, a two-, three-, or four-seater couch, sometimes with no back.

Chareau also made variations on a single model. An article of bathroom furniture may be left bare, or transformed by a mirror. Tables of similar structure may differ in size without their overall equilibrium being disturbed. The same is true of the M-shaped stools which may be enlarged or elongated, upholstered or made of several exotic woods.

Each variation testifies to the coherence of his repertoire of forms, as well as to his success at matching furniture to its context. It also reflects the endless explorations the designer made along lines considered to be stable, if not commonplace. Chareau rarely gave up on a design. He would never forget them either. When he went on to a new phase, he continued to use items designed years before in new settings. There is a discreet belief expressed in many ways all through his work that is founded on his attachment to original designs and on the idea that a successful piece of furniture is suited to modern life in general and thus may be used in different circumstances.

NATURAL AND ARTIFICIAL LIGHT

Another of the designer's preoccupations was lighting. It was not so much a response to the needs of his time as an abiding interest, to be seen in all the projects he undertook. The importance he gave to redefining space in the apartments he fitted out after the war has already been looked at. Natural light and its exploitation for certain effects played a part in this. But from that time on Chareau also became interested in artificial lighting.

Although never a specialist in lighting like Salomon—he hardly had the scientific training—he was a practical innovator in the field.

As early as 1925, he conceived of a single strong source for the Embassy study which would be diffused by a domed ceiling above. Given the advantages of being able to regulate light when required, he devised a fan partition of palm-wood panels to go with this, which worked like a shutter when opened out.

In his estimation, lighting was one of the elements, one of the tools needed to create the harmonious interiors that he sought.

But beyond this, electric light was a way of transforming a lifestyle. It gave a new freedom, new dimensions to the architect's work as well. The final fruits of his research in this field, as in many others, are to be found in the Maison de Verre. Here he combined natural and artificial, blue and yellow light. He foresaw his clients' needs, matching the light sources, their brilliance and location to the moments in a day each room was used. From the intimate lighting of the bedrooms to the floods of light bathing the façade, he provided for the whole gamut of gradations that correspond to every situation of life, winter and summer, day and night. In doing this, he entered into a world that he knew indirectly. Re-creating daylight at night, with a light source outside, using Nevada bricks to reflect the light from four projectors, he created an atmosphere redolent of the theater and film set. Seen from inside, at nighttime, the figures moving along the glass wall in front of the lights are like Chinese shadow players. Bathed in light reflected by the façade, the hostess receives visitors at the top of the main staircase. A black silhouette, haloed in light, she welcomes the guests, inviting them onto the great stage of the reception room.

It is worth noting that Chareau's inventiveness did not stop with the lighting effects. He turned his attention to the wiring and to the most suitable locations for switches.

Although there is no record of his thoughts on maintenance problems and architectural decay, it seems likely that he had strong opinions on the subject. One example serves to indicate this. In the Maison de Verre he covered over the electric wiring with metal tubing positioned vertically at about 15 centimeters

EZ 431. Exhibition display at the Pavillon de Marsan, 1927. Reutilization of one of the fan partitions in the "Study-library of a French embassy." Desk 6, chair MF 275, stool MT 1015, lamp LA 555.

EA 296. Entrance hall of an apartment, spring 1924. The design of this apartment
was shared between Pierre Chareau and Francis Jourdain.

EA 283. Apartment with sliding fan door on a curved guiding rail. Lamp LP 166, couch MP 169.

EB 207. Design for the entrance to the ''Study-library of a French embassy,''
1924.

"Study-library of a French embassy," Exposition Internationale des Arts
Décoratifs et Industriels Modernes, Paris, 1925. The sliding fan partitions in
palm-wood marquetry can screen off the light reflected from the cupola.

LP 180, 181

(6 inches) from the walls. Over these tubes he fitted small box-shaped brackets with clearly marked switches on them. Each switch corresponds to a room or lighting system. At night, dimmed guiding lights pick the switchboards out. Lighting selection was, as a result, made easier, and electricians could get to the wiring without damaging walls or partitions.

Chareau was quite aware of the guiding power of light. In the doctor's practice on the ground floor of the Maison de Verre, he used it to direct patients towards the receptionist behind whom they could catch a glimpse of the garden. It also guided visitors up the main staircase so that they could cope without a banister or stair risers. And at night, automatic time switches lit the path from the entrance right up to the bedrooms.

But the relationship between daily life, lighting, and architecture was not the only field he explored. Like his furniture design, the light fittings he created reveal the powerful unified thought behind them. Devoid of superfluous decoration, the lamps are strong three-dimensional forms and often testify to his interest in Cubism. He treated the alabaster shades like pieces of sculpture in their own right, each volume answering or opposing another in a rhythmic way. His form of Cubism had four dimensions to it. Unlit, his lamps reveal the lyrical side to his nature. When switched on, they are once again examples of his taste and logical reasoning. And Dalbet's artistry with iron meant that he could perform new feats of daring. The alabaster plaques are generally mounted on lightweight, slender metal supports that give an overall impression of airiness, as seen for example in the bracket lamps designed for the Grand-Hôtel at Tours. Sometimes the metal is more apparent, forming the main body of the standard lamps. Of varying sizes, these lamps are more like statues than anything else. "La Religieuse" is a good example, with a Cubist-inspired "coiffe" perched on a tall mahogany or wrought-iron stand, or again, a desk lamp that stares at you with its two black clasps supporting a "face" made up of two alabaster quadrants.

These astonishingly sculptural designs that seem so free of the constraints the architect set himself, were not the end of his research. As early as 1923, in conjunction with his work on metal, he began to integrate lighting into specific items of furniture. He worked out the lighting for some of his mirrors. His long cheval mirrors were designed with a device to alter light on the face by turning the metal cylinder surrounding the light source. He had electrical fittings built into the writing tables of the Grand-Hôtel writing room, and the small desks at La Semaine à Paris. It was a preoccupation that led him even further, designing a library with Rose Adler, exhibited at the Salon de la Lumière as a Union des Artistes Modernes contribution. It had a system of automatically controlled dimmer-switch lighting which made it easier to look for books.

From the architectural planning of a building down to the details of a furniture accessory, there were thus few areas left unexplored by Chareau. He could design anything from a building of some size to a grape dish. He was just as capable of setting himself the hard task of preparing an old building for something new and

Bathroom of the Maison de Verre, coat hangers in the form of mustaches.

utterly different and keeping it all in a fine balance, as he was of giving it a comic touch like the coat hangers that take the form of mustaches in the bathroom of the Maison de Verre. *

What is most striking is not the amount he produced—although in certain areas this was by no means negligible—but its breadth of vision, its quality, and the unfailing consistency of his approach. The overall significance of Chareau's work could be ascribed to the undying and committed attention he gave everything he did, whatever the circumstances, so that "our minds, and the feelings we have that arose out of, and are part of, the wondrous beauty of existence, are more fully satisfied."[2]

2. Pierre Chareau, cited by Léon Moussinac in *Intérieurs I*, Paris 1924.

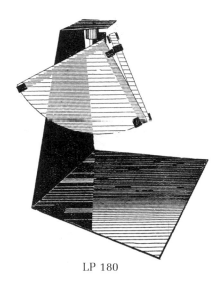

LP 180

<hr />

*His underlying attention to the aging and upkeep of buildings is seen in other components in the Maison, for example, the removable and replaceable steps made of grating on the stairs from the doctor's office to the small upstairs study. It is worth noting that Piano and Rogers followed Chareau's example on a larger scale, exteriorizing the functional or utility systems ("the guts" or "les tripes") of the Paris Centre National d'Art et de Culture Georges Pompidou.

ES 165, bearing inscription, "Salon d'Automne 1924." Armchair MF 732 (version with floor skirting), standard lamp "La Religieuse," firedogs and bas-relief by J. Lipchitz.

31, standard lamp known as "La Religieuse."

Desk MB 388, armchair MF 1050, 1050 bis.

ARTISTIC DESIGN AND COMMERCIAL IMITATION

By Pierre Chareau.
L'Architecture d'Aujourd'hui,
no. 9, Paris, September 1935,
pp. 68–69.

When confronted with a creation of the human mind, most people are, as a general rule, unaware of all the stages in the process between the original conception of the work and its final realization.

Every human being has these creative powers within him; they are part of his very nature.

If the original conception of a work is divorced from Society and nature, which are essential to its nourishment, then creativity itself is endangered.

I do not think it necessary to examine what "made the Architectural truths of the past great," to draw attention to the interdiction there is, now, not only on the creator expressing himself, but also on every man practicing a craft with a professional conscience.

For many, success means bringing a plan to fruition by overcoming opposition and vested interests of the basest and most selfish kind.

Individual creative efforts are losing ground. What there are will be used for photographic records which will quickly be stripped of their identity, distorted, and shamelessly commercialized.

The creative designer is a dangerous man.

The craftsman is an obstacle and not versatile enough.

Architecture is a social art. It rules over all the other arts and at the same time arises out of the mass of humanity; the architect can only operate if he listens, if he understands what millions of men are saying, if he suffers what they suffer, if he joins their fight for freedom, if he gives voice to their hopes, form to their dreams. He uses the iron that they have forged. He gives substance to their theories. He helps them live, produce, create, consume. He guides them toward the future because he knows what has passed is past. Yet he lives for them alone. Architecture is determined by the lives of these men, though it can guide them, deceive them, or send them to sleep.

Between architecture and men lies money: that all-powerful monster that needs to grow, grows to live, and grows by subjugating people to it.

An architect can only be approached with it acting as an intermediary. And he can only work for the benefit of man if there is money at his disposal.

But those who have money are not the kind of people the architect can represent. They are not of the masses. They belong to a group whose function is to conserve money. They had needs once. All they need now is prudence.

They commissioned works of art.

Now they are afraid of them and can no longer inspire them.

They can feel the money moving out of their grasp. They want to keep it. They had their Art once. They believe that the time has come to profit from it by exploiting it commercially. But their Art was designed and made by individuals and thus is not "commercializable."

A hundred thousand examples of a good armchair will not bring them any business since there are no longer a hundred thousand people with enough time to sit down and no one sits down for a good smoke of a cigar anymore, and besides, there are only two cigars per hundred thousand people...

What are needed are hospitals, laboratories, swimming pools, libraries, places to relax in, theaters, restaurants, but none of these things pay because those who are sick, the scientists, sportsmen, writers, tired people, actors, and the starving, have no money to spend. And needs are not copied, not to the extent that they could be turned into something CREATIVE.

The sad plight of the majority of Parisian Architects and Designers, who should not be blamed for the vulgarity and ugliness of most of current production, which is accelerating fast, is not only a result of the economic crisis.

The figures for production in the construction industry have fallen from one hundred in 1929 to thirty-six in 1934, but business transactions with Architects have decreased even more markedly than this, by sixty-four per cent.

While the Architect despairs because of the lack of work, what still remains to be built is falling increasingly into the province of trusts and real estate companies who plan and supervise the building of entire neighborhoods.

Firms specializing in houses "to order" have, with their powerful financial backing, pushed the Architects who could still exercise their craft in this field, right out of the market.

They have also set up offices where they employ draughtsmen to do the work of a whole team of Architects.

And we stand by, unable to do anything but watch the progress of a form of Architectural production with no human or social values, having as its sole purpose material profit.

The material situation of the young is simple: unemployment.

And we have a highly productive tool at our command.

The speed at which discoveries are made, in art even, means that every need can be satisfied and the ever-improving standard of life which man wants can be guaranteed.

As far as our profession goes, there are certain groups who are putting forward solutions which are founded on a misapprehension of the causes of the problem.

For example, the solution that proposes regulating the professional status of Architects is based on the false idea that by placing certain restraints on the profession and limiting access to it, there will be fewer Architects and therefore more work! Such regulations would do nothing to alter the general crisis. There would not be one extra cubic meter to build. The scant work that there is will continue to be done by business enterprises with no Architects, or by Architects with varying degrees of independence, who are now dealing with the business that a few trusts have monopolized. And the mass of Architects, accepted as such by the regulations, will be left empty handed, as ever.

Another consequence would not do much to improve the lot of thousands of other colleagues; which is, that an unqualified architect for one of the biggest real estate trusts which has acquired a virtual monopoly on building from the Paris municipal council, would be replaced by an Architect with an accepted status. The lucky man would not have much of a reward: he would be nothing more than a man of straw.

Other solutions, such as a ban on certain Architectural tendencies or a lowering in interest rates, are even easier to expose for what they are: fallacies, or deliberate attempts to deprive the Architects and Designers hit by the crisis of the real means of improving their situation.

Forming a corporation would be no more effective.

Who would set up such a corporation?

It is not an overproduction crisis.

It is not an underproduction crisis.

To improve the situation, the Architect should take a stand: against monopolizing work; for the abolition of patents, replacing them with a progressive tax on profits; for obliging the public powers-that-be to set up a vast programme of work in the public interest, sharing the work out to the Architects hit by the slump, under their supervision; for the imposition of a code of conduct in competitions ensuring some minimal guarantees; against personal favors and corruption so that professional merit is justly rewarded (Manifesto of the Assembly of Architects, 1935).

Architects must not join the conspiracy of silence. They should relentlessly pursue and expose all suspect activities, knowing the extent of them as they do

The respect for Order and their love of Peace will soon cease to work as soporifics; their training and their profession has prepared them for social work. "To build the highest Tower with the noblest of purposes," such is, and will be, their rallying cry.*

PIERRE CHAREAU

*Words have been capitalized in accordance with the original French text.

LIST OF PIERRE CHAREAU'S SUBMISSIONS TO SALONS AND EXHIBITIONS, AND THE CRITICAL RESPONSE TO THEM

1919 Pierre Chareau takes part for the first time in the Salon d'Automne, with the small study and bedroom designed for the Dalsace's apartment, 195 Boulevard Saint-Germain, Paris (nos. 370, 371 in catalogue).

1920 Exhibits at the Salon d'Automne: no. 441, bathroom; no. 442, part of a bedroom; no. 443, some furniture.

"Relying on the qualities of the material he has chosen, M. Chareau has constructed a bathroom that is extremely practical. The towel racks and the stand to the wash basin are in a kind of honeycomb design through which air can circulate freely. The artist provides us here with a twofold example that is highly relevant; he has a logical understanding of practical requirements and discounts stylistic pretensions."

(Guillaume Janneau, "L'Art décoratif," *Art et Décoration*, July–December 1920, Vol. XXXVIII, p. 154.)

"Certain select recruits seem to be backing up the valuable work of this master (this was Gallerey).... M. Chareau designing a bathroom has wisely confined his project to an extremely practical use of natural wood. Furniture in a bathroom is, of course, minimal. Here, there are towel racks and a wash stand, and M. Chareau has replaced the outmoded bathtub with a pool. Answering practical needs, the artist has seen to it that the air can circulate freely through the lattice panels of the furniture. The solution is a logical one. It is also right that such furniture should not be decorated. A light molding on the crossbars is all the indication we have of his artistic bent. The beauty of it really lies in his loyal observance of a practical requirement. For Viollet-le-Duc's idea still applies, in that true decoration is not the addition of ornament to a form; it comes from the thought given to that form."

(Guillaume Janneau, "Le Mouvement Moderne, le meuble au Salon d'Automne," *La Renaissance de l'Art Français*, no. 1, January 1921, p. 40.)

1921 Pierre Chareau becomes a member of the Salon d'Automne, where he exhibits: no. 429, dining room; no. 430, part of a boudoir.

"Among the dining rooms, there is M. Chareau's in red and brown wood; the seats and table testify to an enviable sense of design, although the accessories are less attractive. There is a couch and a Cubist rug and it is hard to know which to sit on and which to walk over, and a ceiling frieze which I cannot even begin to explain."

(L.C. Watelin, "L'Art décoratif au Salon d'Automne,"*L'Art et les Artistes*, nos. 20–24, October 1921–February 1922, p. 112.)

1922 Exhibits at the Salon des Artistes Décorateurs: no. 53, a desk.

(*Art et Décoration*, January-June 1922, Vol. XLI, p. 192.)

Yvanhoé Rambosson mentions "M. Chareau's geometric furniture."

Exhibits at the Salon d'Automne: no. 451, three rooms in a villa. These were a boudoir, a bedroom, and a dressing room with furniture in amourette wood and palisander, and a reinforced-concrete table for a conservatory.

("Le Salon d'Automne (III), Les Arts appliqués," *L'Amour de l'Art*, 1923, p. 750.)

"I would advise the designers of the Studium-Louvre who appear to be moving in the same direction as M. Chareau, to familiarize themselves with the reasons behind the rather unusual architecture of his furniture. I would like to point out to them that the quest for structural volumes and lines does not mean that Pierre Chareau denies himself the expressive eloquence of a curve; witness the boudoir-bedroom he has exhibited."

(Gaston Varenne, "L'Art urbain et le mobilier au Salon d'Automne," *Art et Décoration*, July-December 1923, Vol. LXIV, pp. 181–182.)

"I've referred to Sognot's bedroom, one of the most original in this Salon, along with Chareau's, who is so generous with his ideas. His colleagues do, on occasion, exploit Chareau's generosity. His latest invention is the fan partition. This means that a bedroom can be separated from the dressing room, or left together if one so wishes. It is a new practical method of combining three rooms, bedroom, dressing room, and boudoir in one. The limited space we have now, and the difficulties of life today, make this imperative for a good many people."

1923 Becomes an associate member of the Salon des Artistes Décorateurs (S.A.D.) and exhibits several items of furniture and ensembles (no. 158, Children's Corner, no. 159, a house for scholars).

(René Chavance, "Le XIVème Salon des Artistes Décorateurs," *Art et Décoration*, January-June 1923, Vol. XLIII, p. 186.)

"Also of a practical nature, I recommend the children's furniture designed by M. Pierre Chareau who has not altogether escaped the Cubist influence as we see in the standard and bracket lamps with their disturbing contours, but who has come up with some amusing novelties: the puppet theater, the painted cane swing, the sturdy table under which there is a net to put toys in, the bed and wide armchairs."

(Guillaume Janneau, "Le Mouvement Moderne, le Salon des Décorateurs," *La Renaissance de l'Art*, p. 430.)

"M. Pierre Chareau, that bold designer who has drawn up a house for a scholar."

He is on the 1922 jury for the Applied Arts section of the Salon d'Automne (no. 324, boudoir, bedroom, and dressing room). Works with Mallet-Stevens, Cavalcanti, and Léger on sets to Marcel l'Herbier's film, *L'Inhumaine*.

(*Art et Décoration*, January-June 1923, Vol. XLIII, p. 112.)

At the Exposition d'Art Décoratif Contemporain organized by the Union Centrale des Arts Décoratifs, he exhibits an "amusing dwarf occasional table with a book tray held between its curved legs."

(Guillaume Janneau, "Le Mouvement Moderne, 1ère exposition d'art décoratif contemporain," *La Renaissance de l'Art Français*, no. 4, April 1923, pp. 203, 206.)

"There is, in fact, not much to say about the selection; it is eclectic and provides us with what could be called a 'taste' of various contemporary tendencies: the precious furniture by Ruhlmann; Sue and Mare is to be found alongside the work of Robert Poulet and Joubert; the commercialized furniture of Lucie Renaudot and Chauchet-Guilleré alongside the dramatic armchairs by Pierre Chareau... and Chareau, a bold designer, with a thirst for the new, looking to these effects, which are sudden, rhythmic, and violent and, in some way, cinematographic, for the secret of a new style, a style which he is the man to come up with.''

1924 Becomes a member of the Salon des Artistes Décorateurs and is exempt from the jury. Collaborates on the ''public and private areas of a modern apartment'' with Mallet-Stevens, Pierre Legrain, Ruhlmann, Paul Poiret, Tony Selmersheim, Eileen Gray, Jean Burkhalter, among others.

''Here an architectural spirit predominates...and especially so in the work of that willing leader who has pointed out the unexplored paths for his band of young followers to take. I refer to M. Pierre Chareau whose ideas are the most salient of those currently developing. Everyone is talking of volumes now, often without rhyme or reason. But Chareau knows what he is talking about. Furthermore, he uses them in giving concrete expression to his ideas, designing the space to fit an individual. He is perhaps the first to have raised this question in such a specific way.''

(Yvanhoé Rambosson, ''Le Salon des Décorateurs,'' *L'Amour de l'Art*, 1924, pp. 190–194.)

At the Salon d'Automne, exhibits: no. 351, article of furniture in palisander and macassar ebony, and in the Urban art section, boutique no. 9, on which he worked with Burkhalter, Survage, Lurçat, and Dalbet.

''Surely it is only natural that our furniture designers reserve their new ideas for international competition.... There is no doubt that many of the designers, not just the lesser known ones, have simply sent in their visiting cards.... Chareau's is a cupboard in palisander and ebony.''

(Henry Clouzot, ''Les arts appliqués au Salon d'Automne,'' *La Renaissance de l'Art Français*, no. 1, January 1925, p. 5.)

''The shops that seem to have been built with a wave of the New fairy's magic wand, by Guévrékian, Djo-Bourgeois, Rigault, Nathan, Burkhalter, Poiret, Chareau, and Le Même, are worth noting, despite their resemblance to the film of Dr. Caligari. With architecture, like art, you have to take risks, and even risk being wrong.''

(Clouzot, *ibid.*, p. 10.)

''We would be hard put to it to commission a lounge; this year there is not one to be found. For lack of a totally unified ensemble, a pleasant reception room could be assembled out of the small palisander and ebony cupboard by Chareau, the exotic-wood desk by René Prou, the fine, perfectly balanced cupboard by Sue and Mare, and the attractive chest of drawers by Bagge.''

(Gaston Varenne, ''Le Salon d'Automne, l'Art Décoratif et L'Art Urbain,'' *L'Amour de l'Art*, no. 11, November 1924, p. 374.)

Pierre Chareau exhibits a dressing table at the second Exposition d'Art Décoratif Contemporain, at the Pavillon de Marsan, Paris.

1925 Takes part in the Exposition Internationale des Arts Décoratifs et Industriels Modernes, where he collaborates with Mallet-Stevens and Francis Jourdain, among others, on part of the project for a French embassy.

He designs the embassy study-library and part of the sportsroom. He also produces a dining room for the Indochinese pavilion and meets Bijvoët.

Absent from the Salon des Artistes Décorateurs.

Admitted to the administration of the Salon d'Automne but does not exhibit.

Film sets for Marcel l'Herbier's *Le Vertige*.

1926 Exhibits a desk and two seats at the Salon des Artistes Décorateurs.

(Gaston Varenne, "Le Salon des Artistes Décorateurs," *L'Amour de l'Art*, no. 6, June 1926, p. 214.)

"Pierre Chareau only too modestly exhibits two small ensembles, a wrought-iron fireplace in an amusingly antiquated style, which is somewhat unexpected from Chareau, with two low seats designed for fireside reading, and a simple and practical desk."

(L.C. Watelin, "Le Salon des Artistes Décorateurs," *L'Art et les Artistes*, no. 38, June 1923, pp. 351–352.)

"For this (a child's bedroom), Pierre Chareau is possibly the man to see, as he concentrates on the practical application of furniture with an unfailing alertness and ingenuity. This designer has decided that the naked flame is still one of the best decorative elements and as such, he presents it to us, framed by his fireplace. Nothing is particularly straightforward about fire, and there is interest to be had here in the home comforts that keep it under control. These applications of Chareau's talent reveal his underlying good sense, which I am sorry to see him abandon when he supports the outdated posturings of Max Ernst for example."

Salon d'Automne: exhibits furniture for a reading and correspondence room made for the Grand-Hôtel de Tours.

1927 Member of the S.A.D. committee but does not exhibit.

(Léon Werth, "Le XVIIème Salon des Artistes Décorateurs," *Art et Décoration*, January-June 1927, Vol. LI, pp. 167–168.)

"The absence of Francis Jourdain and Pierre Chareau, among others, is to be regretted (Chareau's only exhibit in Ruhlmann's stand being a metal plant stand)."

Salon d'Automne: no. 381, bar and smoking lounge.

(Claude-Roger Marx, "Le Salon d'Automne," *Art et Décoration*, July-December 1927, Vol. LII, p. 170.)

"There are no less than three bars in the Salon d'Automne. The most ingenious of them—and the intelligence and sense of purpose characteristic of Chareau is also to be found here—is intended for a grand hotel."

1928 Does not exhibit at the S.A.D.

(Gaston Varenne, "Les 'Décorateurs' de 1928," *L'Amour de l'Art*, July 1928, p. 242.)

"Activity in the past two Salons has centered on the question of lighting. Now most architects have turned their attentions to metallic furniture. The idea started with Chareau, who did not want to make it into any sort of formula and limited its use to specific needs, and also with Le Corbusier on a more widespread level, and Ruhlmann who used it with a good deal of caution and is still interested in it, though not unduly so."

Does not exhibit at the Salon d'Automne.

1929 Does not exhibit at the S.A.D.

(Gaston Varenne, "Les ensembles mobiliers au Salon des Décorateurs," *L'Amour de l'Art*, no. 7, July 1929, p. 246.)

"A regrettable split, which we hope is not definitive, has deprived us this year of contributions from René Herbst, Pierre Chareau, Mallet-Stevens, Madame Perriand, and a few others who come up with often daring and unfailingly original ideas. Talents of this kind are essential for a salon to be a success...."

Salon d'Automne: exhibits a metal table (unnumbered) for a typewriter and calculator (leather-covered top and metal stand), along with furniture for La Semaine à Paris.

"As always, Pierre Chareau adds a touch of his own, using metal strips of specified widths in the austere furniture of a theater agency."

(Léon Deshairs, "Le mobilier et les arts décoratifs au Salon d'Automne," Art et Décoration, July-December 1929, pp. 189–190.)

"Pierre Chareau is among the first to have understood the potential of metal in furniture. Close to the entrance, he exhibits the hall of La Semaine à Paris, where he uses iron and wood, as he does in the library, with not a trace of dogmatism; sometimes he uses metal alone, as in the small chairs and tables that complete the ensemble, each table being supplied with a very well designed lamp.... Chareau's inventiveness, his dislike of a purely aesthetic approach, are both very much in evidence here. It is this strong dislike that gives Chareau's work its distinctive character. Under the guiding principle of Chareau's taste, a new and bold beauty is achieved in such work, and despite the initial shock it may provoke, it is totally convincing."

(Gaston Varenne, "Les ensembles mobiliers au Salon d'Automne," L'Amour de l'Art, January 1930, p. 71.)

1930 Does not exhibit at the S.A.D., joining the splinter group that was to become the Union des Artistes Modernes (U.A.M.).

Participates in the first Salon des Artistes Modernes as a guest member, exhibiting a desk in pear-tree wood with a metal frame, a table-and-bookcase, one side of which is a circular tabletop on a large chrome metal sphere, and, finally, a desk for a young man.

Salon d'Automne: Pierre Chareau leads the jury in the Applied Arts section. Does not exhibit.

1931 Does not exhibit at the S.A.D., but appears in the annual of the Society up to 1933.

At the second U.A.M. exhibition, he exhibits a corner couch and a metal and wood bookcase (shelves and lockers), a low table, and a stool.

Salon d'Automne: exhibits no. 348, "Une Maison de verre" (maquette and plans).

1932 Third U.A.M. exhibition: exhibits a tea table in metal tubing and glass, and a metal stand for floral arrangements.

1933 Ceases to appear in the S.A.D. annual.

Fourth U.A.M. Salon: exhibits a metal-framed wardrobe, a "cosy corner," and a table in glass and metal tubing.

1934   Salon d'Automne: exhibits no. 340, a stainless-steel unit for a ship's cabin, commissioned by the OTUA.

U.A.M. exhibition in the Salon de la Lumière.

(Gaston Varenne, "L'exposition de l'U.A.M. au Salon de la Lumière".)

"With the help of Salomon and Rose Adler, who did the bindings, Pierre Chareau has come up with an ingenious lighting system for a library; the lights go on automatically and in succession, enabling the books to be ordered alphabetically and titles to be clearly seen. Chareau's inventive and practical turn of mind is easy to recognize. His discoveries always arouse interest because they are bold and new, but also because they are so rational that it seems odd that no one thought of it before. To give us such an impression when coming up with something so new, is rare indeed."

1936   Salon d'Automne: exhibits steel schoolroom furniture.

1937   At the Exposition Universelle (Paris World Fair), his only contribution is to the pavilion of the U.A.M.: a country retreat ("une maison de week-end").

1939   Plans for a soldier's mess in the colonies.

(preparatory text for Un Inventeur, l'Architecte Pierre Chareau, Paris, ESAM, 1954.)

"His last project in France before the war was the colonial soldier's mess, shown at the Grand Palais. It was planned so that the book crates and logs that the soldiers provided, could serve as tables, seats, and bookshelves for the mess. Appointed director in charge of their construction, circumstances intervened to put an end to the project."

Dining room of the Indochinese Pavilion at the Exposition Internationale des Arts
Décoratifs et Industriels Modernes, Paris, 1925.

Lounge next to the sportsroom of the French embassy. Table MB 2, swing bed
MP 369, lamp "La Petite Religieuse" 32, stool 1, cupboard MB 82.

Exhibition display at the Galerie Barbazanges. Dressing table MS 1009 bis, high-back armchair MF 1002, stool 1, carpet from a design by J. Lurçat.

Salon d'Automne 1926. Display of furniture for the reading and correspondence
room made for the Grand-Hôtel at Tours. Desk MB 405, writing table MB 1049,
chairs MF 275, nest of tables MB 106, padded seat MF 313, lamps LA 550.

Exhibition display at the Pavillon de Marsan. Desk 6, chairs MF 275, stool MT 1015, lamp LA 555, armchair MF 1050.

Exhibition display at the Pavillon de Marsan, 1927. Desk 6, desk with shelves
MB 388, couch MP 273, stool MT 1015.

ES 1052

Salon des Artistes Décorateurs, 1926. Armchair MF 1050, fireguard, screen, and
log bins made by Dalbet in wrought iron and metal netting.

Desk MB 113, 808, 810, armchair MF 172, couch MP 174 bis, lamp LP 180, 181.

Desk 6, armchair MF 219.

pp 217–227; 230, 231. The Maison de Verre, showing the Dalcases's living room with furniture by Chareau in place; details of the ventilation mechanism by the window; detail of the tubular railing; and the exterior of the building both without the lights turned on and lit up.

Girl's bedroom. Gouache.

Bathroom. Gouache.

Marcel Duchamp. *The Bride Stripped Bare by Her Bachelors, Even (The Large Glass)*, 1915–23. Philadelphia Museum of Art.

VII
PIERRE CHAREAU
AN ECLECTIC
ARCHITECT

It is the paradoxical lot of certain gifted people that they never find their real profession, so that all through their lives they seem haunted by the thought of other careers that they could have chosen. Pierre Chareau seems to have been such a character. Studying at the Paris École des Beaux Arts from 1900 to 1908, he divided his time between painting, music and architecture before he finally decided on the profession of decorator, becoming an apprentice at the relatively late age of twenty-five in the decoration department of the Paris branch of the English firm Waring and Gillow. This was the beginning of a long and thorough apprenticeship, which lasted from 1908 until the beginning of the First World War.

Chareau's career was in many respects inseparable from the life of a young couple, Jean and Annie Dalsace, who were in the end to be the clients of the Maison de Verre. It was they who entrusted him with his first private commission, the decoration of their two-room apartment at Saint Germain des Près, which was completed at the end of 1918. This commission led Chareau and his loyal collaborator, the metal-worker Louis Dalbet, to design and execute a bed and a desk which were subsequently exhibited at the Salon d'Automne of 1919. These objects established Chareau's reputation as a "decorative artist", and were sufficiently admired to entitle him to membership of the prestigious Société des Artistes Décorateurs.

While he was immediately accepted by his peers, particularly as the creator of well-designed and finished furniture, his reputation as an *ensemblier* was to remain slightly marginal in relation to the canon of quality established by French decorative art after 1925. Chareau's distance from the mainstream can be measured by the fact that Charles Moreau, in his *Interieurs Français au Salon des Artistes Décorateurs*, only chooses him three times for inclusion in the annual selection in the ten years from 1926 to 1936. Each time he seems to have been retained not for his inventive ingenuity and his ability as an architect but above all for his precious and prestigious furniture around which he composed interiors to suit the taste of progressive bourgeoisie. This divide, between inventiveness on the one hand, and taste on the other, is already suggested in the Dalsace apartment of 1918 and appears again in the furnishings of his own apartment on the rue Nollet in Paris. In both cases, a tension is created between the high quality finish of the specially designed wooden pieces and the somewhat austere, poetic "brutality" of the metal-framed screens and the various folding devices (permanent fixtures) which Chareau used to fit out his interiors. Where the former perpetuate the bourgeois sense of quality (an interior within an interior) the latter convey a somewhat utopian ideal of invention, as if these new devices in themselves heralded a new style of life. At the same time, it would be wrong to assume that Chareau's work was entirely separate from the triumph of French decoration which followed the celebrated Exposition des Arts Décoratifs of 1925, Chareau having taken quite as much part as any artist in the evolution of certain aspects of this Art Déco style.

Chareau remained at variance with the total Art Déco aesthetic, as can be seen from his own contribution to the Exposition des Arts Décoratifs, for example the "Study-library of a French embassy" which was entirely lined in palm wood. In its overall atmosphere it is comparable to later interiors, furnished entirely in wood to the designs of such fashionable decorators as Lucie Renaudot, Josef Frank and Gabriel Guévrékian. In this respect, Chareau appeared as a precursor: what was to be decisive here from an architectural point of view was that the woodwork was on the scale of the entire suite, focused about a desk at the center which was the masterpiece of the composition. The work should, however, be judged in terms of taste and invention rather than architecture: the first quality derives above all from the rich hermeticism of the wood panelling; the second results from the revolving cylindrical shutter used to transform the cupola of the ambassador's office from the unfolded position (day) to the folded position (night). In this work two characteristics are noticeable which we will observe on a larger scale in the Maison de Verre: the tendency to design an introverted interior, without regard to context (however appropriate it might have been in the circumstances), together with a tendency to bring dualities into play in the form of surprising and ambiguous reciprocal effects. This tendency appears clearly in the operation of the revolving and folding palm wood shutter, which, when it is totally unfolded, completes the hermeticism of the wood-sealed interior. The shutter had, of course, to be folded away (closed up like a Japanese fan) to reveal the indirectly-lit ceiling at night. In fact, there is the suggestion that this reflected, artificial light is in some way natural, because the shutter folds up in front of the source of light, almost like a curtain in front of a window, so that when it is completely closed, it is possible to imagine that above this seal there is a glass cupola opening to the sky. This ambiguous arrangement harks back once again to Chareau's obsessional preference for enclosed spaces, a preference shared by J. K. Huysman's character, Des Esseintes, who was convinced that the exterior world was less real and more remote than the interior one.[1]

A further feature of Chareau's particular sensibility appears in this context. The shutter was a useless mechanism, because clearly the strength of the light could have been altered more effectively by a dimmer switch than by a fan shutter. It is difficult to judge from the existing photographs, which always show the shutter folded up and the ceiling open, what effects could have been obtained by partially opening the shutter. But, apart from the uneven lighting conditions which would inevitably have been the result, there is every reason to think that, when completely unfolded, the shutter must have been far less efficient from the point of view of space. In other words, we are faced with a modifiable object, where the only possible modification is paradoxically "negative" in its effect.

We can see from the example of this embassy interior that Chareau would readily comply with an established style, with the requirements of a general level of refinement and decorum, just as he would reject it the instant that he sensed that certain details were dictated by considerations of fashion or by the Art Déco tendency towards an over-aestheticized *Gesamtkunstwerk*.* In other words, while he wished to create a hermetic environment, he firmly resisted the temptation to abandon himself to a desultory style. Apart, then, from the curtains and carpet by Hélène Henry, a Jacques Lipschitz sculpture and some Cubist-inspired wall lights in alabaster and metal, designed by Chareau, there is not much here of the Art Déco style, in the sense in which Robert Mallet-Stevens or Louis Süe would have understood it, and least of all in the main pieces of furniture designed by Chareau—the wood framed armchairs, covered with velvet (which evoke the "gondola" style of chairs by Ruhlmann and Van de Velde, more than the abstract manner of Mallet-Stevens) and the extendable desk, made of mahogany and oak, covered with Macassar ebony. Even this last, where the values of *grand bourgeois* decoration are clearly apparent in the costly finish, hardly escapes Chareau's disjunctive impulse. This disjunction can be seen in the tubular metal drawer-handles which are closer to the anonymity of American mass-produced office furniture (compare the modern idea of office furniture in Ronéo metal which Le Corbusier discusses in his 1925 polemic against Art Déco, *L'art décoratif d'aujourd'hui*) [2] than to the cabinet-making tradition to which the object, in the main, clearly belongs.

Chareau's first foray into the field of architecture, in the proper sense, was the only detached building of his career in France apart from the Djemil Anik house of 1937. This was the reinforced concrete club-house designed in collaboration with the Dutch architect Bernard Bijvoët and completed at Beauvallon (near Saint Tropez) in 1920. From an architectural point of view, the principal anomaly of this work is that it looks like an unfinished Cubist composition. From whichever side it is approached, it is always off balance, as if its maker was in some way confused by the need for an exterior form. This last is composed of two main elements: a double-height club-room with a bar and a covered outside terrace, with an assembly of small service rooms situated to the rear (kitchen, cloakroom etc.). Awkward in its external appearance, this building does not even succeed in achieving one of those dynamic spatial relationships that we have come to expect from three-dimensional Cubism, so that the main interest lies, once again, in the furnishing of its volumes. Photographs of the period bring out the curiously disjointed effects achieved by the furnishing and the eccentric treatment of architectural details: the contrast, say, between the exterior treatment of the chimney, and the interior hearth which is built partly from brick and partly from plastered reinforced concrete.

Similar inconsistencies are to be found in the interiors that Chareau and Bijvoët designed in the same years for the Grand Hôtel de Tours (designed by Maurice Boille, 1928–1931), which included a large ballroom, a smoking room, a bar, and a large variety of smaller areas reserved for rest and reading. Here, the Cubist

---

* Gesamtkunstwerk: literally "total work of art". In 1925, it applied more exactly to the notion of uniform decoration as conceived by the furnishers and decorators of the period.

style of the period finds an unequivocal expression in the glyptic surfaces, the unornamented planes of the mezzanine balcony and the orderly concrete beams which flank the three-story high ballroom on every side. However, this first manner is departed from, if not utterly rejected, by the non-architectonic way in which the space is detailed. The rest of the work, reverses to Cubism in the surface decoration of certain areas, in the abstract, orthogonal design of the marquetry floor and in the neo-plastic mosaic decoration of certain columns in the adjoining spaces.

Elsewhere, the tone and the syntactic repertoire owe more to principles borrowed directly from the anonymous tradition of shop fitting or other discrete forms of quality carpentry. For instance, the wood panels which encase the ballroom as far as the level of the cornice are held in place by continuous bands of chrome steel, while the areas of uncovered plaster above are animated by a sprinkling of randomly arranged invisible "luminous stars." This mixed aesthetic seems to swing oddly between the antithetical poles of a post-*Jugendstil* Viennese manner: on the one hand, the deconstructed decorative style crystallized by Josef Hoffmann; on the other, the "silent" interiors of Adolf Loos. The anonymous tradition of shop fitting, as found in the Loos's Knize shop of 1910, sets the tone for the remaining areas, with glass screens framed by black-painted, light metal, with marquetry on nearly all the available wall surfaces, while versions of the English club chair, in the form of a truncated chaise longue without armrests, upholstered in leather, serve to maintain an aura of luxurious austerity. Such, in substance, is the basic interior syntax which was to be adopted two years later in the furnishing details of the Maison de Verre. Other pieces of furniture should, however, be noted in passing, which serve to forestall the already somewhat attenuated elegance of the hotel bar and smoking room. These are the bar stools, summarily built of tubes of encased metal, and the strange high bar tables designed to go with them. One has the feeling that when Chareau designed these pieces of furniture in 1925 he was momentarily more concerned with experimental construction than aesthetic refinement. Whether this peculiar combination of furniture was intentional or not, the effect was the same, namely, a lapse into a kind of "styleless" style, combined with a strange discrepancy between the apparent dimensions of the various pieces of furniture—the stools appear almost too tall and the chairs too low. Taken together, these discordances in style and scale have a Surrealist feel to them, and this characteristic in Chareau's work was pointed out by Paul Nelson in one of the first studies on the Maison de Verre.[3]

In the Maison de Verre, designed in collaboration with Bijvoët and under construction from 1928 to 1932, this disjunctive tendency is resolved at once by a clearly marked opposition between the taste governing the choice of furnishings, whether bought or specially created, and the inventiveness of the house as a whole. This separation between furniture and permanent fixtures was henceforth to be the norm. It is, clearly, close to the distinction made by Adolf Loos when he stated that furniture should never be designed by architects but rather created by craftsmen and arranged by the client according to his taste. Loos claimed that the influence of the architect should not extend beyond permanent fixtures. Chareau could accept responsibility for both sides of this argument, because he was, in a sense, at the same time craftsman and architect. The Maison de Verre is capable of adapting to different types of furniture without compromising its technical and architectural syntax in any way. It is as if this house was suffused with some kind of benevolent mechanism capable of assimilating entirely different works—an antique dining table and chairs, a suite by Chareau, or a decorative tapestry by Jean Lurçat—without its character, or technical qualities, being compromised or contradicted.

Bernard Bijvoët (1976)

It is important to recall the special circumstances which prevailed at the time of the house's construction. In 1928, Madame Dalsace's father bought an eighteenth-century *hôtel particulier* in Paris, at 31 rue Saint Guillaume. The site was enclosed on all sides by party walls of varying heights and contained, besides the three-floor *hôtel particulier*, a forecourt and a garden at the rear. The clients intended to demolish the existing building and build from scratch, but the presence of a protected tenant on the second floor obliged clients and architect to envisage another solution. Out of this came the decision to underpin the second floor with steel and to demolish the unoccupied floors beneath, keeping only the existing access staircase. The resulting volume was sufficiently spacious to make room for three new floors of normal height, each level being set aside for a different purpose: the first floor to the practice of medicine; the second floor to daily living, and the third for sleeping quarters. A narrow service wing of three floors was built as an extension on one side of the forecourt to house the kitchen, a work room and a maid's room, etc. Once this idea had been perfected and the steel frame erected, all that was needed was to enclose the house in a protective envelope and to furnish the interior. In this respect it was not unlike the embassy exhibited by Chareau in 1925, in that the latter was conceived as an exhibit of permanent fixtures of an exceptional size and complexity, constructed within an enclosing volume provided by an existing site. Dr Dalsace was to write on this subject:

"In order to spare an old lady who didn't want to leave her dingy second floor apartment, Pierre Chareau has performed the extraordinary feat of building three floors full of light, in the ground and first floor of a small *hôtel particulier*... The light circulates freely through this block, the first floor of which is devoted to medicine, the second floor to social life and the third to nighttime privacy. The problem this raised was enormously difficult to resolve. Interconnecting rooms, certain of which occupy two floors, make the problem of soundproofing very difficult... The first floor, the professional section of the building, facilitates work and, with their initial uneasiness overcome, calms the patients down considerably. The whole house has been created under the influence of friendship, in complete affectionate understanding." [4]

From the first perspective sketches of the interior (the only drawings which remain) it may be deduced that the subdivisions and fittings were worked out little by little, as the work proceeded. These rather hasty drawings are the only evidence existing of the methodology of the project and construction. And thus, once the main idea had been laid down, the entire operation unfolded like a montage, bit by bit. In fact, we know that no working drawings in the general sense of the term were done. [5] On the contrary, the procedure usually consisted of moving from on-site drawings and sketches straight to fabrication as the craftsman Dalbet was on hand to build the prototypes and execute the final work. A rather crude model exhibited in 1931 shows the basic volume of the house after the structural work. It also shows the floors in place and the glass block curtain walls which comprised the two façades of the house. Site photographs taken in 1930 show more or less the same state of affairs.

Chareau used this commission to invent and perfect new prototypes of components, and in a sense the creator of the Maison de Verre seems to have regarded the work as a laboratory for the development of a hypothetical industrial architecture. Materials and techniques were either derived from industrial practice or from new combinations which were rich with industrial possibilities when the ideas were new. Chareau evidently had a passion for new materials as is clearly seen in the first perspective sketches. In this context, it is quite characteristic that bent duraluminum sheeting was the first material considered for the balustrade of the main staircase. Even though this deployment was, in the end, reduced to a low, psychologically reassuring, tubular-steel guard-rail, bent duraluminum was to reappear in the cylindrical broom cupboard placed behind the staircase and in the free-standing clothes closet designed for the master bathroom.

In spite of the one-off experimental objects which abound throughout, the Maison de Verre is also built along rational lines. Thus, because of the standardization of its components, the house was to take on a wealth of implications which place it beyond the limits of a bourgeois domestic space. Although by definition limited in its realization to specialized craftsmen (it is almost unthinkable that the house could have been built without the many talents of Dalbet) it postulated nonetheless by virtue of its modular nature, to a form of high quality mass-production. Doors, stair rails, bookshelves, and cupboards as well as the curtain wall fenestration are treated like the modular components of a grid which crosses the entire house from back to front and, to a certain extent, from side to side.

Apart from this industrial potential, which even today remains largely unexploited in society as a whole, the Maison de Verre was the total machine object, elegantly conceived and executed with precision. In many instances, in line with the economical spirit of the French construction industry, the resistance of a material or a given component was pushed to its limits, as illustrated by the rolling-sliding mobile library ladder which moves on a carriage made from a single piece of bent tubing. It is significant that the railway carriage windows, made of vertically sliding plate glass, the clerestoreys and remote-control ventilation shutters are, apart from the side-hung doors, the only openings of the outer envelope. From this we can conclude that the concept of "mobility" impregnated nearly all the details of the house, from sliding or swiveling windows to detachable staircases, from rotating cupboards to pivoting bidets, from sliding partitions to rotating screens.

In this respect the Maison de Verre is the transformable plan *par excellence*, to the extent that the ultimate motive of each transformation can appear completely variable, passing from necessity in one case to convenience in the next, or let us say this "poetry of equipment" has a more overtly symbolic significance in one instance than in another. The glass door pivoting on its axis on the first floor landing of the main staircase is necessary to separate the social areas from the medical premises, and vice versa, while the service hatch for serving tea in Madame Dalsace's boudoir may be viewed as a straightforward convenience. Similarly, the hinged, perforated, zinc screens which are attached to the pivoting glass door can be regarded as pure "poetry of equipment," in opposition, say, to the play between fixed and folding staircases at the rear of the house which have to be seen as having certain mythical connotations to which we will return. Differences of this sort are clearly presented as concrete phenomena. In fact, the Maison de Verre appears to be organized homologically so that paired oppositions and reciprocal relations are found at every instance (compare the analysis of the Berber house by Pierre Bourdieu).[6] This is nowhere more pronounced than in the treatment of light, in which *natural* is noticeably opposed to *artificial* light, *translucent* to *transparent*, and so on. Depending on the hour of day, the light is now natural, now artificial; and the house is now illuminated externally or is itself the source of light. This homology appears in the course of time as a circumstantial sequence in which the components and the positions change place reciprocally. In the first case, the house is lit from the outside by the natural light penetrating to the interior through a translucent enclosure. In the second, the house is lit from inside by artificial lighting, some of which filters out through the glass block façades, so that the house glows like a Chinese lantern. In the third case, the house is lit from outside by the artificial light, penetrating to the interior through these same façades—the house now being lit from the front and back by floodlights mounted on cantilevered brackets and free-standing ladders.

A homology of a similar, though less complex, nature, may be observed in the interior fittings; specifically in the correspondence established between the layout of the library staircase (the mind) and the layout of the serving hatch from the kitchen to the dining area (the body). On the whole, this structural homology predominates in the design of all the mechanical services. For instance, throughout the house, all the electric cabling and interconnections run in separate vertical tubes which rise from one floor to another. At suitable points, these tubes are fitted with steel-covered consoles on which are placed all the necessary switches and sockets, so that the walls are kept clean. While energy and communication are conveyed in vertical tubes which cross the body of the house like a grid, heat in the form of air conditioning circulates in ducts. In the first instance, invisible, modern energy is transported vertically and rendered visible; in the second, palpably antique energy (Roman) is conveyed horizontally and rendered, almost inevitably it seems, invisible. Essentially, the adjustable polished-metal vents, set in black laquered manifolds are the only signs of the presence of this channelled air.

The Maison de Verre was recognized in its day as a functionalist work and as an integral part of the avant-garde of the Modern Movement, especially by Alberto Sartoris in his book *Gli elementi dell' architettura funzionale*—published in 1931, the year of the Maison de Verre's completion. Otherwise, it has in the main been left out of general works which discuss the Modern Movement, with the exception of the French edition of my book: "Modern Architecture: A Critical History."[7] The reasons for this strange omission are not hard to find, because, while the Maison de Verre was both functional and machinist, it was hardly a pure example of these approaches. On one hand, its functionalism exceeded the minimum necessary to satisfy certain material requirements, leading to a certain redundancy in terms of both form and mechanical device. On the other, it was furnished in such a way as to exemplify the homogeneity of the interior and its capacity to assimilate different components of varied origin. In this respect, one would have no doubt mistrusted the non-transparent, but translucent walls and the taste for highly upholstered interiors as in the curtained walls of Dr. Dalsace's study. All these ambigious characteristics would surely have been anathema to the fresh-air and hygiene cult of the mainstream Modern Movement.[8]

In fact, the Maison de Verre is just as difficult to classify according to accepted genres or common ideologies as is Marcel Duchamp's equally atypical work, *Le Grand Verre*, his famous glass construction created during the years 1915–1923, more accurately known as *The Bride Stripped Bare by her Bachelors, even*. This comparison goes much further than the seemingly trivial fact that the two works were based on an obsessional and superfluous use of glass, since the two objects break all the classificatory rules which accord with a traditional understanding of their respective disciplines. Similar problems of classification abound in each. Should the Maison de Verre be looked on as architecture or as a furnishing operation on a large scale? Should *Le Grand Verre* be seen as a painting or a relief construction? In both cases, the works are unclassifiable in any conventional sense; they are "other" in the deepest sense of the word and this "strangeness" is a consequence of their opposition to the mainstream of Western art after the Renaissance. In this respect, both are "anti-" works, the Maison de Verre being a piece of anti-architecture and *Le Grand Verre* an anti-painting. The more or less continuous translucent covering of the Maison de Verre at one stroke does away with the counterpoint between solid and void which one finds in all architecture including the Modern Movement. The same is true for *Le Grand Verre* which utterly undermines all established ideas on the fundamental nature of painting, that is to say, that it is about an image and a surface to be looked at, rather than looked through. As Duchamp was to say, " 'retained in glass' doesn't mean 'painting on glass.' It is simply a means for no longer regarding the thing in question as a painting."[9]

But the comparison does not stop there, because the two works are homologically structured in a way that has more to do with pre-Renaissance magic or alchemic culture than with the Cartesian civilization. Of course, this is not to pretend that the conceptual structure of *Le Grand Verre* and the Maison de Verre are in any way identical, or that there is any proof of a direct influence by the one on the other. But nevertheless, in the two works, certain common themes become apparent which are worth noting. In the first place, the two works display in different ways a sort of excessive and needless mechanization; secondly, the two works are arranged in ways which, to some extent, at least, have erotic or sexual implications. In the case of *Le Grand Verre*, all this is well established and generally accepted; in the case of the Maison de Verre, we have little data except that the plan of the house lends itself to a reading which makes it appear as a "bachelor machine," according to the definition that Michel Carrouges has given of these contrivances:

"To the contrary of real machines and even the larger part of imaginary but rational and useful machines such as Jules Verne's *Nautilus* or the rockets of science fiction, the bachelor machine appears first and foremost as a machine that is impossible, useless, incomprehensible, delirious...

"Each bachelor machine is a system of images composed of two equal and equivalent *ensembles*. One of these is the *sexual ensemble*. By definition this is comprised of *two elements: masculine* and *feminine*...

"The other part, is the *mechanical ensemble*, also composed of two *mechanical elements*, which correspond respectively to the two masculine and feminine components of the sexual ensemble.

"This duality and correspondence appear very distinctly in Duchamp's *Le Grand Verre* which places the "bride" alone at the top, while the masculine "bachelor machine" is isolated at the bottom."[10]

With the gynecological suite entirely occupying the first floor, the scheme of the Maison de Verre corresponds rather paradoxically with the first condition of this definition, and not only as far as the first floor is concerned, since the second and third floors follow a similar hierarchical order. In this way, the first floor can legitimately be analysed as the "bachelor" or male part of the house, above all because it is in fact Dr Dalsace's sacred domain and necessarily consecrated to celibacy; the third floor, which is that of the family bedrooms, can be taken as the "bride's" domain or the feminine area. Between these two floors, of course, lies the complex interface of the *piano nobile* which is in part public and social, and in part private and intimate, and it is a fact that the second floor seems to comply with this code on more than one level.

This second floor is divided, quite intentionally, it would seem, into two sections. The eastern section combines the privacy of the boudoir, the domestic space of the kitchen and the sociability of the dining area and can therefore conventionally be considered as the domain of the bride. The western section combines the privacy of the study and the public status of the drawing room and, as such, is under the conventional sign of the bachelor. While it is quite reasonable to suggest that this layout simply responded to functional needs as expressed in the project, the way in which these divisions are coded homologically by the varied floor coverings and by mechanical devices, such as the service stairs, only go to demonstrate the mythic status of the house as a bachelor machine.

Firstly, the rubber tiling of the first floor gynecological suite continues via the main staircase to become the floor covering of the lounge and is further prolonged along an inconvenient, almost inelegant, route which stops at the threshold of the boudoir. This coding is completed by the use of different floor coverings in other areas. Both the boudoir (female) and the study (male) are distinguished as intimate spaces by a flooring of mat black ceramic tiles, while the dining room and the service passage which leads to the kitchen are finished in parquet flooring, the warmth of the wood indicating their obvious character as domestic spaces.

Secondly, the "mechanical" side appears in the reciprocal disposition of the service staircases, which set up a discreet but precise relationship between the intimate spaces of the second floor—the boudoir and the study—and the respective spheres of the male and the female on the other floors, the bride being above and the bachelor below. The specific form of the stairs is not without significance in this regard. Firstly because the bride's staircase is quite explicitly a mechanical device, an open ladder that can be lowered and retracted into the soffit of the ceiling separating the boudoir from the main bedroom above which is evidently the bride's domain; and second because the bachelor's staircase is fixed although still mechanical in that it winds around a telephone cabin as it descends from the study to the medical suite. This implicit movement is emphasized by the way in which the handrail in tubular steel climbs in an unbroken zigzag from the ground to the *piano nobile*.

The homologous disposition of the private areas in the bride's and bachelor's domains on the first floor reads then as follows: the boudoir (the bride) is linked by a detachable "rising" staircase to the main bedroom above, while the study (the bachelor) is linked by a fixed "descending" staircase, to the gynecologist's consulting room below. An indication of this homology is encountered in the same area of interface in plan, as an exchange, so to speak, between the coding of the second and third floors. This exchange transpires between the study and the boudoir on the one hand, and the bathroom and the main bedroom on the other. In the first case, a double set of staggered sliding doors, set at right angles, creates a valvular passage between the study and the boudoir. In the second, a similarly valvular arrangement is involved in the division of the main bathroom into a male and a female zone: between the rectangular bath (female) and the circular shower cubicle (male) situated on opposite sides of the bathroom. The fact that these different arrangements conform to Madame and Dr Dalsace's respective preferences for ablution reinforces rather than undermines the symbolic organization of the Maison de Verre according to the myth of the bachelor machine.

Such a combination is further confirmation of the astonishing intimacy, "the friendship, the complete affectionate understanding," which existed at the creation of the Maison de Verre. It is clear that, as in all first-rate houses, the client shares the responsibility equally with the architect. In fact, there are times when the entire work seems to be an exact reflection of the personality of Annie Dalsace: a subtle homage that Chareau pays to his client. Subtly, but with a curious insistence, the house appears to be dedicated again and again to the "bride," from the gynecological suite itself to the multiplicity of bidets arranged on the bedroom floor. Moreover, in spite of the functional motifs, a dominant feminine image (which is nevertheless paradoxically submissive) is twice placed at the panoptic centre of a space; the first in the axis of the entrance hall, which appropriately falls under the eye of the nurse who supervises the medical floor, the second on the third floor, where the maid's work and control room looks down on the entire volume of the lounge. It may be added that these two panoptic control positions are assumed by the servants of the "bachelor" and "bride" respectively.

Although the relationship (or rather the absence of relationship) between Le Grand Verre and the Maison de Verre must almost certainly remain as one of the enigmas of twentieth-century avant-garde culture, a comparison of this sort cannot completely ignore the consideration of certain specific correspondences between the two works. For instance, we can ask ourselves whether there is not some justification in comparing the detachable staircase of the Maison de Verre with the *pendu femelle* ("swinging this way and that") of Le Grand Verre, or if it is not correct to see the staccato climb of the study staircase or the revolving clothes cupboard of the main bathroom as transpositions of Duchamp's *Chocolate Grinder* of 1914, of which he was to write in *La Boîte Verte*, 1934: "The bachelor grinds his chocolate himself...." [11]

The thing which is clear in all this, is that Chareau was perfectly *au fait* with the vicissitudes of Cubism and Futurism and must therefore without any doubt have had knowledge of Duchamp's Le Grand Verre and the different paintings in his production from which it was derived. Moreover, it is significant that Chareau resorted to Cubist devices—changes of level and of material—to differentiate the areas of the various floors. These differences were juxtaposed in a way which strongly recalls Synthetic Cubism, above all the Cubist collage, and marked, as we have seen, changes in the real and mythic status of the volumes.

Throughout his career, at least until the Maison de Verre, the work of Chareau wavered continually between the cult for the "ready-made," which he owed in part to the influence of Dadaism, and the standards of quality craftsmanship of the Salon des Artistes Décorateurs. There is without doubt only one work from his period of greatest activity in which this opposition is for a moment abandoned in favor of a normative, functional approach that is entirely rational. This is the offices for the LTT Telephone Company in Paris (1931–1932), which was notably the only commission in Chareau's career that was not a domestic but a utilitarian building. Of a mechanical precision throughout, with its concrete mosaic floors, tubular steel chairs, standardized steel office furniture, glass-tiled partitions, mirror screens and metal windows, the interior of the LTT was a *tour de force* in steel and glass construction. This austere work was illuminated by large windows and sparkling with light. In it Chareau seems finally to have abandoned his predeliction for enclosed interiors. Under the influence of International Constructivism, via his daily dealings with Bernard Bijvoët, he comes closer than ever in this work to the hyper-functionalism of the *Neue Sachlichkeit*.* Indeed, two years later, he was to choose an even more "sachlich" approach in the project for a boat cabin, an exhibition piece destined for the fifth exhibition of the Union des Artistes Modernes as part of the Salon d'Automne.[12]

The swan song of Chareau's career in France was the little weekend house that he built for the dancer Djemil Anik in the Paris suburbs in 1937.[13] This work seems to announce a fundamental break in the nature of Chareau's approach, a break as definitive as that undergone by Francis Picabia in his career as a painter, after 1924. While such ruptures were not in themselves connected in any way, they are comparable in the sense that after having reached a certain pinnacle of success, the work of each of the artists was irremediably changed. In the case of Picabia, it is the set designs for *Relâche* and *Entr'acte*, both of 1924, which seem to have been the decisive factors; in Chareau's case it is the completion of the Maison de Verre. The rupture between the Maison de Verre and the Anik house is so complete that René Herbst chose to exclude any illustration of it in his monograph of 1954 in memory of Chareau, even though his text proves that he knew of its existence.[14] It is equally significant and even understandable that Herbst should have discriminated between Chareau's work in France, which is well represented, with large photographs, and his production in America, to which he accords only small illustrations as pointers.

Apart from the Depression and the further shock of the Second World War, which obliged him to exile himself in the United States, not to mention the modest sums that were subsequently placed at his disposal, there seem to be only two plausible explanations for this sudden change in his work. The first is that Chareau was psychologically burnt out after the energy spent on the Maison

*   Die Neue Sachlichkeit: the new objectivity. Exhibition organized from June 14 to September 13 1925 at the Kunsthalle in Mannheim. This movement particularly influenced the painters (for example, Christian Schad, Otto Dix) and the photographers (for example, Albert Renger-Patzch, August Sander).

de Verre. The second is that, in the middle of the thirties, he lost his principal collaborators, Bijvoët, who returned to Holland in 1935, and Dalbet, who was left exhausted and ruined after the work on the Maison de Verre. At any event, Chareau seems to have consciously decided that a certain epoch had come to an end and that there was no other alternative but to continue a kind of *degré zero* architecture. Partly from necessity, partly from choice, after 1932 Chareau opted for ordinary, low-cost constructions, in which the only poetic qualities that could be found came from subtle inflections imposed on the common necessities of everyday life.

Influenced possibly by the house that Le Corbusier built at Mathes in 1935, the Anik house is an attempt to return to a modern rustic style, the architectural emphasis passing from the body of the house to the structure, and to a deliberate interplay between two gently sloping roofs which were to cover respectively the main dwelling and the out-house with the toilets, etc. Chareau seems to have attempted to accentuate the rustic effect by giving these roofs different slants. In other respects, the organization of the house could hardly be simpler, the first floor being given over to a garage and a shower room, and the second floor consisting of a large room facing west over a covered access gallery. The only interruption in the main volume was a steep staircase climbing to two attic bedrooms and a small enclosed kitchen. The structure consists of a three-story framework set on low stone walls and pillars. Above this stone base, the building is covered with panels of heraclite. Something of Chareau's fondness for the Japanese attention to detail (clearly apparent in the steel objects lacquered in black and painted with red oxide of the Maison de Verre) is again present here, above all in the naïve orientalism of the revealed wooden skeleton. In other respects, the woodwork is typically western with bolted, centered window frames. Little, in fact, remains of the inventiveness that was peculiar to Chareau and still less of his taste, except perhaps for the metal grill balustrade in the gallery and the portholes which light the garage. In the main, the Anik house seems like a disenchanted reflection on the impossibility of preserving architectural culture, a sort of compensatory worship of "the dumb and the ordinary" thirty years *avant la lettre*.

This feeling undoubtedly persisted in the American houses that Chareau designed at the end of his life, the house and studio built for the painter Robert Motherwell in corrugated metal shells of military quonset huts, and in the rather anonymous one-story house built for himself on the same East Hampton site. In these simple buildings, and in a scarcely more important work built in New York State for Germaine Monteux and Nancy Laughlin, and known as *La Colline*, neither invention nor taste really survive, because the whole thing was reduced to variations on an American pseudo-vernacular. Everything about these houses was decided either by the tightness of the budget or by the prevailing circumstances, so that all that remained was a hidden nostalgia, expressed in crude material, which brought back in one way or another the memory of the lost glories of the Maison de Verre. This nostalgia appears perhaps even more poignantly in the mezzanine of the Motherwell house, where the floor is covered in sawn-off logs set in concrete and where once again there is a metal grill balustrade, even though, unlike in the Anik house, the grill is the cheapest kind of chicken wire. In the Motherwell house, the Maison de Verre is still present in the exposed columns and the steel I-beams supporting the upper floor, in the collapsable canvas canopy and the continuous flower box which both occupy and articulate the space between the fenestration of the long greenhouse window and the semi-circular structure of the hut itself. At East Hampton, everywhere there are brief flashes of the old mastery: the sliding entrance door, the open plan, the free-standing fireplace of the Motherwell house, and in the strange doors and oblique windows of Chareau's own one-story house. But in the main he had thrown in his hand and little remained to be done in the last decade of his life, in those twilight years in New York where he worked on the exhibitions that he was asked to present for the French Cultural Center. He surely knew what was lost when he wrote to René Herbst a few months before his death: "I cannot tell you the emotion which I feel from a distance at all the touching gestures and expressions of friendship. I feel it all the more because I am certain of your support in the pursuit of my duties here. I would give so much for us to meet before long, but what can you do, I have to choose to be of some use and I believe that I am."

These laconic words testify more than anything else, perhaps, to Chareau's stoicism and modesty: the architect as bricoleur before the deluge.

NOTES

1 Huysmans, J.K. A Rebours. Paris, 1884.
2 Le Corbusier. "L'art décoratif d'aujourd'hui" in L'esprit nouveau collection. Paris, 1959.
3 Nelson, Paul. "Maison de Verre" in L'Architecture d'Aujourd'hui, no. 9, November-December 1933, p. 9.
4 Cited by René Herbst in Un inventeur, l'architecte Pierre Chareau. Paris, 1954, pp. 7 and 8.
5 In an interview with Robert Vickery in 1965 Bernard Bijvoët stated that no real working drawings were ever done for the house.
6 Bourdieu, Pierre. "La maison ou le monde renversé" in Esquisse d'une théorie de la pratique précédé de trois études d'ethnologie Kabyle. Paris, 1972.
7 Frampton, Kenneth. Modern Architecture: A Critical History. London, 1980.
8 For some, the house was too functional. See the account by Julien Lepage in L'Architecture d'Aujourd'hui, no. 9, November-December 1933, pp. 14 to 15.
9 Duchamp, Marcel. Boîte Verte. New York, 1960.
   One may equally refer to another text by Duchamp where he writes: "This is no longer a painting: the transparent surface of the glass ceases to play the role of an imaginary screen; the erotic machinery operates in the empiric space".
10 Carrouges, Michel. "Mode d'emploi" in Les Machines célibataires. Venice, 1975, p. 21.
11 Duchamp. Boite Verte.
12 L'Union des Artistes Modernes (UAM) was founded by René Herbst; the first executive committee in 1930 was composed as follows: Hélène Henry, René Herbst, Francis Jourdain, Robert Mallet-Stevens, Raymond Templier. Pierre Chareau appeared as a "guest member" in 1930.
13 See: Philippe Bourgeois, Jean-Marc Dutrevis, Robert Ecoiffier and Rémi Leberre. "Un projet inédit de Pierre Chareau" in Architecture, Mouvement, Continuité, no. 51, December 1980, pp. 45 to 54.
14 Herbst, Un inventeur.

Picabia
Scénario de Relâche
1924

Rideau blanc, à plat. Projection cinématographique à déterminer, de trente secondes environ, accompagnée de musique. Le rideau se lève ; la scène se présente comme une voûte de forme ovoïde, entièrement tapissée de gros ballons blancs. Tapis blanc. Au fond, porte tournante articulée. La musique dure encore trente secondes après le lever du rideau.

Une femme se lève aux fauteuils d'orchestre : elle est en grande toilette de soirée, elle monte en scène à l'aide d'un praticable.

Musique : 35 secondes. Au moment où elle apparaît en scène, la musique cesse.

La femme s'arrête au milieu de la scène et examine le décor, puis elle s'immobilise. A ce moment la musique reprend pendant une minute environ. Lorsqu'elle cesse, la femme se met à danser. Chorégraphie à régler. La musique reprend pendant une minute et demie ; la femme remonte au fond de la scène et tourne trois fois avec le battant de la porte tournante, puis s'arrête face à la salle. Pendant ce temps, trente hommes, en habit noir, cravate blanche, gants blancs et chapeau claque, quittant l'un après l'autre des places de spectateurs montent tour à tour sur la scène par le praticable. Durée de la musique : une minute et demie.

La musique s'arrête au moment où par une danse à régler, ils entourent la femme revenue au milieu du plateau ; ils tournent autour d'elle pendant qu'elle se dévêt et apparaît en maillot de soie rose, entièrement collant. Musique pendant 40 secondes. Les hommes s'écartent, se rangent contre le décor ; la femme reste immobile quelques secondes, pendant que la musique reprend durant trente-cinq secondes. Quelques ballons éclatent au fond. Danse générale.La femme est enlevée dans les cintres.

RIDEAU

Pas d'entracte, à proprement parler ; la musique dure cinq minutes avec projections cinématographiques des auteurs assis face à face, échangeant une conversation dont le texte s'inscrira à l'écran durant dix minutes. Pas de musique pendant la projection écrite.

DEUXIEME ACTE

Le rideau se lève. Musique de une minute. Sur un fond noir, sont disposées des enseignes lumineuses et intermittentes où dominent alternativement les noms de Erik Satie, de Francis Picabia, de Blaise Cendrars, en couleur.

Deux ou trois projecteurs puissants, très puissants, sont dirigés de la scène sur la salle : ils éclairent le public et produisent des effets de noir et blanc à l'aide de disques percés de trous. Les hommes rentrent un par un et se placent en rond autour de la toilette de la femme, posée à terre, au milieu de la scène. Musique de 20 secondes.

La femme redescend des cintres toujours en maillot ; elle porte sur la tête une couronne de fleurs d'orangers ; elle se rhabille tandis que les hommes se dévêtissent à leur tour et apparaissent en maillot de soie blanche. Musique de vingt secondes. Danse à régler.

Les hommes un à un regagnent leur place où ils retrouvent leurs pardessus. Musique de trente secondes. La femme, restée seule, prend une brouette, y entasse les vêtements laissés par les hommes et va les verser dans un coin en tas ; puis s'approchant le plus près possible de l'avant-scène, elle enlève sa couronne de mariée, et la jette à l'un de ses danseurs qui ira la déposer sur la tête d'une femme connue se trouvant dans la salle. Musique : quinze secondes.

Puis la femme va à son tour rejoindre son fauteuil ; on baisse le rideau blanc devant lequel apparaît une petite femme qui danse et chante une chanson. Musique : 45 secondes.

250

Picabia
Lettre à René Clair
Scénario d'Entr'acte
1924

Mon cher ami, je vous envoie inclu, la partie cinématographique du ballet.
Bien sympathiquement votre.

> Francis Picabia.

LEVER DU RIDEAU
Charge d'un canon au ralenti par Satie et Picabia, le coup devra faire le plus de
bruit possible.
durée totale : 1 minute.

PENDANT L'ENTRACTE
1°) Assaut de boxe par des gants blancs, sur écran noir : durée 15 secondes. Projection écrite pour l'explication : 10 secondes.

2°) Partie d'échecs entre Duchamp et Man Ray, jet d'eau, manoeuvré par Picabia, balayant le jeu : durée 30 secondes.

3°) Jongleur et "père Lacolique" : durée 30 secondes.

4°) Chasseur tirant sur un oeuf d'autruche sur jet d'eau, de l'oeuf sort une colombe,
elle vient se poser sur la tête du chasseur, un deuxième chasseur tirant sur elle,
tue le premier chasseur ; il tombe, l'oiseau s'envole : durée 1 minute.
Projection écrite : 30 secondes.

5°) 11 personnes couchées sur le dos, présentent le dessous de leurs pieds : 10 secondes. Projection manuscrite : 15 secondes.

6°) Danseuse sur une glace transparente, cinématographiée par en-dessous : durée 1
minute, projection écrite : 5 secondes.

7°) Gonflage de ballons et paravents de caoutchouc, sur lesquels seront dessinés des
figures accompagnées d'inscriptions, durée : 35 secondes.

8°) Un enterrement ; Corbillard trainé par un chameau, etc. durée : 6 minutes, projection écrite : 1 minute.

Drawing by Jean Lurçat. Armchair MF 172.

Studio-house built for the painter Robert Motherwell with sections of a greenhouse and an American army Quonset hut.

Robert Motherwell's studio-house, interior. East Hampton, 1948.

"La Colline" ("The Hill"), 1948.

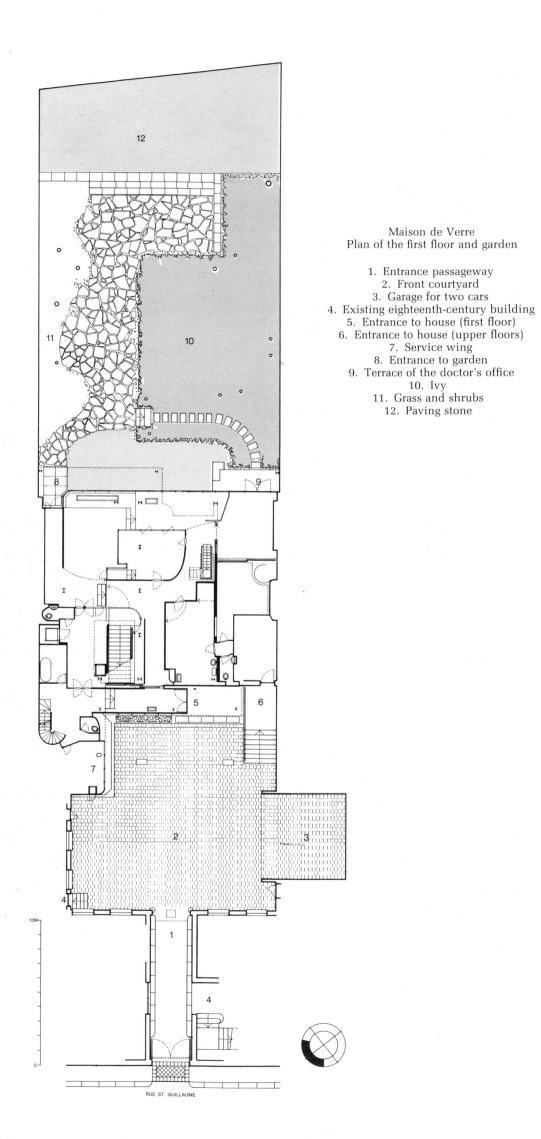

Maison de Verre
Plan of the first floor and garden

1. Entrance passageway
2. Front courtyard
3. Garage for two cars
4. Existing eighteenth-century building
5. Entrance to house (first floor)
6. Entrance to house (upper floors)
7. Service wing
8. Entrance to garden
9. Terrace of the doctor's office
10. Ivy
11. Grass and shrubs
12. Paving stone

RUE ST. GUILLAUME

The courtyard and garden front of 31 rue Saint-Guillaume, early 1928.

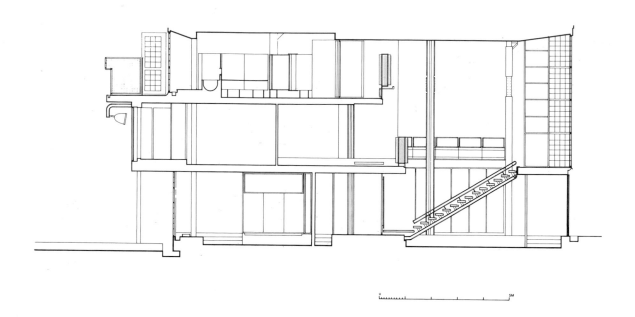

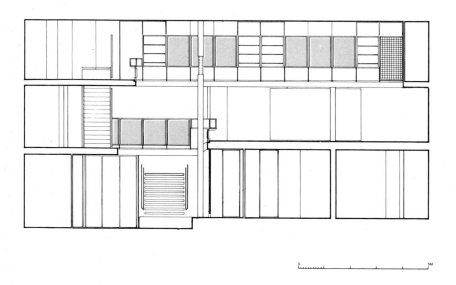

Maison de Verre: Longitudinal section
                    Transverse section

AR 1032. Maquette for the Maison de Verre exhibited at the 1931 Salon
d'Automne, as no. 348. Made by Dindeleux.

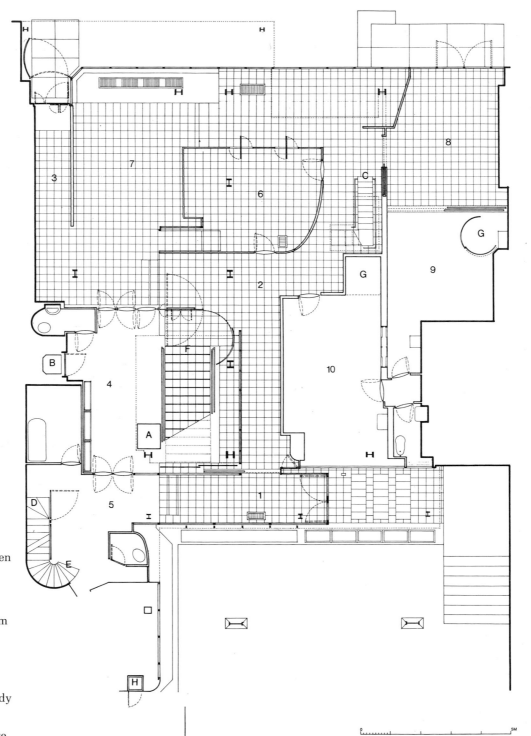

Plan of the first floor

1. Entrance
2. Main corridor
3. Corridor leading to garden
4. Servants' quarters
5. Tradesmen's entrance
6. Reception
7. Waiting room
8. Doctor's consulting room
9. Examination room
10. Surgery

A. Dumbwaiter
B. Elevator
C. Side staircase to the study
D. Staircase to kitchen
E. Staircase to basement
F. Main staircase to lounge
G. Cloakroom
H. Garbage bins

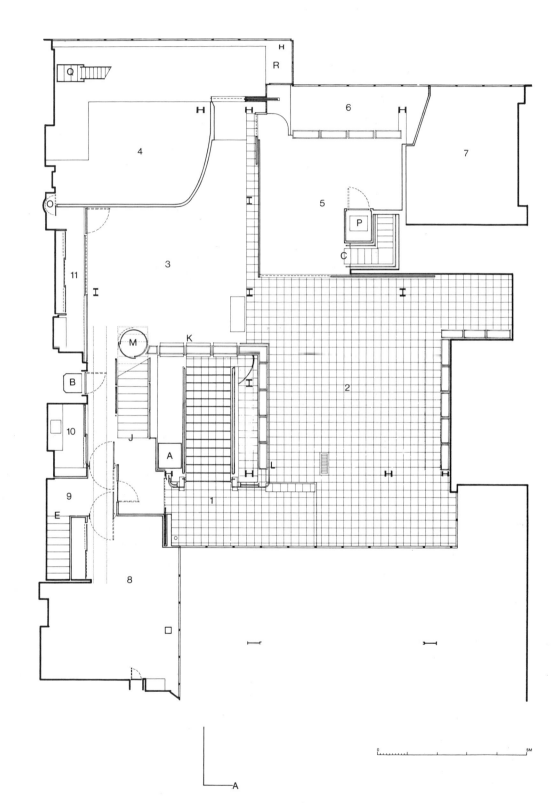

Plan of the second floor

1. Landing
2. Main lounge
3. Dining room
4. Small sun room
5. Study
6. Area above waiting room
7. Area above consulting room
8. Kitchen
9. Entrance to kitchen
10. Pantry
11. Storage room

A. Dumbwaiter
B. Elevator
C. Staircase down to consulting room
E. Staircase to kitchen
J. Staircase to third floor
K. Storage units
L. Low bookshelf units
M. Revolving broom cupboard
O. Passageway
P. Telephone cabin
Q. Removable stairs to main bedroom
R. Conservatory

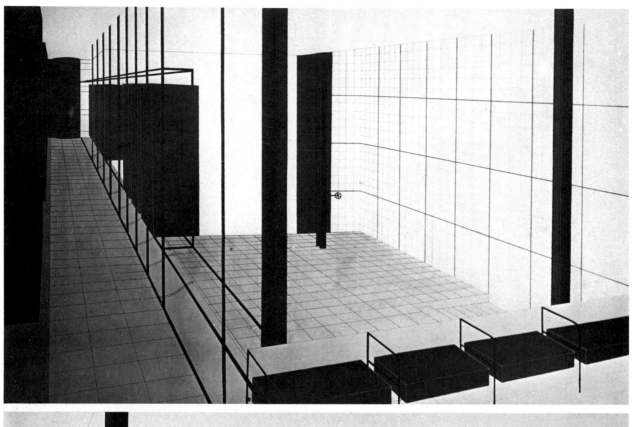

Maison de Verre

Top: Study for the bedroom corridor on the third floor.

Bottom: Study for the main entrance hall of the Maison de Verre. Several
changes are worth noting: the banisters on the main staircase were to disappear;
the folding partition screening the stairs to the third floor was not executed,
neither were the mobile units shown here on the right.

Maison de Verre. Study of the passageway from the waiting room to the doctor's consulting room.

The future Maison de Verre, seen from the courtyard (above) and the garden
(below), around April-May 1928.

AR 1048, courtyard of 31 Rue Saint-Guillaume, July 24, 1928.

AR 1043, view from the garden, July 24, 1928.

Maison de Verre, first floor of the service wing seen from the courtyard.

Maison de Verre, glass wall of the façade from the kitchen (second floor).

Maison de Verre

Top: Main hall on the second floor. The two nearest pillars are now covered over. The method of supporting ceilings and floors is clearly visible. The metal base to the curved wall of the dining room is in place.

Bottom: Third floor, façade and terrace around 1930. The highly refined structures of the future curtain wall on the left and the thickness of the ceiling are quite apparent.

First floor. Swing doors between the waiting room and the library stairwell. Black convex metal and untreated duralumin.

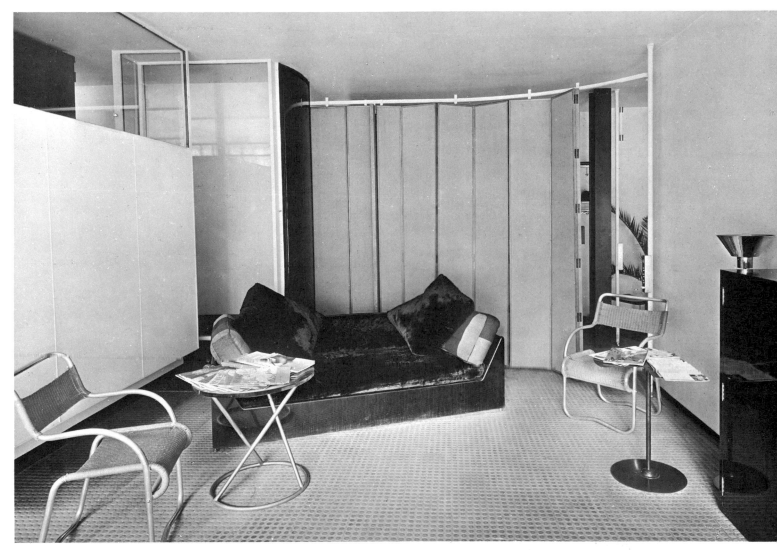

Maison de Verre, first floor. Waiting room.

his use of untreated duralumin
again undecotrive (pure - truth)

Maison de Verre, first floor, doctor's consulting room. First exhibited at the Salon
d'Automne of 1919, the furniture established Chareau's reputation and he
became a Salon member as a result. Furniture in macassar ebony.

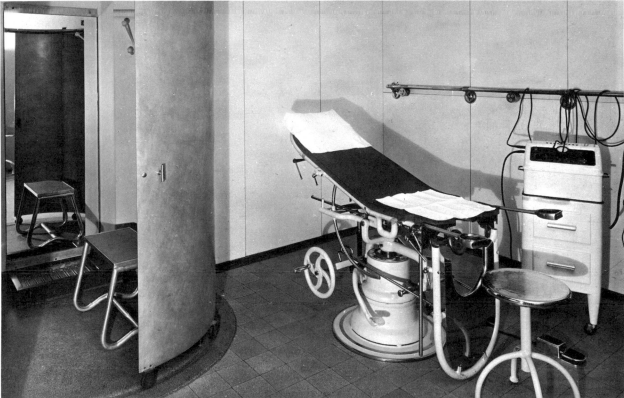

Maison de Verre, medical examination room seen from doctor's consulting room.
The sliding partition door is floor to ceiling height.

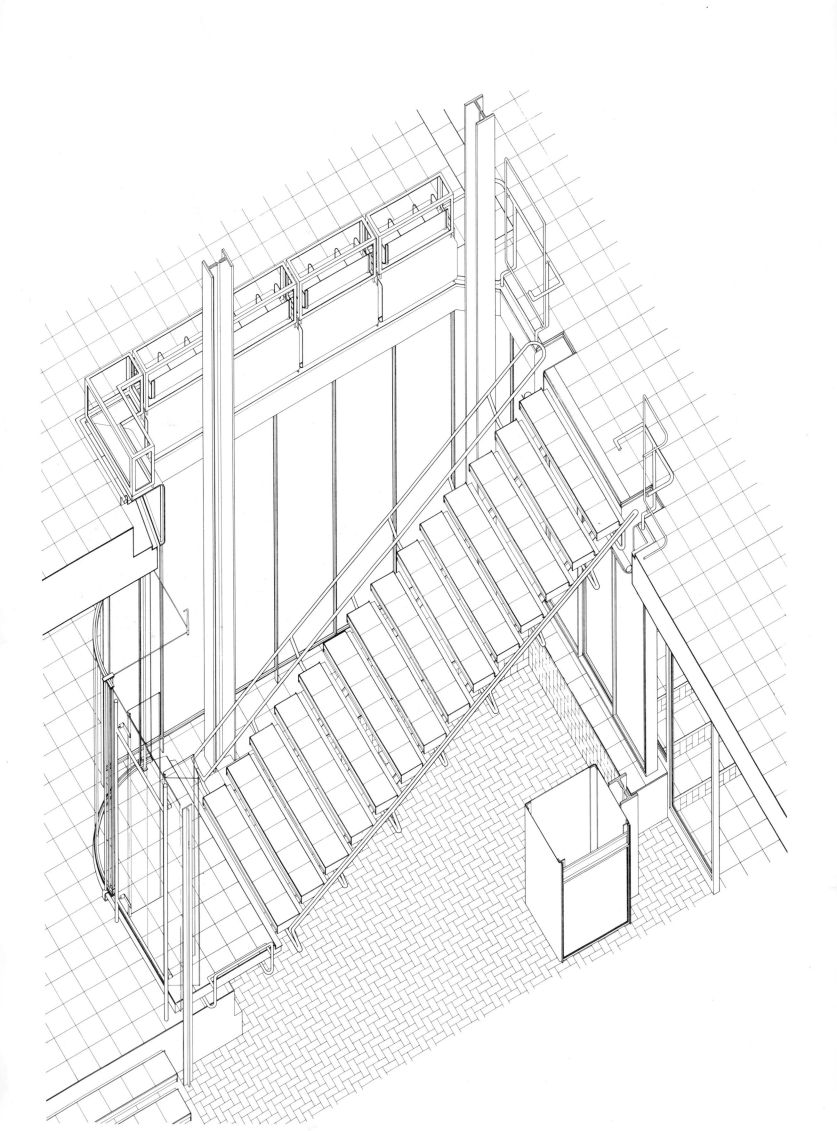

Maison de Verre, main staircase seen from the first floor.

Maison de Verre, first floor, passageway from the waiting room to the doctor's consulting room. On the floor is the slate-framed air vent. The façade windows open by turning handles which were inspired by industrial designs of the period.

Maison de Verre, first floor, passageway from the waiting room to the doctor's consulting room. View of the glass partitions separating the secretary's office. Spatial continuity is well illustrated here. The balustrade bookshelves of the second floor can be seen.

Maison de Verre, dining room just after construction, c. 1933.

Maison de Verre, second floor. Main hall, dining room and doctor's study. Above
are the balustrade bookshelves and cupboards of the third floor.

Maison de Verre, third floor bathroom. Detail of shower and bath. Sliding
partitions in perforated sheet metal, soap tray in brass. Gray glass mosaic on wall
and around pillars.

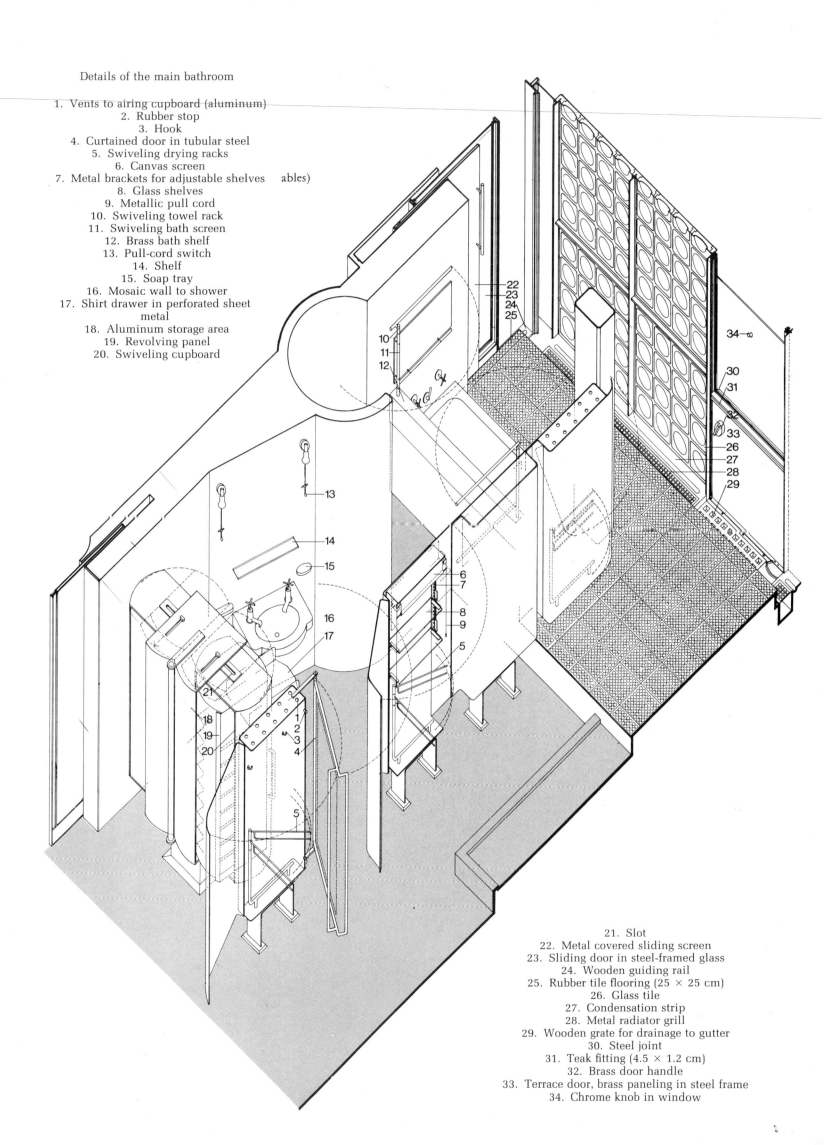

Details of the main bathroom

1. Vents to airing cupboard (aluminum)
2. Rubber stop
3. Hook
4. Curtained door in tubular steel
5. Swiveling drying racks
6. Canvas screen
7. Metal brackets for adjustable shelves   ables)
8. Glass shelves
9. Metallic pull cord
10. Swiveling towel rack
11. Swiveling bath screen
12. Brass bath shelf
13. Pull-cord switch
14. Shelf
15. Soap tray
16. Mosaic wall to shower
17. Shirt drawer in perforated sheet metal
18. Aluminum storage area
19. Revolving panel
20. Swiveling cupboard

21. Slot
22. Metal covered sliding screen
23. Sliding door in steel-framed glass
24. Wooden guiding rail
25. Rubber tile flooring (25 × 25 cm)
26. Glass tile
27. Condensation strip
28. Metal radiator grill
29. Wooden grate for drainage to gutter
30. Steel joint
31. Teak fitting (4.5 × 1.2 cm)
32. Brass door handle
33. Terrace door, brass paneling in steel frame
34. Chrome knob in window

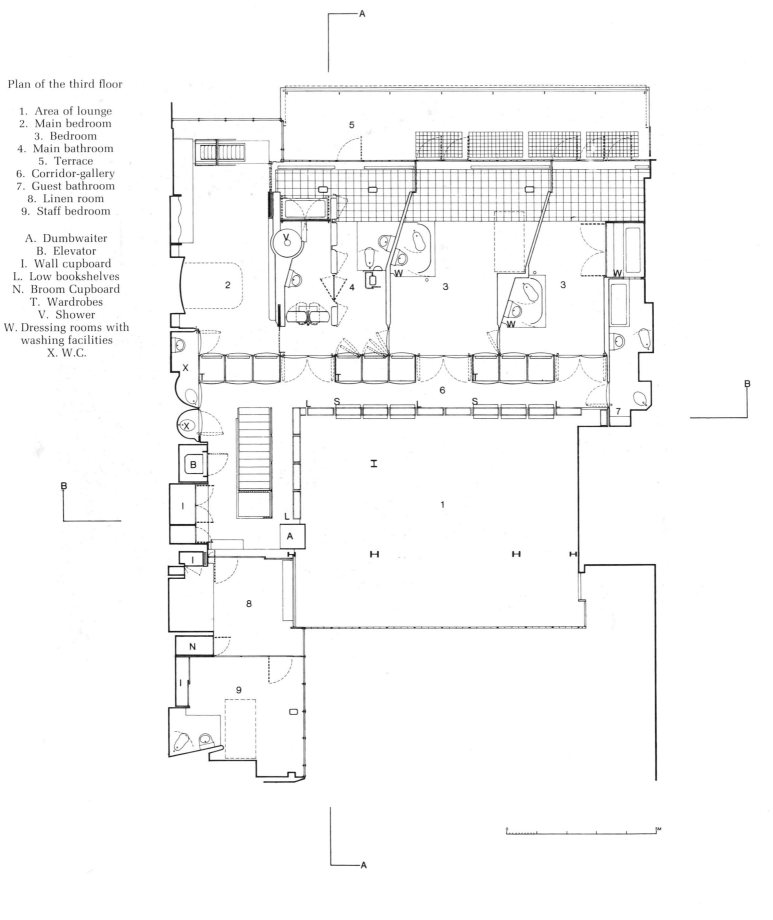

Plan of the third floor

1. Area of lounge
2. Main bedroom
3. Bedroom
4. Main bathroom
5. Terrace
6. Corridor-gallery
7. Guest bathroom
8. Linen room
9. Staff bedroom

A. Dumbwaiter
B. Elevator
I. Wall cupboard
L. Low bookshelves
N. Broom Cupboard
T. Wardrobes
V. Shower
W. Dressing rooms with
   washing facilities
X. W.C.

Maison de Verre, third-floor bathroom. Duralumin joinery. Terrazzo or natural-
rubber tile flooring. Walls in gray glass mosaic.

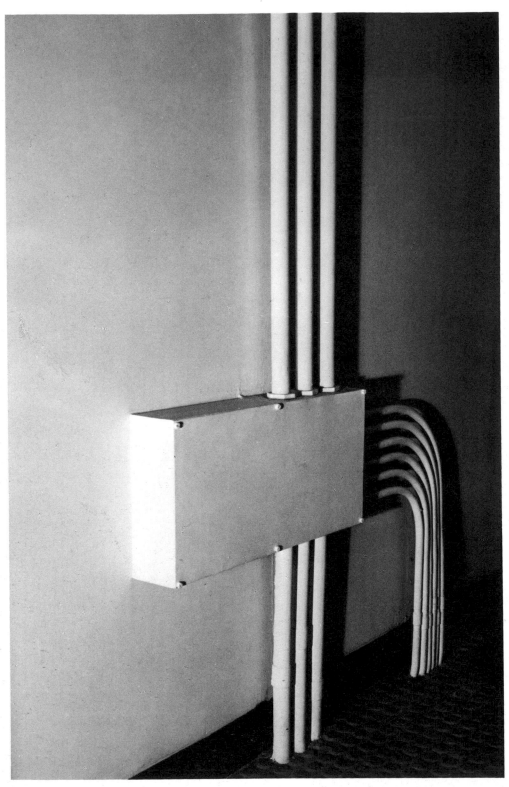

Maison de Verre. Electric conduits and switchboard. An electrician can do his work without touching the walls.

Maison de Verre, second floor. Corridor between kitchen and dining room. Pantry designed to receive dishes from a trolley linked to ceiling rails. Main switch and fuse board. The service hatch was dismantled.

Overleaf: Maison de Verre, perforated metal screen in corridor of third floor. ▷

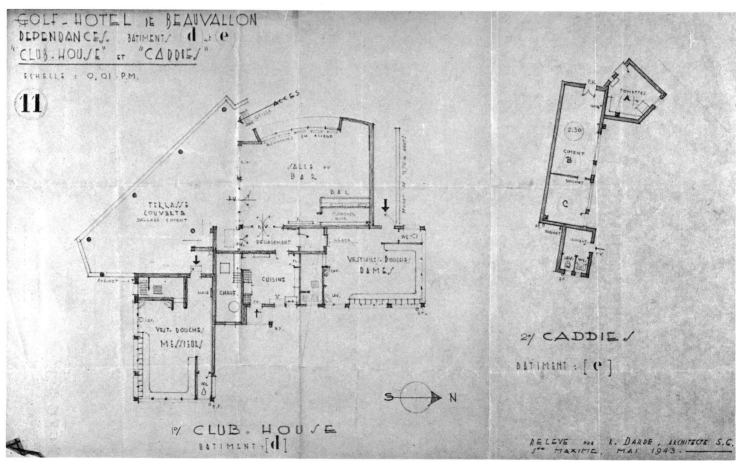

Top: Maquette for the "Vent d'Aval" villa. Chareau's design was built in his absence during World War II. It was planned to house three generations of the family.

Bottom: Plan of the clubhouse at Beauvallon.

Clubhouse at Beauvallon.

AR 685. Clubhouse at Beauvallon. Terrace and façade.

AR 684. Clubhouse at Beauvallon. Court and terrace.

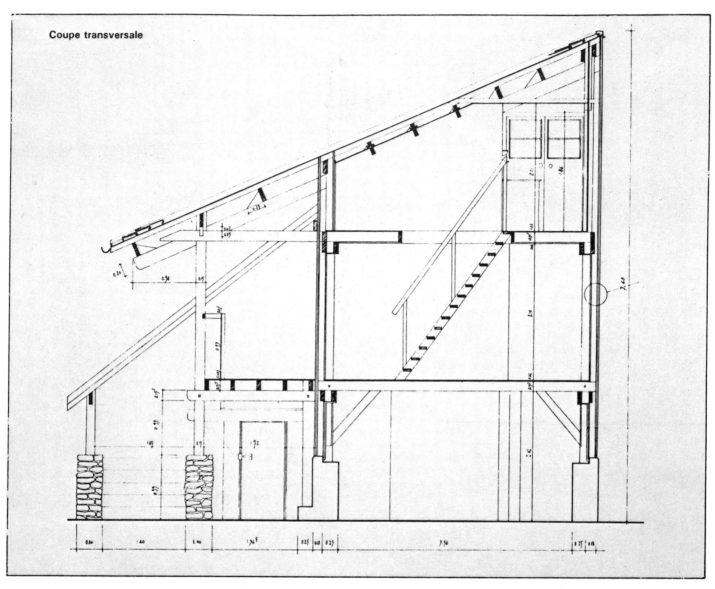

Coupe transversale

Cross-section of Djemil Anik's house.

Djemil Anik's house in the Paris region, 1937.

292

FOREWORD TO CATALOGUE

TITLE

This is the original name given to an item of furniture (such as "La Religieuse"), or a classification used by contemporary critics. Failing this, there is a simple indication of its nature. Where the English translation lacks precision, the original French term has been given in parentheses.

DATE

This is either the date given on the original photographic document, when it is certain, or the date of the first publication in which the item appeared. In the absence of a specific dating, an informed approximation (such as c.1927: circa 1927) will be given, or an indication of the period (such as 1927–9). When there is no information whatsoever as to the date of an item, it is omitted.

DESCRIPTION

This is given only when necessary. The wood used is specified when known for certain, although this does not imply that the item was made exclusively with this wood.

DIMENSIONS

All measurements are given in centimeters.

h.	height	*w.*	width
l.	length	*d.*	depth
diam.	diameter		

VERSIONS

Different versions of an item are described when their common source is known. It was impossible to locate every variation in size.

WHEREABOUTS

The current location of an item is given only when of a public nature.
The abbreviation *p.c.* indicates that the item or version is known to exist in a private collection. The abbreviation C. refers to items belonging to an identified collection. Whereabouts unknown means that no example of the item has been found to date.

REFERENCES

The reader will find abbreviated references (titles and dates) to articles and books in which the item is cited. Further details of the most important will be found in the bibliography.

EXHIBITIONS

Exhib: is followed by abbreviated references to exhibitions that are listed in full at the end of this book.

SALES

Location (in France unless otherwise stated), date, sales number, and price in French francs.

ABBREVIATIONS USED

C.	Collection of original owner
p.c.	Private collection
EIADIM	Exposition Internationale des Arts Décoratifs et Industriels Modernes, Paris
LdA	Louvre des Antiquaires, Paris
M.A.D.	Musée des Arts Décoratifs, Paris
S.A.D.	Salon des Artistes Décorateurs
Sd'A	Salon d'Automne, Grand Palais, Paris

CATALOGUE

EA 752 Music cabinet, 1928. *C. Reifenberg.*
Mobilier et Décoration, no. 5, April 1928,
p. 168.

EF 596 Cf. MT 344.

EF 610 Table. Cf. MB 170, 770. C. Mme G.

EF 928 Hung bed (Lit balancelle), 1925.
Black wrought-iron frame. High wall
suspension. *h.* 200, *l.* 230, *w.* 93. Three
versions: for the lounge next to the French
embassy sportsroom (1925, fabric by Hélène
Henry, cf. ET 249, 253); for the Villa
d'Hyères built by Mallet-Stevens for the
Noailles family; for Hélène Bernheim. C.
Comtesse de Noailles, Bernheim, *p.c. Les
Arts de la Maison*, Fall 1925, pl. VI. *Art et
Décoration*, July-December 1928, Vol. LIV,
p. 17. Ed., *R. Mallet-Stevens*, p. 198.

EH 52 Bed. Amboyna wood veneer. *La
Renaissance de l'Art Français*, G. Janneau,
"Le mouvement moderne: les salons d'art
décoratif," p. 700.

EH 176 Tub chair, 1923. Bergère with floor
skirting. Back top edged in wood. C.
Dalsace, *p.c. La Renaissance de l'Art
Français*, no. 4, April 1923, p. 203. *L'Amour
de l'Art*, no. 5, April 1924, p. 116. *Les Arts
de la Maison*, Winter 1924, p. 19 (plan).
Herbst, *Un Inventeur*, p. 33. *Exhib*: M.A.D.,
1923.

EN 12 Three armchairs, 1923. Painted
wickerwork. The first has a gondola back
with six sloping panels, the two center
panels forming the backrest, the two
hollowed-out panels on each side forming
armrests. Floor skirting except, sometimes,
at front (cf. EN 741, 742, 752). The second
is a rocking-chair version of the above, with
short or floor-length skirting. The third is a
tub chair, with full arms and floor skirting
except at front. Part of the Children's Corner
displayed at the 15th S.A.D. (cf. EN 161). C.
Dalsace, *p.c. L'Art et les Artistes*, no. 46,
April 1924, p. 283. *Mobilier et Décoration*,
no. 8, July 1928, p. 227 (floor skirting, no
rocker). *La Renaissance de l'Art Français*,
no. 7, July 1923, p. 433. *L'Amour de l'Art*,
no. 5, May 1923, p. 559. *Art et Décoration*,
January-June 1923, Vol. XLIII, p. 173. *Exhib*:
15th S.A.D., 1923.

ET 47, 48, 49 and ET 50, 523 Two
bathrooms, 1920 and 1925. *L'Art et les
Artistes*, no. 46, April 1924, p. 285. *Art et
Décoration*, July-December 1920, Vol.
XXXVIII, p. 152. *La Renaissance de l'Art
Français*, no. 1, January 1921, p. 40. *Art et
Décoration*, January-June 1923, Vol. XLIII,
pp. 134–136. *Les Arts de la Maison*, Winter
1924, pl. VII (gouache). *Art et Décoration*,
May 1925, p. 159. *Art et Décoration*, January
1931, Vol. LIX, p. 107. Moussinac, *Intérieurs
I*, pls. 9, 10, 11 (gouache), 12 (photo). *Exhib*:
First bathroom shown in Sd'A, 1920.

ET 508, c.1920. C. Dreyfus. *Art et
Décoration*, July-December 1920, Vol.
XXXVIII, p. 152. *Les Arts de la Maison*,
Winter 1924, pl. VII, bathroom (gouache).
Art et Décoration, 1932, p. 131.

EZ 849 Small writing table, 1930.
Rectangular surface with one edge bent over
to accommodate light fitting. Tubular stand
on circular base. Metal. Designed for
entrance hall of La Semaine à Paris, Rue
d'Assas. *L'Amour de l'Art*, January 1930,
p. 72. Herbst, *Un Inventeur*, 1954, p. 94.
Exhib: Sd'A, 1929.

LA 164 Wall lamp (Lampe appliqué) 1923.
A quarter-circle alabaster plaque supported
by three metal attachments. Appeared in
sets of Marcel l'Herbier's film, *L'Inhumaine*,
1923. *L'Amour de l'Art*, no. 4, April 1924,
p. 123. *Les Arts de la Maison*, Winter 1924,
pl. 1 (gouache). Ed., *R. Mallet-Stevens*, 1980,
p. 133.

LA 250, 252 Lamp, c.1925. Three wedge-
shaped alabaster blocks mounted on the end
of an extending arm consisting of three
hinged metal blades. Made for the "Study-
library of a French embassy," EIADIM,
1925. *Les Arts de la Maison*, Spring 1926,
pl. XVII, figs. 5, 6. *Exhib*: EIADIM, 1925.

LA 254 Bracket lamp, c.1926. Fixed version
of LA 250, C. G. Reifenberg. *Mobilier et
Décoration*, no. 5, April 1928, pp. 167–168,
no. 8, July 1928, p. 226. Herbst, *Un
Inventeur*, pp. 75, 98–99.

LA 271, LP 625 (front and back, electric
fitting) of LA 665 Bracket lamp, c.1926.
Five-sided section of a near parallelepiped
in alabaster held by a metal attachment
connected to the electric fitting. *h.* 14.5, *l.*
16, *w.* 11. Model used for several other
bracket and hanging lamps (cf. LA 250, LA
252, LA 254, LA 271 in doubled form, LA
321, LA 550, LT 314, LT 753). Herbst, *Un
Inventeur*, p. 73. Double version with one
light shade above the other in *Les Arts de la
Maison*, Summer 1926, pls. XXIX, XXX.
Triple version LA 254. Hinged triple
version, LA 250, LA 252. *Sale*: Monaco, 24–
25 October, 1982, no. 360, 362.

LA 292 Bracket lamp. Alabaster triangle
held by two metal clips. Herbst, *Un
Inventeur*, p. 98.

LA 315 Bracket lamp, 1923. Two segments
of a circle in alabaster joined at their radius
to form a corner angle. *L'Amour de l'Art*,
no. 1, November 1923, p. 748; no. 4, April
1924, p. 123. *Exhib*: Sd'A, 1923. LA 188
double version of above, on metallic
support.

LA 317 Lamp. Cf. LA 548.

LA 321 Composite lamp. Two alabaster
blocks (as in model LA 665) set back to
back and hung on cross-shaped metal strips.

LA 415 Bracket lamp. Cf. LA 548.

LA 548 Bracket lamp, c.1924. Three
alabaster plaques, two trapezoidal and one
rectangular, fixed by metal attachments. C.
Dreyfus. *Art et Décoration*, 1932, Vol. LXI,
p. 129. Herbst, *Un Inventeur*, pp. 63, 74, 99.
Version on metal plate support, LA 317.
Version with four alabaster plaques, LA 415.

LA 550 Bracket lamp, c.1927. Two alabaster
blocks as model LA 271, set back to back on
either side of an upright metal T-bar. C.
Reifenberg. *L'Art International
d'Aujourd'hui*, no. 6, pl. 13. Herbst, *Un
Inventeur*, p. 101.

LA 555 Bracket lamp, c.1927. Six
rectangular alabaster plaques distributed
symmetrically either side of the upright and
under the horizontal of a metal T-bar.
Mobilier et Décoration, no. 2, January 1927,
p. 101. *Exhib*: M.A.D., 1927.

LP 133, LP 414 Lamp, 1924–5. Metal.
Appeared in sets of Marcel l'Herbier's film,
L'Inhumaine, 1923, for which it may have

been designed. *Les Arts de la Maison*,
Spring 1926, pl. XVIII. *L'Art International
d'Aujourd'hui*, no. 10, pl. 15. Herbst, *Un
Inventeur*, p. 85. Ed., *R. Mallet-Stevens*,
p. 131.

LP 166 Lamp, c.1924. Several rectangular
alabaster plaques arranged around and
above a cylindrical base. *Les Arts de la
Maison*, Winter 1924, p. 18; Spring 1926, pl.
XVII, fig. 2. Herbst, *Un Inventeur*, p. 73.

LP 180, 181 Lamp, 1922–4. Base composed
of a triangular strip of wrought metal folded
in upon itself at two right angles, with a
tube inserted into its uppermost surface
supporting a counterweight, a metal strip
bent into an S shape bearing shades formed
by two alabaster quadrants. Another version
consisting simply of the base and shades.
Appeared in sets of Marcel l'Herbier's film
Le Vertige, 1925. C. Bernheim, Dalsace, *p.c.
Les Arts de la Maison*, Winter 1924, p. 18;
Spring 1926, pl. XVII, fig. 1. *Mobilier et
Décoration*, no. 2, January 1927, p. 103.
Herbst, *Un Inventeur*, p. 78. Ed., *R. Mallet-
Stevens*, p. 223. 1930,..., 1981, no. 126.
Version with metal bar on the vertical side
of the base and detachable reflectors. *Les
Arts de la Maison*, Spring 1926, pl. XVII,
fig. 3; Winter 1926, pl. XL. Tall version with
same base but with upright metal bar
crossing the upper fold of the wrought-
metal triangle and supporting a hinged
bracket on which the alabaster shades are
fixed. *Les Arts de la Maison*, Winter 1924,
pl. II (in gouache); Spring 1926, pl. XIX.
Bracket lamp version, 1923. *Art et
Décoration*, January-June 1923, Vol. XLIII,
p. 173. *Exhib*: 15th S.A.D., 1923.

LP 270 Ceiling light, c.1923. Eight or more
rectangular alabaster plaques clustered
around the end of a metal T-shaped or flat
bar. Made for the Indochinese pavilion at
EIADIM, 1925, and for the Grand-Hôtel at
Tours. *L'Art et les Artistes*, January 1928,
no. 83, p. 132. *Art et Décoration*, January-
June 1923, Vol. XLIII, p. 173. *Mobilier et
Décoration*, no. 2, January 1927, p. 105. *La
Renaissance des Arts Français*, no. 8,
August 1925, p. 358. *L'Amour de l'Art*, no.
8, August 1925, p. 315. *Les Arts de la
Maison*, Spring 1926, pl. XVIII.
Encyclopédie des Métiers d'Art, Vol. I, pls.
59, 61. Herbst, *Un Inventeur*, pp. 89, 99.
Exhib: S.A.D., 1923. LP 166, version with
cylindrical base.

LP 998 Lamp, 1930–2. Spherical globe of
opaline glass resting on a transparent glass
base formed by two plates of glass crossing
at right angles. C. Fleg. *Art et Décoration*,
1932, p. 139.

LP 1003 Bedside lamps. A cylinder that has
been cut to form a spiral. Nickel-plated
metal and frosted glass. *h.* 20. *Sale*: Cornette de
Saint-Cyr, 12/5/83, no. 51, 20,000 FF.

LT 314 Composite lamp. Cf. LA 321, LT
753.

LT 753 Composite lamp. Version of LA 321
in a horizontal pair. Two alabaster reflectors
as in model LA 271 set back to back and
held by metal attachments. Made for the
Grand-Hôtel at Tours, 1928. C. Reifenberg.
Mobilier et Décoration, no. 5, April 1928,
p. 167. Herbst, *Un Inventeur*, p. 100. LT
314, version suspended from the end of a
strip of wrought metal.

MA 69 Chair, 1922–8. Floor skirting except at front. Two small rectangular spaces in upper back. Wickerwork. h. 80, w. 40, d. 38. C. Dalsace, p.c. Sale: Monaco, 6 March, 1983, no. 161 (in group MF 18 × 2, MB 595, and large couch).

MA 99 Chest of drawers (Commode), c.1919. Bow-fronted side columns of six drawers, top drawer of which is smaller, either side of a flat central block of six drawers of equivalent size, diamond-shaped locks, ivory threading at top of each drawer. Knotted elm. Made in 1918 for Doctor and Madame Dalsace. h. 111, w. 151, d. 58. C. Dalsace, p.c. Herbst, Un Inventeur, p. 87.

MA 109 Cupboard (Meuble de rangement), c.1925. Three flattened columns separating two single-panel doors. Central column has four drawers decorated with geometric motifs, side columns have one top drawer. Raised on eight small circular metal feet. Palisander and thuya wood. Mobilier et Décoration, no. 2, January 1927, p. 100.

MA 112 Armoire. Two single-panel doors set over four drawers. Doors and drawers edged with lighter wood. Raised on four light-wood ball feet. Knotted elm or walnut.

MA 205 Commode (Commode a doucine). Single row of drawers between two doors. Square drawer knobs in ivory, two side flaps. Amboyna and palisander on oak core. Version omitting upper area. h. 80, l. 95, w. 56. C. Dreyfus, p.c. Sale: Cornette de Saint-Cyr, 12/5/83, no. 83.

MA 333, 334 Low cupboard (Bahut). Inscribed 1925. Main storage area divided in two and enclosed by two double doors. Above this, a line of five drawers over which two sliding doors open onto a single shelf. Small door opening onto box area at either side of shelf.

MA 374, 420, 1992 Small linen cupboard, c.1927. Sometimes called linen chest ("coffre à linge"). Box chest with single door, encased in wrought-iron mount. MA 374, version V1: five linen shelves on a pivot situated on the same side as the chest hinge. Sycamore with mahogany interior. MA 1092, version with mirror above. Version V2: cabinetwork chest supported by wide wrought-iron strip that encloses it on three sides and terminates in inward-turned angles. 3 shelves and 8 drawers on one side, 15 small compartments and 5 shallower drawers on the other. Knotted walnut with sycamore interior. h. 99, l. 70. C. Reifenberg, Simon. V2: Michel Souillac coll., p.c. Art et Décoration, January-June 1927, Vol. LI, p. 108. Mobilier et Décoration, no. 5, April 1928, p. 169. Nouveaux Intérieurs Français, Paris, 1933, pl. 13. L'Art International d'Aujourd'hui, no. 7, pl. 31. Encyclopédie des Métiers d'Art, Vol. I, pl. 17, m. 8. Herbst, Un Inventeur, p. 86. V2: 1930,..., no. 97. Florence Camard, "Mobilier Art Déco; la rencontre du bois et du métal," Guide de la XIème Biennale des Antiquaires, Paris, 1982, p. 111.

MA 384 Armoire. Nursery armoire. Two cupboards with double doors separated by three rows of shelves over a mantelpiece.

MA 537, 538, 539, 540. Armoire. The front section of a cylinder recedes into the wall to reveal two rows of drawers, a wardrobe or

mirror which can be swiveled round into use at will. Designed for M. and Mme Reifenberg's apartment, Rue Mallet-Stevens. C. Reifenberg.

MA 567 Low cupboard bookcase (Bahut-bibliothèque). Double door. The cupboard surface forms a shelf of the bookcase which extends down the left side.

MA 788 Sideboard (Bahut), c.1928. In two units: the larger resting on stand with two sliding doors, the smaller suspended above, elongated, with three sliding panels and a cabinet below, the top of which has a hinge attachment towards the back. Square locks. C. Bernheim. Mobilier et Décoration, no. 8, July 1928, pp. 228–229. L'Art International d'Aujourd'hui, no. 7, pl. 42.

MA 866 Low cupboard (Bahut). Three single doors. Woodwork covered in shagreen?

MA 1005 Commode, c.1927. Two storage areas enclosed by single doors and separated by a row of four drawers. Palisander. Mobilier et Décoration, no. 2, January 1927, p. 102.

MA 1055 Lady's writing desk with sloping sides (Bureau de femme á pans coupés). Cf. MB 1055. Ebony. Herbst, Un Inventeur, p. 88.

MB 14, 16 Nursery dressing table (Table à langer), 1922–3. Circular tabletop on four cylindrical legs linked by a crossbar, sliding net drawer under top. Oak. Exhib. in the Children's Corner at the 15th S.A.D. C. Dalsace, p.c. Les Arts et Les Artistes, no. 46, April 1924, p. 283. La Renaissance de l'Art Français, no. 7, July 1923, p. 433. L'Amour de l'Art, no. 5, May 1923, p. 559. Art et Décoration, January-June 1923, Vol. XLIII, p. 173.

MB 97 Table, c.1923. Oval top resting on four slightly buckled leaves of wood, joined at base by two crescent-shaped feet. Cf. MB 110, MP 102. Designed for the Indochinese pavilion. Exhib: EIADIM, 1925, and S.A.D., 1925(?). L'Amour de l'Art, no. 1, January 1926, p. 315.

MB 98 Small pedestal table bookcase (Petit guéridon bibliothèque), c.1923. Shelves enclosed by wings forming cross over oval pedestal. C. Simon, p.c. Palisander and amourette wood, marble plaque. Art et Décoration, July-December 1923, Vol. XLIV, p. 179. L'Amour de l'Art, no. 4, April 1924, p. 117. Art et Décoration, May 1925, p. 155. Herbst, Un Inventeur, p. 95. Exhib: Sd'A, 1923(?). Version alongside single bed EH 300 (1925), MP 102.

MB 106 Occasional tables (Tables basses), c.1924. Nest of four triangular-surfaced tables that fan out around an axis through the acute angle of each triangle. h. 55/64, l. 65, w. 40. Palisander, palm wood, or mahogany, bronze hinge. Appeared in Pierre Chareau's apartment (EB 408). C. Bernheim, Dalsace, Chareau, Dreyfus, G., p.c. Les Arts de la Maison, Winter 1924, pp. 20, 26; Winter 1926, pl. XXXIX. Mobilier et Décoration, no. 2, January 1927, p. 99. Good Furniture Magazine, January 1927, p. 30. Vogue, May 1927, p. 41. Mobilier et Décoration, no. 8, July 1928, pp. 215–221. Parures, no. 27, 15 September 1928. Foreign Trade, no. 12, December 1928, p. 42. Art et

Décoration, 1932, p. 134. Architecture d'Aujourd'hui, November-December 1933, p. 4. Art et Décoration, 1934, Vol. LVIII, pp. 50, 55. L'Art International d'Aujourd'hui, no. 6, pl. 6. Herbst, Un Inventeur, pp. 9, 20, 25. 1925, p. 211. Global Architecture, no. 46, 1977, pp. 28–31. Exhib: Sd'A, 1926.

MB 110 Small table (Petit guéridon), c.1923. Oval top, resting on slightly buckled leaves of wood, joined at base by two crescent-shaped feet, cf. MB 97, MP 102. h. 52, l. 60, w. 48. C. Bernheim, Reifenberg. Art et Décoration July-December 1923, Vol. XLIV, p. 179. Mobilier et Décoration, no. 5, April 1928, p. 169. Encyclopédie des Métiers d'Art, Vol. II, pl. 76, 77. L'Art International d'Aujourd'hui, no. 6, p. 12. Herbst, Un Inventeur, p. 76.

MB 113, 808, 810 Work desk (Bureau de travail), 1921. Top resting on two side pedestals each of which houses a pull-out cabinet with storage areas. At either end an extension leaf on two legs can be pulled out from the main body of the desk. Central drawer under top surface. Cf. EB 54. Palisander or walnut, cabinet interiors in sycamore. h. 78, l. 175, w. 89. C. Bernheim, p.c. L'Amour de l'Art, no. 3, March 1922, p. 86. MB 808, version with wider handles. Les Arts de la Maison, Winter 1924, pp. 21, 26, pl. II (gouache).

MB 130 Low table (Petite table basse), 1923–5. Oval top on full floor stand with small drawer and inside shelf. Two wings with rounded triangular tops open out from pivot either side. Walnut and knotted walnut, Cuban mahogany or palisander. Appeared in sets of Marcel l'Herbier's film Le Vertige, 1925. h. 55, l. 63, w. 47/80. C. Dalsace. Michel Souillac coll. p.c. Nouveaux Intérieurs Français, 1933, pl. 15. Art et Décoration, 1934, Vol. LXIII, p. 52. Mobilier et Décoration, no. 2, January 1937, p. 105. Herbst, Un Inventeur, pp. 29, 84. Global Architecture, no. 46, 1977, p. 28. R. Mallet-Stevens, p. 225. Exhib: LdA, 1981, no. 83.

MB 152 Low table, c.1925. Nest of four triangular-surfaced tables, swiveling from the right of a column, the hollow upper area of which can be used as a bookcase. Cf. MB 277, single table version. Art et Décoration, no. 2, May 1925, p. 155. Les Arts de la Maison, Summer 1926, pl. XXIX (studio II).

MB 170 Table, c.1923. Hexagonal top over tulip-shaped stand with six sides on hexagonal base. Cf. MB 770, EF 610. Made for the Grand-Hôtel at Tours, and elsewhere. h. 60, l. 79, w. 77.5, h. 60, l. 92, w. 80. Sycamore, palisander, macassar ebony, or walnut. C. Dreyfus, Fleg, Grumbach, Bernheim, l'Herbier. L'Amour de l'Art, no. 3, March 1923, p. 487. Les Arts de la Maison, Summer 1926, pl. XXVI, XXVII. Art et Décoration, January-June 1928, Vol. LIII, p. 35. Mobilier et Décoration, no. 8, July 1928, pp. 222–225. P. Olmer, L'Art Décoratif en 1928, Paris, n.d., p. 22. Art et Décoration, 1932, p. 129. Encyclopédie des Métiers d'Art, Vol. I, pl. 59. Herbst, Un Inventeur, pp. 74–75. Sale: Monaco 24–25 October, 1982, no. 366. Enghien, Champin, 15 November, 1981.

MB 180 Table, c.1924 (Straight-legged version). Lux, April 1924, p. 440.

MB 186 Table. Rectangular top with rounded corners resting on eight legs, four outer legs, the lower part of which form a base, four other legs on narrower cubic feet. Cf. EM 911, smaller version, four full square-sectioned legs.

MB 212 French embassy desk, 1925. Flat work surface between two sloping surfaces concealing lockers. Raised inclined back containing a removable letter file, covered in pigskin, behind two sliding flaps. Supported in front by two pedestals with three drawers either side, and behind by two detached side-opening cupboards. Polished steel handles. Palisander veneer on mahogany and oak. *h.* 76, *l.* 140, *w.* 77. Designed and made for the French embassy exhibit in EIADIM, 1925. Bought from the artist in 1926, by the M.A.D. for 1,200 francs (no. 25480). Another example known to exist. C. M.G. Whereabouts unknown. *Les Arts de la Maison*, Fall 1925, pl. IV. *Beaux Arts*, June 1925, p. 26. *Vogue*, September 1925, p. 40. *L'Amour de l'Art*, no. 8, August 1925, p. 313. *Art et Décoration*, July-December 1925, pls. XXXVII–XXXVIII. *Mobilier et Décoration*, no. 8, July 1928, p. 218. Herbst, *Un Inventeur*, p. 90. 1925, p. 67 (gouache). *Exhib*: Paris, 1925, p. 98. M.A.D., 1937, no. 688. M.A.D., 1966, no. 577. Milan, 1966, 1975. M.A.D., 1983.

MB 233 Table, c.1920. Rectangular top with lowered rounded sides, on full lateral supports resting at either side on two parallelepipeds. Version with full feet. C. Dalsace. Whereabouts unknown. *Les Arts de la Maison*, Winter 1924, pl. I (gouache).

MB 241a Folding game table (Table de jeu mouchoir), c.1926. Long narrow surface with rounded ends along the central axis of which the diagonal line of a square-top surface rests. The corners of the latter fold in to form a smaller square. Rounded outer supports made up of three strips at inward facing angles. The two outer corners of the unfolded game table are supported by wooden legs, oval in cross-section, which fold back into the main body. Cuban mahogany or walnut. Brass ashtrays. Bronze hinges. *h.* 65/69, *l.* 140, *w.* 52. C. Dalsace, *p.c. Les Arts de la Maison*, Summer 1926, pls. XII, XXI–XXV. *Architecture d'Aujourd'hui*, November-December 1933, p. 4. *Art et Décoration*, 1934, Vol. LVIII, p. 50. Herbst, *Un Inventeur*, pp. 19–20. 1925, p. 211. *Global Architecture*, no. 46, pp. 24–31.

MB 277 Table, c.1926. Low table with a hollowed-out column that can be used as a bookcase. Tabletop curves round and back at one end, with rounded lateral support beneath. *h.* 80. Sycamore or dark wood. C. Reifenberg, B. (EL 565), *p.c. Les Arts de la Maison*, Winter 1924, p. 20. *Mobilier et Décoration*, no. 5, April 1928, p. 167. *Encyclopédie des Métiers d'Art*, Vol. II, pl. 76. *Exhib*: LdA, 1981, no. 81. Version without column, EH 400. Version without column, three drawers, MS 1009. Version without column, three drawers, mirror, and metal shelves on right side, MS 1009.

MB 345 Bar table. High table with solid rectangular top on full lateral supports. Base a triangle in cross-section. Mahogany or palisander. *h.* 91, *l.* 44.5, *w.* 34.5. C. Bernheim, Dalsace, *p.c.* High version with bar stool and low version with mahogany and green leather upholstered armchair made for the Grand-Hôtel at Tours.

Encyclopédie des Métiers d'Art, Vol. I, pl. 66. Herbst, *Un Inventeur*, pp. 64–66, 93.

MB 388 Desk. Rectangular top surface in wood, encased in wrought-iron strip. Wrought-iron supports, extending at right, over the tabletop, with a locker mounted at right angles to the surface, and below the surface, on the same side, a shelf hung parallel to the locker. On the left, a small table swivels out from under the work surface. Version with metal cube (light) in the extension to the support. C. Dreyfus *p.c.* Cf. ES 856, 857, 858. Version with cubic locker in metal, open on two sides, that swivels out from under the rectangular tabletop, on an axis parallel to the right-hand support, the L-shaped top of which supports a shelf; swivel side table on left.

MB 405 Desk, 1927. L-shaped work top, with frame and feet in wrought-iron strips, forming inverted T base on left-hand side, and side table swiveling out from under work surface above. On right, a shelf mounted in the metal strip extending from feet below. Wrought iron and palisander. *h.* 82/93, *l.* 161, *w.* 40/103. Cf. MB 388, 405, 673, 744; MS 877/8. C. Bonney (EL 852), Chareau (EB 408), Dalsace. *Vogue*, 1 May, 1927, p. 41. *L'Art International d'Aujourd'hui*, no. 7, pl. 42. *Art et Décoration*, no. 15, 1950, p. 49. Herbst, *Un Inventeur*, pp. 9, 25, 29, 72. Version in metal, palisander veneer, with metal lamp. *Sale*: Monaco, 24–25 October, 1982, no. 358. Mallet-Stevens version, 1927; L-shaped work surface bearing a metal cabinet with domed front flap at right and swivel side table on left. Chareau had this example made for his friend and colleague Robert Mallet-Stevens, giving him the choice of wood and metal. Black-glazed beech and polished steel. *h.* 62, *l.* 102, *w.* 93. C. Mallet-Stevens. Michel Souillac coll. *Exhib*: M.A.D., 1977, no. 310. LdA, 1981, no. 79. M.A.D., 1984. *L'Art International d'Aujourd'hui*, no. 6, pl. 22. 1925, p. 217. Ed., *R. Mallet-Stevens*, p. 281. *1930…*, 1981, no. 79. EB 754, 756, version with metal or wood parallelepiped locker. Wrought iron with black patina, walnut or mahogany. C. Dalsace, *p.c.*

MB 410 Wall table. Wrought iron and wood. C. Dreyfus. Whereabouts unknown. *Art et Décoration*, 1932, p. 130.

MB 413 Table, c.1927. Rectangular beveled tabletop on supports joined beneath surface on three sides, square-sectioned legs linked with base, at opposite ends. Knotted walnut and walnut. C. Bernheim. Whereabouts unknown. *Mobilier et Décoration*, no. 2, January 1927, p. 105. *Mobilier et Décoration*, no. 8, July 1928, p. 229. Herbst, *Un Inventeur*, p. 80. Version with rectangular-sectioned legs. C. Reifenberg. *Mobilier et Décoration*, no. 5, April 1928, pp. 164–166. Herbst, *Un Inventeur*, p. 69.

MB 512 Herbst, *Un Inventeur*, p. 88.

MB 595 Low table, c.1924–8. Table in the form of a bobbin. Wickerwork and bamboo. Cf. EN 740, 741, 742. C. Fleg. Whereabouts unknown. *L'Art et les Artistes*, no. 83, January 1928, p. 130. *Mobilier et Décoration*, no. 8, July 1928, p. 227 (Nursery). Herbst, *Un Inventeur*, p. 67. *Sale*: Monaco, 6 March, 1983, no. 161.

MB 629 Bedside table. Rectangular surface with sliding flap. The stand, forming a T in

cross-section, is made up of two orthogonal strips, resting on a rectangular base. Two shelves on the right side of the upright bar of the T. Sycamore. MB 794: version with four drawers (cubic handles) on the left of the upright bar of the T. Ebony or palisander? C. M.G. Whereabouts unknown. *Mobilier et Décoration*, no. 8, July 1928, p. 226.

MB 673 Desk, c.1927. Rectangular work surface, set in wrought-iron strip on three sides. To the left side, an inverted T-shaped leg, with swivel table under the work surface. To the right, two legs, at side and front, in wrought-iron strips, linked at top to form an L shape, supporting a shelf above the work surface. Below, two swivel tables. Sycamore or palisander and wrought iron. C. Bonney, Dalsace, Fleg, *p.c. h.* 69/97, *l.* 126, *d.* 45. *Art et Décoration*, 1932, p. 139. *Mobilier et Décoration*, no. 8, July 1928. Herbst, *Un Inventeur*, p. 92. Version with locker above, palisander. *Mobilier et Décoration*, no. 2, January 1927, pp. 99, 106. *Art et Décoration*, January-June 1927, Vol. LI, p. 138.

MB 744 Desk, 1927. As MB 673, metal locker with single door suspended beneath the work surface. Swivel table at left. Wrought iron and wood. Cf. MB 405, MB 673. *L'Art International d'Aujourd'hui*, no. 7, pl. 27. *Mobilier et Décoration*, no. 8, July 1928, p. 230.

MB 770 Table (known as tulip table). Cf. MB 170. Hexagonal top and base. Top sometimes beveled. Stand sometimes a six-sided tulip shape, sometimes composed of two orthogonal metal strips. *h.* 60, *l.* 79, *w.* 77.5 Macassar ebony, palisander, or dark wood (for top surface) and light wood (for stand). C. Mme B., Fleg, X. (ES 859). *Sale*: Monaco, 24–25 October, 1982, no. 366.

MB 771, 773, 774 Table/desk, c.1928. Consisting of a table with one rectangular work top resting on full side stands; to the right, a nest of attached triangular-surfaced tables that can be fanned out, the highest of which is on a level with the main work top. A fourth triangular-surfaced unit is slightly lower, on the left side. Preparatory sketch exists. Cuban mahogany. Cf. MB 106. *Mobilier et Décoration*, no. 8, July 1928, p. 221. *L'Art International d'Aujourd'hui*, no. 7, pl. 2.

MB 794 Bedside table, cf. MB 629.

MB 808, 810 Desk. Two pull-out lockers and two flaps that can be pulled out from the main body of the desk. Cf. MB 113.

MB 812, 813 Table for phonograph, c.1928. Two record cabinets, flat surface for phonograph with adjustable height. Walnut and metal. Designed for Dollie Chareau. C. Chareau. Whereabouts unknown. *Art et Décoration*, 1950, no. 19, p. 49. Herbst, *Un Inventeur*, p. 88.

MB 864 Ashtray on stand, c.1930. Removable ashtrays. Tubular stand on circular base. Black patinated wrought metal and brass. Whereabouts unknown.

MB 920 Table. Cf. MS 423, MD 73.

MB 960 Table/bookcase, c.1930. Made up of a bookcase unit curved in at one end, with central shelf, hinged to a low round table resting on a chrome or nickel-plated metal sphere which renders it mobile. Pear or sycamore and vellum. *Art et Décoration*, July–December 1930, L. Werth, p. 50. *Nouveaux Intérieurs Français*, 1933, pl. 16. *Exhib*: 1st U.A.M. Salon, 1930.

MB 1049 Writing table (Table de correspondance), 1926. Two work surfaces separated by a frosted glass and metal panel. Rectangular top with sloping sides, each of which contains two pigeonholes. Four oxidized tubular metal legs linked by side and cross bars. Designed and made for the Grand-Hôtel at Tours. *Exhib*: Barbazanges. *Sale*: Paris, Champin, 8 April, 1979, no. 358, 26,100 FF. Cf. EB 707, long desk version, two pull-out slides cover pigeonholes. C. Van Melle-Henry.

MC 767 Chair, c.1927. Cf. MC 769 (1929). Metal, metal and leather cushion or cane seat and back. Made for the clubhouse at Beauvallon and for the entrance hall at La Semaine à Paris. *h*. 80, *l*. 35, *d*. 48. C. Dalsace, *p.c. L'Amour de l'Art*, no. 1, January 1930, p. 72. *Architecture d'Aujourd'hui*, no. 3, April 1934, p. 89. *L'Amour de l'Art*, no. 9, November 1935. *Art et Décoration*, 1930, p. 47. *L'Art International d'Aujourd'hui*, no. 7, pl. 2. *Art et Décoration*, 1950, no. 19, p. 49 (iron and cane). Herbst, *Un Inventeur*, p. 50, 94. *Domus*, no. 443, October 1966. *Exhib*: Sd'A, 1929.

MC 769 Folding chair, c.1929. Rectangular back. Seat made up of three interlocking units, the supports for which fan out from joints in the rectangular frame base. Registered patent no. 659330 for a "folding chair with fan-shaped structure" applied for on 25 June, 1928. Made for the clubhouse at the Beauvallon Golf-Hôtel. C. Dalsace, *p.c.* U.A.M., 17 July, 1929, p. 4. *Art et Décoration*, January–June 1930, Vol. LVII, p. 47. Herbst, *Un Inventeur*, p. 50. *Domus*, no. 443, October 1966.

MD 73 Cf. MS 473, MB 920.

MD 234 Sideboard (Meuble d'appui pour une salle à manger), 1925. Tabletop on four tapered legs. Two serving hatches at either side extend work-surface area and frame lower central unit, with double doors. Orange wood, violet wood, and walnut. Made for the Indochinese pavilion at EIADIM. *La Renaissance des Arts Français*, no. 8, August 1925, p. 353. *L'Amour de l'Art*, no. 8, August 1925, p. 315.

MD 237 Buffet, 1925. Upper area, two storage compartments, with double doors above, and fall flap below. Beneath this, a heavy rectangular table, the narrow ends of which curve up slightly. Four tapered legs support whole structure. Made for the Indochinese pavilion, EIADIM, 1925. *L'Amour de l'Art*, no. 8, August 1925, p. 315.

MD 362, 407 Radiator cover/bookcase/magazine rack, 1922–6. Cf. MT 407. Three swiveling tabletops (rectangular with one corner indented) hinged onto a wrought-iron strip at right angles to the wall, under which are three fixed shelves. Wrought iron and mahogany. *h*. 100. Tabletop: *l*. 86, *w*. 36. Total *h*. 132.5, *l*. 95, *w*. 63. C. Bernheim, Dalsace, F., *p.c. Exhib*: Sd'A, 1926, with other furniture for the Grand-Hôtel at Tours. LdA, 1981, no. 96. *Sale*: Monaco, 19 April, 1982, 200,000 FF.

MF 8 Armchair.

MF 11 Gondola chair (Fauteuil gondole), 1922. Sycamore or mahogany, upholstered. *h*. 90, *l*. 56, *w*. 45. C. Bernheim, *p.c. Les Arts de la Maison*, Summer 1926, pl. XXXI.

MF 15 Bergère, 1920–2. Photo dated 1922. Walnut, beech, leather, with metallic struts. *h*. 73, *l*. 66/74, *d*. 60. C. Dalsace, Simon, *p.c.* Herbst, *Un Inventeur*, p. 29, 72. *Global Architecture*, no. 46, 1977, p. 35.

MF 18 Armchair, c.1920. Gondola back with six sloping panels. Floor skirting raised at front. Slender supports. Black-painted wickerwork. *h*. 70, *l*. 77, *d*. 84. C. Dalsace, X., *p.c. L'Art et les Artistes*, 1924, no. 46, p. 283. *Sale*: Monaco, 6 March, 1983, no. 161.

MF 19 Armchair, c.1920. Version of MF 18, with higher elbow rests widening down to floor. Black-painted wickerwork. Herbst, *Un Inventeur*, pp. 22, 37, 95 (floor skirting). 1925, p. 211.

MF 75 Armchair. Curved elbow rests. Walnut. L. Cheronnet, "Cabine de travail et salon de réception de l'administrateur du Collège de France," pp. 113–118.

MF 168 Armchair with low back.

MF 172 Armchair, c.1920. Gondola back with six sloping panels. Full seat with solid wood base. Palisander and padouk, or sycamore, ebony(?). *h*. 65, *l*. 77, *d*. 56. Photo dated 1920. Figured in sets for Marcel l'Herbier's film *Le Vertige*, 1925. C. Bernheim, Dalsace, Dreyfus, F., G., Reifenberg. *Les Arts de la Maison*, Winter 1924, pp. 19 (plan and elevation), 22, pl. II (gouache). *Mobilier et Décoration*, no. 2, January 1927, p. 99; no. 5, April 1928, p. 169; no. 8, July 1928, p. 226. *Art et Décoration*, 1932, p. 129. *L'Art International d'Aujourd'hui*, no. 6, pl. 12. Ed., R. Mallet-Stevens, pp. 223–224. Herbst, *Un Inventeur*, p. 79. *Sale*: Monaco, 10 February 1981, no. 1440.

MF 182 Armchair. Oak or mahogany. Part of the nursery ensembles. Chair version in oak. *h*. 103, *l*. 40, *d*. 39. C. Dalsace, *p.c. L'Art et les Artistes*, 1924, no. 46, p. 286 (dark wood, mahogany).

MF 208, 217 Bergère, c.1923. Lyre-shaped legs. Wood at front of armrests. Extension supports to broadened back legs. Palisander or walnut, beech framework, sometimes upholstered in leather. *h*. 81/85, *w*. 70, *d*. 49/55. *Exhib*: as part of the "Study-library of a French embassy," EIADIM. Made for the Grand-Hôtel at Tours. C. Dalsace, X., *p.c. Beaux Arts*, June 1925, p. 27. *Les Arts de la Maison*, Summer 1926, pls. XXVI, XXVII. *Encyclopédie des Métiers d'Art*, Vol. I, pl. 59. *Art et Décoration*, 1934, Vol. LVIII, pp. 50, 54. Herbst, *Un Inventeur*, pp. 20–21, 25, 55. *Global Architecture*, no. 46, 1977, pp. 26–31. *Sale*: Monaco, 8 October, 1977, no. 68, 20,000 FF; 24 October, 1982, no. 365, 70,000 FF the pair. Paris, Laurin, 10 April, 1979, 24,000 FF.

MF 219. Armchair with reclining back, c.1923. Lyre-shaped legs, cf. MF 208, 217. Adjusts to two positions by means of moving bar. Palisander or walnut. *h*. 83, *l*. 74, *d*. 95. C. Dalsace, Dreyfus, Homberg, Reifenberg, Van Melle-Henry. *p.c. Beaux*

Arts, June 1925, p. 27. *L'Amour de l'Art*, no. 6, June 1926, p. 213. *Les Arts de la Maison*, Summer 1926, pl. XXIV, XXVI, XXVII. *The Studio Yearbook*, 1927, p. 81. *Mobilier et Décoration*, no. 2, January 1927, p. 99. *Art et Décoration*, 1932, Vol. LXI, p. 134. *Architecture d'Aujourd'hui*, November–December 1933, p. 4. *Art et Décoration*, 1934, Vol. LVIII, pp. 50–54. Herbst, *Un Inventeur*, pp. 19, 20, 54, 84. *Global Architecture*, no. 46, 1977, p. 32.

MF 220 Armchair, c. 1922. Back adjusts to two positions. Visible wood at front and back of armrests. Supports below seat are upright, splay out above. Chrome or nickel-plated metal bun feet. Leather and walnut or leather and palisander or brown velours and walnut. *h*. 80, *l*. 68, *d*. 79/84. C. Bernheim, Dalsace, G., Simon. *p.c. Mobilier et Décoration* April–May 1924, p. 27. *Les Arts de la Maison*, Winter 1924, pl. 1. *Mobilier et Décoration*, no. 8, July 1928, pp. 219–222. *Nouveaux Intérieurs Français*, Paris, 1933, pl. 15. *Art et Décoration*, 1934, Vol. LVIII, p. 50. *L'Art International d'Aujourd'hui*, no. 6, pl. 6. *Encyclopédie des Métiers d'Art*, Vol. I, pl. 60; Vol. II, pl. 76. 1925, p. 211. *Global Architecture*, no. 46, 1977, p. 32. *Exhib*: 15th S.A.D., 1923. Cf. ES 193, Bergère (exhib. at the Sd'A, 1924).

MF 232 Armchair, c.1922. Rectangular back with bar adjusting to three positions. Rectangular sides. Wood frame, fabric panels on solid base. Ebony. *h*. 76, *w*. 105, *d*. 68. *Sale*: Monaco, 24–25 October, 1982, no. 363.

MF 276 Chair, c.1924. Straight block or tapered legs. Walnut, with or without knotted walnut, sycamore or palisander, oak or stained beech, plus leather or fabric. *h*. 86, *l*. 52, *d*. 38. Made for the Indochinese pavilion, EIADIM, 1925, the Grand-Hôtel at Tours, 1928, the Noailles' Villa d'Hyères. C. Bernheim, Dalsace, Dreyfus, Fleg, Comtesse de Noailles, Reifenberg. *L'Amour de l'Art*, no. 6, June 1926, p. 215. *Art et Décoration*, January–June 1927, pp. 101, 105. Vol. LI, p. 110. *Mobilier et Décoration*, no. 2, January 1927, pp. 101, 105. *L'Amour de l'Art*, no. 2, February 1928, p. 59. *L'Art et les Artistes*, no. 83, January 1928, pp. 132–133. *Art et Décoration*, January–June 1928, Vol. LIII, p. 33; July–December 1928, Vol. LIV, "Une villa moderne à Hyères." *Mobilier et Décoration*, no. 5, April 1928, pp. 164–166; no. 8, July 1928, pp. 221–229. *Art et Décoration*, 1932, Vol. LXI, pp. 134–138. *Encyclopédie des Métiers d'Art*, Vol. I, pls. 53, 62, 63, 65. Herbst, *Un Inventeur*, pp. 66 (GHT), 69. *Exhib*: EIADIM, 1925; M.A.D., 1927(?). Version without arms: sycamore or macassar ebony. *Lux*, April 1924, p. 440. *L'Art International d'Aujourd'hui*, no. 6, pl. 12. Herbst, *Un Inventeur*, pp. 73, 75, 80, 96. *Sale*: Cornette de Saint-Cyr, 12/5/83, no. 80, pair for 9,000 FF.

MF 310 Armchair, 1923–8. Wickerwork and green leather or fabric. Technique used for back of wicker chair MP 13 reutilized here. Made for the Grand-Hôtel at Tours (1928). *L'Art et les Artistes*, no. 83, January 1928, p. 130. *Art et Décoration*, January–June 1928, Vol. LIII, p. 34. *Encyclopédie des Métiers d'Art*, Vol. I, pl. 52. Herbst, *Un Inventeur*, p. 67. Version in black cane with no cushion or arms appeared in sets of Marcel l'Herbier's film *Le Vertige*, 1925. Ed., R. Mallet-Stevens, p. 225. Version as corner (seats 6). Wickerwork and green leather.

Made for the Grand-Hôtel at Tours. Known to be destroyed.

MF 313 Fireside chair (Chauffeuse), c.1926. Bolster back. Velours or tapestry by Lurçat. Green leather upholstery for the Grand-Hôtel. *h.* 57, *w.* 90. Made for the Grand-Hôtel at Tours (1928). C. Bernheim, Bonney, G., *p.c. Good Furniture Magazine*, January 1927, p. 30. *L'Amour de l'Art*, no. 2, February 1928, p. 60. *Art et Décoration*, January-June 1928, Vol. LIII, p. 36. *Foreign Trade*, Vol. 3, no. 12, December 1928, p. 42. *Mobilier et Décoration*, no. 8, 1928, pp. 218–220. *Encyclopédie des Métiers d'Art*, Vol. I, pl. 66, Vol. II, p. 77. Herbst, *Un Inventeur*, pp. 64–76. *Exhib:* Sd'A, 1926. *Sale:* Paris, Laurin, 7–8 July, 1982, 17,000 FF.

MF 389 Bed. *Les Arts de la Maison*, Summer 1928, pl. XXXI. Cf. MF 1050, MP 389.

MF 732 Armchair, c.1924. Same supports as MF 220. Walnut or macassar ebony. Made for the Grand-Hôtel at Tours, 1928. C. Reifenberg. Version with floor skirting. Metal bun feet (in nickel-plated bronze?). *Mobilier et Décoration* April-May 1924, p. 27. *L'Amour de l'Art*, no. 6, June 1924, p. 193; no. 2, February 1928, pp. 60–62. *L'Art et les Artistes*, no. 83, January 1928, pp. 121–122. *Art et Décoration*, January-June 1928, Vol. LIII, p. 35. *Mobilier et Décoration*, no. 5, April 1928, pp. 161–162. *Encyclopédie des Métiers d'Art*, Vol. I, pls. 59, 61. *Nouveaux Intérieurs Français*, Paris, 1933, pl. 15. Herbst, *Un Inventeur*, p. 51. *Exhib:* 15th S.A.D., 1923. Version with raised skirting. Herbst, *Un Inventeur*, pp. 72, 80. *Sale:* Cornette de Saint-Cyr, 12/5/83, no. 87, 60,000 FF the pair.

MF 980 Chaise longue, c.1931. Metal tubing and rubber. C. Dreyfus. Whereabouts unknown. *Art et Décoration*, January-June 1931, Vol. LIX, p. 107; 1932, Vol. LXI, p. 130.

MF 1002 High-back armchair, 1924–7. Frame covered with fabric or tapestry designed by J. Lurçat. One example was, in 1927, covered in a fabric based on a motif designed by J. Burkhalter. *h.* 95, *w.* 69, *d.* 44. C. Dalsace, L'Herbier, *p.c. Art et Décoration*, July-December 1927, Vol. LII, p. 44. *The Studio Yearbook*, 1927, p. 117. *Encyclopédie des Métiers d'Art*, Vol. II, pl. 76. Herbst, *Un Inventeur*, pp. 28–29. *Global Architecture*, no. 46, 1977, p. 34. *Domus*, no. 443, October 1966. *Exhib:* Barbazanges.

MF 1050, 1050 bis, 1051 Armchair, c.1926. Palisander or palisander and pigskin, or macassar ebony. Cf. MF 389, MP 389. C. Dreyfus, Reifenberg, Michel Souillac coll. *L'Amour de l'Art*, no. 6, January 1926, p. 215. *Mobilier et Décoration*, no. 2, January 1927, pp. 99, 103, 106; no. 5, April 1928, pp. 162–163. *Art et Décoration*, 1932, Vol. LXI, p. 134. Herbst, *Un Inventeur*, pp. 74–76. *1930 . . .*, 1981, no. 88. *Exhib:* S.A.D., 1926; LdA, 1981, no. 88.

MG 7 Mirror. Oval hung with braided silk thread inserted in two ivory hooks.

MG 311, 312 Mirror, c.1928. Metal-framed square mirror sliding on a pleated metal strip attached to the lighting system. Ivory handle. *h.* 80, *w.* 25/35, *d.* 7. Made for the Grand-Hôtel at Tours. C. Dreyfus, Dalsace. Former coll. Lise Deharme, Michel Souillac.

coll., *p.c. L'Art et les Artistes*, no. 83. January 1928, p. 131. *L'Amour de l'Art*, no. 2, February 1928, p. 61. *L'Art International d'Aujourd'hui*, no. 10, pl. 15. *Encyclopédie des Métiers d'Art*, Vol. I, pl. 59. Herbst, *Un Inventeur*, p. 97. *Exhib:* LdA, 1981, no. 98.

MG 820, 821 Triple mirror. The two side mirrors slip behind the central mirror. Electric socket below, lighting system with frosted glass shade above. Herbst, *Un Inventeur*, p. 97.

MK 297 Fireplace, 1926. *Mobilier et Décoration*, no. 2, January 1927, p. 101. *L'Amour de l'Art*, no. 6, June 1926, p. 215; no. 10, December 1932, p. 342. *Exhib:* S.A.D., 1926; M.A.D., 1927.

MK 751 Fireplace, fireguard, coal shovel and tongs. Pink brick interior, stone and metal. Designed and made for the Reifenberg's home, Rue Mallet-Stevens, Paris. *Mobilier et Décoration*, no. 5, April 1928, p. 167. *Art et Décoration*, October 1932, Vol. LXI, p. 308.

MK 940 Corner fireplace with extending fireguard, shovel and tongs. Pink brick and metal. *Art et Décoration*, October 1932, p. 304.

MP 13 Chaise longue, c.1922. Back with four sloping sides. Floor skirting. Black-painted wickerwork. Cf. MF 18, 19, 310 EN 12, 22. Whereabouts unknown.

MP 23 Child's cot, 1921–4. Drop side for easy access to bed. Precious or white-painted wood. C. Fleg. *Mobilier et Décoration*, no. 8, 1928, p. 227 (with drawers and cupboard forming ship's prow, EN 740). *L'Art International d'Aujourd'hui*, no. 7, pl. 43.

MP 102 Bed, 1923. The bed ends, slightly buckled leaves of wood on crescent bases, derive from the forms used in the tables MB 97 and MB 110. Palisander and amourette wood. Photo EH 300 dated 1925. *Art et Décoration*, July-December 1923, Vol. XLIV, p. 179. *Mobilier et Décoration*, p. 22. *Exhib:* Sd'A, 1923.

MP 108, Child's cot, 1923. Four wooden barred sides, the longer of which are drop sides for easy access. Raised on castors. Version with one dark and one light wood, MP 116. *La Renaissance de l'Art Français*, no. 7, July 1923, p. 433. *Art et Décoration*, January-June 1923, Vol. XLIII, p. 173. *Exhib:* 15th S.A.D., 1923.

MP 115 Bed. Cf. Armchair MF 8.

MP 167 Curved sofa (Méridienne galbée), c.1923. Gondola back rest with four sloping panels. Palisander, ivory feet, velours. *h.* 81, *l.* 182. Model designed and made for H. Bernheim's sitting room (known as the "salon de coromandel"). C. Bernheim, *p.c. L'Amour de l'Art*, no. 3, March 1923, p. 487. *L'Art et les Artistes*, 1924, no. 46, p. 281. *Les Arts de la Maison*, Winter 1924, p. 22, pl. V. *L'Art Vivant*, no. 32, 15 April, 1926, p. 304.

MP 169 Couch (Sofa canapé), 1923. Long oval seat, enclosed by level back sloping to armrests each side at front. Velours and leather, or velours and tapestry designed by J. Lurçat. Appeared in sets of Marcel L'Herbier's films *L'Inhumaine* (1923) and *Le Vertige* (1925). *h.* 57/60, *w.* 192/197, *d.* 83.

C. Bernheim, Dalsace, G., *p.c. Les Arts de la Maison*, Winter 1924. *Art et Industries*, no. 8, 10 August, 1927, p. 26. *Mobilier et Décoration*, no. 2, January 1927, pp. 97–106; no. 8, July 1928, pp. 215, 217. *Art et Décoration*, February 1934, Vol. LXIII, p. 52. Herbst, *Un Inventeur*, pp. 25, 78. *Domus*, no. 443, October 1966. *Global Architecture*, no. 46, 1977, pp. 26–30. Ed., *R. Mallet-Stevens*, pp. 133, 223.

MP 174 bis Couch (Canapé). Back made up of six sloping panels. Palisander, sycamore, or ebony. Cf. MF 172, MP 167. C. Bernheim, *p.c. L'Amour de l'Art*, no. 3, March 1923, p. 487. *L'Art et les Artistes*, no. 46, 1924, p. 281. *L'Art Vivant*, no. 32, April 1926, p. 304.

MP 214, 215 and MP 262 Couch, 1923–32. The curved armrests/front legs were adopted from 1923. One version has an adjustable back rest. Walnut or palisander, beech frame. *h.* 64, *w.* 139, *d.* 66. C. Dalsace, Homberg, *p.c. L'Art et les Artistes*, no. 83, January 1928, p. 131. *Art et Décoration*, 1932, Vol. LXI, p. 134. Extra long version, C. Dreyfus, *p.c. Art et Décoration*, 1932, Vol. LXI, p. 136.

MP 230 Corner couch (Canapé d'angle). Two units. Macassar ebony. Whereabouts unknown.

MP 273 Couch, c.1926. Two low chairs with bolster backs either side of a higher couch with no back. Cf. MF 313.

MP 287 Couch, 1924. Cf. MF 230, MF 1050. Walnut and velours, or sycamore(?). C. Dalsace, Dreyfus, Reifenberg, *p.c. L'Amour de l'Art*, no. 6, June 1924, p. 193. *Les Arts de la Maison*, Summer 1926, pl. XXVIII. *Mobilier et Décoration*, no. 2, January 1927, pp. 97–106; no. 5, April 1928, p. 69.

MP 287 Couch, version c.1926. Palisander, macassar ebony, or walnut and yellow velours. *The Studio Yearbook*, 1927, p. 118. C. Dalsace, Dreyfus, *p.c.* Cf. MF 1050.

MP 369 Hung bed (Lit balancelle), c.1925. Cf. EF 928.

MP 389 Bed, c.1926. Palisander, rosewood, macassar ebony. C. Reifenberg. Whereabouts unknown. *Les Arts de la Maison*, Summer 1926, pl. XXXI. *The Studio Yearbook*, 1927, p. 115. *Mobilier et Décoration*, no. 5, April 1928, p. 167. *L'Art International d'Aujourd'hui*, no. 6, pl. 13.

MP 526 Raised corner couch (Estrade et canapé d'angle), c.1923. Sycamore C. Fleg. *L'Amour de l'Art*, no. 3, March 1923, p. 487.

MP 671 bis Bench (Banquette), c.1930. Upright back made up of three rectangular units. Seat a single unit forming an arch in cross-section. Flat wrought-iron strip elbow rest on right. On the left, a tabletop in wrought metal mounted on a tube with circular base, and an ashtray on a tripod, both of which are detachable. Rectangular base, criss-cross slats. Composite piece, cf. MC 767 and ashtray table. *h.* 81, *l.* 114, *w.* 5. Metal, wicker-back "ban-mouc" seat in beige and brown, or metal and leather or metal and wickerwork. *Art et Décoration*, 1930, p. 34. Version with no back or tabletop, C. Dalsace. Whereabouts unknown. *Architecture d'Aujourd'hui*, November-December 1933, p. 14. *Art et Décoration*, 1934, Vol. LVIII, p. 52. Version with no tabletop. *Sale*: Monaco, 7 December 1981, no. 262, 78,000 FF.

MP 747 Bed.

MP 761 "Cosy corner." With an upright unit, two shelf tops and two bookcase units either side, one with one shelf, one with two. Palisander.

MP 764 Bed, c.1927. For young person. To the right of the bed head, a flap door cabinet and shelf.

MP 812 Phonograph table. Cf. MB 812, 813.

MP 901 Bed.

MP 906 "Cosy corner."

MP 1029 Corner couch/bookcase, c.1931. *Art et Décoration*, July-December 1931, Vol. LX, p. 28. Rounded version, with bookcase. *Art et Décoration*, 1933, Vol. LXII, p. 228. *Nouveaux Intérieurs Français*, Paris, 1933, pl. 14. *Exhib*: 4th U.A.M. Salon, 1933. Version without back. *L'Art et les Artistes*, no. 46, 1924, p. 284. Herbst, *Un Inventeur*, p. 70.

MS 14 Corner dressing table, c.1923. Quarter-circle surface on two columns of three drawers, set together at right angles. Three oval feet. Oval mirror (version with rectangular mirror, rounded at top). Conical pendent (or semicircular) handles. Knotted elm and oak, or palisander. C. Dreyfus (EH 387), *p.c.* Moussinac, *Intérieurs I*, 1924, pl. 7 (gouache). Version omitting mirror. *Art et Décoration*, January-June 1923, Vol. XLIII, p. 130.

MS 80 Dressing table, 1926. Cf. MS 423.

MS 417 Mirror on stand.

MS 418, 419, bis, ter. Dressing table, jewelry box. Made up of two jointed units. Upright vertical mirror in wooden frame, on right. On the left, a unit consisting of a box with two sliding doors and a shelf beneath, set in a wrought-iron strip which supports the structure. Swivel table below the shelf. Metal and treated mahogany, or sycamore. h. 116/167, w. 95/66, d. 30/40. C. Dalsace, *p.c. Art et Décoration*, January-June 1927, Vol. LI, p. 109, January-June 1931, Vol. LIX, p. 107. *L'Art International d'Aujourd'hui*, no. 7, pl. 27. Herbst, *Un Inventeur*, p. 89. *Exhib*: Barbazanges.

MS 423 Dressing table with lit mirror, 1926-7 or before. Rectangular top with slightly sunken center and bow front. Solid side supports. Inclining mirror with adjustable light fittings that can illuminate mirror or observer. Copy of a model made in 1923, with two drawers in the flat-fronted top surface, an oval mirror between two square-ended posts, in knotted elm. Cf. MB 820. Veneered palisander or sycamore, and silvered metal. C. G. Whereabouts unknown. *Mobilier et Décoration*, no. 8, July 1928. *Art et Décoration*, January-June 1927, Vol. LI, p. 138. *1950*, no. 19, p. 49. Version MS 80, 1926, three drawers in top surface, of which the largest in the bow-fronted central area, oval mirror on stand.

MS 877, 879 Dressing table, 1927-9. Rectangular top surface. Two shelves at right, one above, one below surface. On the left, a swivel table with a rectangular mirror hinged onto a wrought-iron strip. Side

supports. Wrought iron and wood. (Version MB 744 without flap or locker). Version in metal and sycamore. Herbst, *Un Inventeur*, p. 92. Version in metal and pigskin-covered wood. Signed. *p.c. Guide de la xième Biennale*, 1982, p. 115. *Exhib*: LdA, 1981.

MS 1009, 1009 bis Dressing table, 1926-7. Top surface curving around and inwards at left, over full side support, and at right rests on column of four drawers. Metal case can be fixed to back of item, with a door opening to reveal storage space and a mirror. Cf. MB 277. Palisander. C. Fleg. Whereabouts unknown. *Mobilier et Décoration*, no. 2, January 1927, p. 97. *Art et Décoration*, 1932, p. 139. Version omitting mirror. *Mobilier et Décoration*, no. 2, January 1927, p. 103. Herbst, *Un Inventeur*, p. 78.

MS 1013 Bathroom cupboard, 1926. Cf. MD 73.

MT 25 Small cupboard. Oval surface, with upright back around three sides. Sides and base extend to floor from this surface, except at front where two doors open to reveal storage space. Painted wickerwork. Wide version with two doors. *L'Art et les Artistes*, no. 46, 1924, p. 283. *La Renaissance de l'Art Français*, no. 7, July 1923, p. 433. *L'Amour de l'Art*, 1923, p. 559. *Exhib*: 15th S.A.D., 1923. Small version with one door. *L'Art et les Artistes*, no. 46, 1924, p. 283. *La Renaissance de l'Art Français*, no. 7, July 1923, p. 433. *L'Amour de l'Art*, 1923, p. 559. *Exhib*: 15th S.A.D., 1923.

MT 286 Stool, c.1923. Belongs to series of models with lyre-shaped legs, cf. MF 208, 219, MP 214, 215, 262.

MT 344 and EF 596 Bar stool, 1926. Concave seat in solid wood on tubular legs in oxidized metal, standing on round wooden feet, cross-bars. Mahogany. h. 90, l. 35, d. 35. Designed and made for the clubhouse at Beauvallon and the Grand-Hôtel, Tours. C. Bernheim, Dalsace, X, *p.c. L'Amour de l'Art*, no. 2, February 1928, p. 60. Herbst, *Un Inventeur*, pp. 64, 65, 66, 93. *Sale*: Monaco, December 7, 1981, 264, 13,000 F.F. the pair.

MT 407, MD 362 or 407 Radiator cover / Bookcase or magazine rack, 1922-6. Three rectangular tabletops, with one corner rounded, swinging on hinges fastened to a bar of wrought iron attached to the wall at right angles, below which are three fixed shelves. Wrought iron and mahogany or palisander. h. 100, shelf: l. 86, w. 36. h. 132.5, l. 95, w. 63. *Les Arts de la Maison*, Winter 1926, pl. XXXVIII. *Good Furniture Magazine*, January 1927, p. 30. *Encyclopédie des Métiers d'Art*, Vol. I, pls. 59, 61, 62. *Art et Décoration*, 1932, p. 139. *Exhib*: Sd'A 1926, with other furniture for the Grand-Hôtel, Tours. *Sale*: Monaco, April 19, 1982, 200, 200,000 F.F.

MT 876 Office table—metal table for typewriters and calculating machines, c. 1929. Made up of two units: at right, a rectangular tabletop and side support bearing a metal cabinet with domed front flap; at left, a work surface, also rectangular, resting on a wrought-iron bar and turning on a central support. Metal and pear wood or wood covered in red leather. h. 60, w. 155, d. 40. C. Dalsace, *p.c. Art et Décoration*, July-December 1929, Vol. LVI,

p. 186; July-December 1930, Vol. LVIII, p. 49. *L'Amour de l'Art*, no. 1, January 1930, p. 68; no. 10, December 1932, p. 342. Herbst, *Un Inventeur*, p. 91. *Exhib*: 1st U.A.M. Salon 1930.

MT 1004 Stool, c. 1930. Leather seat, legs in the form of a bobbin consisting of three tubes of metal twisted and welded to three tubular rings. Cf. MB 595 and table.

MT 1015 Stool, c. 1923. Curule type, concave seat, solid side supports, resting on four parallelepipeds. h. 35, l. 49, w. 30, or h. 40. Macassar ebony. C. Bernheim, Reifenberg, *p.c. Art et Décoration*, January-June 1923, Vol. XLIII, pp. 136, 137. Moussinac, *Intérieurs I*, 1924, pls. 9 (gouache), 12 (versions top and bottom). *Mobilier et Décoration*, no. 2, January 1927, p. 101. *Art et Décoration*, January-June 1927, Vol. LI, p. 110. *Vogue*, May 1, 1927, p. 41. *Mobilier et Décoration*, no. 8, July 1928, p. 226. *L'Art International d'Aujourd'hui*, no. 6, pl. 13. *Exhib*: M.A.D. 1927, Barbazanges, Ld'A 1981, no. 85.

MU 871 Bookcase, 1930. At left, the principal unit, three shelves above a cabinet with two sliding doors; below this a small swivel table and a lower shelf; at right, five narrower shelves; the two units are hinged together. Wrought iron and palisander. Designed and made for the hall of *La Semaine à Paris*. *L'Amour de l'Art*, no. 1, January 1930, p. 72

MU 959 Bookcase, c. 1930. Pink pear wood and plate glass. *Art et Décoration*, July-December 1930, Vol. LVIII, p. 49. *L'Amour de l'Art*, no. 10, December 1932, p. 342. *Exhib*: 1st U.A.M. Salon.

MU 1030, c. 1930. Composite piece of furniture, consisting of an armoire on the left attached to unit MU 871. Palisander and metal. C. Dreyfus, *p.c. L'Amour de l'Art*, January 1930, no. 1, p. 72. *Art et Décoration*, July-December 1931, Vol. LX, p. 29; 1932, Vol. LXI, p. 134. *Exhib*: Sd'A 1929, 2nd U.A.M. Salon.

MT 344 and EF 596 Bar stool, 1926. Concave seat in solid wood on tubular legs in oxidized metal, standing on round wooden feet, cross-bars. Mahogany. h. 90, l. 35, d. 35. Designed and made for the clubhouse at Beauvallon and the Grand-Hôtel, Tours. C. Bernheim, Dalsace, X, *p.c. L'Amour de l'Art*, no. 2, February 1928, p. 60. Herbst, *Un Inventeur*, pp. 64, 65, 66, 93. *Sale*. Monaco, December 7, 1981, 264, 13,000 F.F. the pair.

MT 407, MD 362 or 407 Radiator cover / Bookcase or magazine rack, 1922-6. Three rectangular tabletops, with one corner rounded, swinging on hinges fastened to a bar of wrought iron attached to the wall at right angles, below which are three fixed shelves. Wrought iron and mahogany or palisander. h. 100, shelf: l. 86, w. 36. h. 132.5, l. 95, w. 63. *Les Arts de la Maison*, Winter 1926, pl. XXXVIII. *Good Furniture Magazine*, January 1927, p. 30. *Encyclopédie des Métiers d'Art*, Vol. I, pls. 59, 61, 62. *Art et Décoration*, 1932, p. 139. *Exhib*: Sd'A 1926, with other furniture for the Grand-Hôtel, Tours. *Sale*: Monaco, April 19, 1982, 200, 200,000 F.F.

MT 876 Office table—metal table for typewriters and calculating machines, c. 1929. Made up of two units: at right, a rectangular tabletop and side support bearing a metal cabinet with domed front flap; at left, a work surface, also rectangular, resting on a wrought-iron bar and turning on a central support. Metal and pear wood or wood covered in red leather. h. 60, w. 155, d. 40. C. Dalsace, p.c. *Art et Décoration*, July-December 1929, Vol. LVI, p. 186; July-December 1930, Vol. LVIII, p. 49. *L'Amour de l'Art*, no. 1, January 1930, p. 68; no. 10, December 1932, p. 342. Herbst, *Un Inventeur*, p. 91. *Exhib:* 1st U.A.M. Salon 1930.

MT 1004 Stool, c. 1930. Leather seat, legs in the form of a bobbin consisting of three tubes of metal twisted and welded to three tubular rings. Cf. MB 595 and table.

MT 1015 Stool, c. 1923. Curule type, concave seat, solid side supports, resting on four parallelepipeds. h. 35, l. 49, w. 30, or h. 40. Macassar ebony. C. Bernheim, Reifenberg, p.c. *Art et Décoration*, January-June 1923, Vol. XLIII, pp. 136, 137. Moussinac, *Intérieurs I*, 1924, pls. 9 (gouache), 12 (versions top and bottom). *Mobilier et Décoration*, no. 2, January 1927, p. 101. *Art et Décoration*, January-June 1927, Vol. LI, p. 110. *Vogue*, May 1, 1927, p. 41. *Mobilier et Décoration*, no. 8, July 1928, p. 226. *L'Art International d'Aujourd'hui*, no. 6, pl. 13. *Exhib:* M.A.D. 1927, Barbazanges, Ld'A 1981, no. 85.

MU 871 Bookcase, 1930. At left, the principal unit, three shelves above a cabinet with two sliding doors; below this a small swivel table and a lower shelf; at right, five narrower shelves; the two units are hinged together. Wrought iron and palisander. Designed and made for the hall of *La Semaine à Paris*. *L'Amour de l'Art*, no. 1, January 1930, p. 72

MU 959 Bookcase, c. 1930. Pink pear wood and plate glass. *Art et Décoration*, July-December 1930, Vol. LVIII, p. 49. *L'Amour de l'Art*, no. 10, December 1932, p. 342. *Exhib:* 1st U.A.M. Salon.

MU 1030, c. 1930. Composite piece of furniture, consisting of an armoire on the left attached to unit MU 871. Palisander and metal. C. Dreyfus, p.c. *L'Amour de l'Art*, January 1930, no. 1, p. 72. *Art et Décoration*, July-December 1931, Vol. LX, p. 29; 1932, Vol. LXI, p. 134. *Exhib:* Sd'A 1929, 2nd U.A.M. Salon.

MU 1106 Bookcase.

PF 25, 35 Three-legged hinged plant stand, c. 1923. Wrought iron. h. 103, diam. 49. Appeared in sets of Marcel l'Herbier's film *Le Vertige*, 1925. Made for, among others, the Grand-Hôtel, Tours. No doubt appeared at the stand of J.-E. Rulhmann, S.A.D. 1927. C. Bernheim, Dalsace, Dreyfus, Michel Souillac, p.c. *L'Amour de l'Art*, no. 6, June 1924, p. 193. *Les Arts de la Maison*, Winter 1924, Winter 1926, pl. XXXIX. *L'Art et les Artistes*, January 1928, no. 83, p. 130. *Art et Décoration*, January-June 1928, Vol. LIII, pp. 34, 38; January-June 1930, Vol. LVII, p. 5; January-June 1932, Vol. LXI, p. 134. *L'Art International d'Aujourd'hui*, no. 6, pl. 6. Herbst, *Un Inventeur*, pp. 53, 81, 101. Ed., *R. Mallet-Stevens*, p. 225. *Exhib:* S.A.D. 1924, Sd'A 1926.

PF 83 Wall bracket for flower pot. Wrought iron. C. Bernheim. Made for the Grand-Hôtel, Tours. Circular hanging version. *Mobilier et Décoration*, no. 8, July 1928, p. 221. *Art et Décoration*, January-June 1930, Vol. LVII, p. 4; January-June 1932, Vol. LXI, p. 101. *L'Art International d'Aujourd'hui*, no. 6, pl. 6. Herbst, *Un Inventeur*, pp. 74, 76. *Exhib:* 3rd U.A.M. Salon. Version with a

two-bar support. *L'Art International d'Aujourd'hui*, no. 10, pl. 15. *Good Furniture Magazine*, January 1927, p. 30. *Exhib:* Sd'A 1926.
PF 1007 Version with a three-bar support.

PF 213 Vase / Planter. Carved alabaster. C. Dalsace, X, p.c. 1. *Art et Décoration*, January-June 1930, Vol. LVII, p. 4; January-June 1932, Vol. LXI, p. 101. *L'Art International d'Aujourd'hui*, no. 6, pl. 6. Herbst, *Un Inventeur*, pp. 74, 76. *Exhib:* 3rd U.A.M. Salon. Version with a two-bar support.

PT 887 Carpet, 1923-30. From a design by Jean Burkhalter, light brown, dull pink, and several shades of dark brown gray on a beige ground. l. 265, w. 227. *A.B.C. Artistique et Littéraire*, July 1931, p. 176. Produced for La Boutique.

1 Low stool, M-shaped curule type, c. 1925. Concave rectangular seat on four straight rectangular legs, slightly curved and rounded on the sides at the top. The legs can act as a framework for a movable seat covered in tapestry or leather or even for a seat in another wood. h. 35.5, l. 51.5, w. 33. Sycamore or sycamore and tapestry by Lurçat or palisander and tapestry by Lurçat or leather-covered seat. Made for the Grand-Hôtel, Tours, 1928. C. Bernheim, Dalsace, Dreyfus, Fleg, L'Herbier, p.c. *L'Art Vivant*, 1925, p. 27. *Les Arts de la Maison*, Autumn 1925, pl. VI. *L'Art et les Artistes*, 1924, no. 46, p. 282. *Mobilier et Décoration*, no. 2, January 1927, pp. 97, 99, 103; no. 5, April 1928, p. 45; no. 8, July 1928, p. 222. *L'Art Décoratif Français en 1928*, p. 222. *Art et Décoration*, 1932, Vol. LXI, pp. 134, 138. *Nouveaux Intérieurs Français*, 1933, pl. 15. Herbst, *Un Inventeur*, pp. 33, 74, 78, 79. *Exhib:* Version in sycamore with tapestry seat from a design by Lurçat, EIADIM 1925, in the lounge next to the French Embassy sports room. *Sale:* Paris, Loudmer, December 15, 1980, 18,000 F.F.; Monaco, December 7, 1981, 261, 20,000 F.F., October 24-25, 1982, 364, 19,500 F.F

2 U-shaped stool, c. 1920. Base and sides in solid wood, seat covered in fabric and fitted between the two uprights. Made for the Grand-Hôtel, Tours, 1928. *Art et Décoration*, July-December 1920, Vol. XXXVIII; p. 150, January-June 1923, Vol. XLIII, p. 129. *L'Art et les Artistes*, January 1928, no. 83, p. 132. *L'Amour de l'Art*, February 1928, no. 1, p. 62; July 1931, no. 7, p. 312. *Art et Décoration*, 1931, p. 29. *Exhib:* SdA 1920, 2nd U.A.M. Salon. Version with four sharp-angled parallelepiped feet, made for the Grand-Hôtel, Tours. *Encyclopédie des Métiers d'Art*, Vol. I, pl. 59, Moussinac, *Intérieurs I*, 1924, pl. 4, pl. 7 (gouache).

3 Stool, c. 1927. Concave seat in solid wood, supported by a flat strip of beaten iron forming a T-shaped base, the vertical bar bent at right angles, with two round rods connecting the seat to the base at either end. h. 46/49, l. 49, d. 38. Palisander or mahogany and metal. With a mahogany seat, made for the Grand-Hôtel, Tours, 1928. C. Chareau, Dalsace, G., R. Mallet-Stevens (polished steel), Col. Michel Souillac, p.c. *Art et Décoration*, January-June 1927, Vol. LI, p. 138. *L'Art et les Artistes*, January 1928, no. 83, p. 133. *L'Amour de l'Art*, February 1928, no. 2, pp. 59, 60. *Art et Décoration*, January-June 1928, Vol. LIII, p. 36; 1932, Vol. LXI, p. 133; 1934, Vol. LXIII, p. 50. *L'Architecture d'Aujourd'hui*, November-December 1933, p. 4. *Encyclopédie des Métiers d'Art*, Vol. I, pls. 63, 65, 66. *L'Art International d'Aujourd'hui*, no. 6, pl. 22. Herbst, *Un Inventeur*, pp. 26, 28, 65. *Domus*, no. 443, October 1966, p. 211. Ed., *R. Mallet-Stevens*, pp. 279, 281.

Guide de la XIème Biennale des Antiquaires, Paris 1982, p. 109. *Sale:* Monaco, October 24-25, 1982, 358.

4 Table, 1932. Two tabletops, supported by duralumin tubing bent and welded into a T-shape at the bottom; the large semicircular top screwed to three legs, the small semicircular top resting on two welded brackets. h. 60, diam. 63, w. 62. Thickness of the glass: 21 mm. Glass and duralumin. No doubt formed part of the "Conversation center in a lounge and small conservatory" at the 3rd U.A.M. Salon. C. Dalsace, p.c. *Beaux-Arts*, 1932, Vol. II, p. 11. *Acier*, 1934, p. 33.

5 Table, 1932-3. Legs consist of three tubes bent and welded, two of them L-shaped and parallel, connected by tubular cross-bars welded at right angles; large tabletop in glass and two small tabletops supported by the third leg and acting as shelves on the left side. *Art et Décoration*, 1933, p. 228. *Vu*, no. 274, 14 June 1933, p. 894. *Exhib:* 4th U.A.M. Salon.

6 Desk, c. 1927. Wooden top with sloping sides to right and left, each holding two pigeon-holes with independent sliding lids; double metal accordion legs. Palisander(?) and wrought iron. C. Pingusson, p.c. *Mobilier et Décoration*, no. 2, January 1927, p. 101. *Art et Décoration*, January-June 1927, Vol. LI, p. 110. Version with solid wood legs. French walnut. Created for Hélène Henry. Signed. C. Van Melle-Henry, p.c. *Exhib:* LdA 1981, no. 81.

7 Bedside table, small round table, 1922-3. Cf. EH 145. An inscription on the photo gives the date 1922. *Les Arts de la Maison*, Winter 1924, p. 21 (plan and elevation), pl. IV (gouache). *Art et Décoration*, January-June 1923, Vol. XLIII, p. 138.

8 Table, 1925. Rectangular top in wood supported by two U-shaped legs, each resting on a rectangular foot. Made for the dining room of the Indochina Pavilion, EIADIM, 1925. *L'Amour de l'Art*, August 1925, no. 8, p. 315. Herbst, *Un Inventeur*, p. 30. *Exhib:* EIADIM 1925.

9 Small table in wrought iron. Rectangular top with one rounded corner, vertical tubular leg riveted to a flat circular metal base. Version with a single tabletop, tripod ashtray stand and brass ashtray. h. 65, l. 36, w. 20, diam. 33. C. Dalsace, X, p.c. Herbst, *Un Inventeur*, pp. 30, 31. Version with three tabletops, one rectangular with a rounded corner and fixed, the other two segmental and swiveling fanwise. h. 60/65, l. 38, diam 41. C. Bernheim, Dalsace, p.c. Herbst, *Un Inventeur*, p. 40. *L'Architecture d'Aujourd'hui*, November-December 1933, p. 13. *Sale:* Monaco, April 19, 1982, 201, 50,000 F.F.; March 6, 1983, 164, 95,000 F.F.

10 Table, c. 1923. The top wraps down to meet four square legs. Cf. MT 1015. *Art et Décoration*, January-June 1923, Vol. XLIII, p. 137. Moussinac, *Intérieurs I*, pl. 12.

11 Desk, 1931-3. Large double-sided desk with two sets of drawers. Satin mahogany on tubular copper legs. h. 74, l. 220, w. 120. Possibly "created in 1931 for his collaborator Henri Meyer." No doubt designed for the offices of LTT, rue de la Faisanderie, Paris 16e. *Art et Décoration*, 1933, p. 124. *Sale:* Cornette de Saint-Cyr, December 5, 1983, 85, 41,000 F.F. There is a small work table belonging to the same group, with a satin mahogany top and tubular copper legs. *Sale:* Cornette de Saint-Cyr, December 5, 1983, 86.

12 Table, c. 1925. Rectangular top, four square legs ending in spindle-shaped feet. *L'Art et les Artistes*, 1924, no. 46, p. 182. MB 82 Version with an extension leaf concealed below the tabletop. Version with an open storage unit and an extension leaf concealed beneath it. *Les Arts de la Maison*, Autumn 1925, pl. VI. *L'Art Vivant*, 1925, p. 27. *Exhib*: EIADIM 1925, in the lounge next to the French Embassy sports room.

13 Table, 1932. Glass top resting on four tubular metal legs joined at the bottom by tubes of the same diameter forming an X, from the center of which a column made of four vertical tubes rises to meet the center of the table. Glass and black-painted metal. *h.* 63, *diam.* 58 and 54. C. Dalsace, Dreyfus, *p.c. Art et Décoration*, 1932, pp. 132, 138. *L'Architecture d'Aujourd'hui*, November-December 1933, p. 13. Herbst, *Un Inventeur*, p. 36.

14 Table, 1932. Circular top supported by three metal tubes in torque between two tubular rings of unequal diameter. Glass and black-painted metal. *h.* 63, *diam.* 58 and 54. C. Dalsace, Dreyfus, *p.c. Art et Décoration*, 1932, pp. 132, 138. *L'Architecture d'Aujourd'hui*, November-December 1933, p. 13. Herbst, *Un Inventeur*, p. 36.

15 Low table, c. 1930. Rectangular tabletop resting on an offcentered column serving as a bookcase, a shelf and a square base of the same area, two L-shaped feet. Palisander. *h.* 50, *l.* 65, *w.* 55. C. Dalsace, Dreyfus, Fleg, *p.c. L'Amour de l'Art*, no. 7, July 1931, p. 312. *Art et Décoration*, July-December 1931, Vol. LX, p. 29; 1932, Vol. LXI pp. 134, 136. *Exhib*: 2nd U.A.M. Salon.

16 Bed, 1920. Cf. EH 163. *L'Art et les Artistes*, 1924, no. 46, p. 282. *Art et Décoration*, July-December 1920, Vol. XXXVIII, p. 150. Moussinac, *Intérieurs I*, pls. 4, 6, 8 (gouache). *Exhib*: Sd'A 1920.

17 Bed, c. 1928. Cf. MF 75. Made for the Noailles' villa at Hyères. C. Vicomtesse de Noailles. *Art et Décoration*, July-December 1928, Vol. LIV, p. 24.

18 Bedroom corner seat (Coin de chambre), 1938. Wicker. Herbst, *Un Inventeur*, p. 83.

19 Bed, 1921. Dated 1913 on the photo of EH 226 (version with fluted corners, in walnut and ebony). Macassar ebony. *L'Art Vivant*, April 1926, no. 32. p. 455(?). Herbst, *Un Inventeur*, p. 77.

20 Couch, 1932-4. Perforated sheet-metal painted black and screwed to a metal framework. Possibly designed and made for the Maison de Verre. C. Dalsace, *p.c. Acier*, 1934, p. 64.

21 Couch, 1923-4. Six sloping panels. Sycamore or palisander. Cf. armchair and chaise lounge, MD 18, 19, 172, MP 167. *Les Arts de la Maison*, Winter 1924, pl. II (gouache).

22 Large couch, c. 1928. Back with ten sloping panels, floor-length skirting except in front, three front feet. *l.* 190. Wicker. Part of a drawing-room set in wicker made and sold in 1928 (2 × MF 18, MB 595, and two "Children's Corner" chairs). *Sale*: Monaco, March 6, 1983, 161.

23 Sofa bed (Canapé-lit), 1923-4. Cf. bergère MP 732 and armchair MF 220. *Les Arts de la Maison*, Winter 1924, pl. I. *Mobilier et Décoration d'Intérieur*, April-May 1924, p. 27. *Exhib*: 15th S.A.D. Version with back. *Nouveaux Intérieurs Français*, 1933, pl. 15.

24 Sofa bed (Canapé-lit). Cf. armchair MF 15. Herbst, *Un Inventeur*, p. 36.

25 Couch, 1922-3. Cf. EH 145. *L'Amour de l'Art*, no. 11, November 1923, p. 748. *Exhib*: Sd'A 1923.

26 Storage unit (Meuble de rangement). Four compartments encased with wrought-iron bands like MA 374, assembled to form a square. *Art et Décoration*, 1933, p. 228. *Nouveaux Intérieurs Français*, 1933, pl. 14. *Exhib*: 4th U.A.M. Salon.

27 Armoire, c. 1924. Palisander or palisander and Macassar ebony, keyholes and keys in ivory. *Les Arts de la Maison*, Winter 1924, pl. III. *Mobilier et Décoration d'Intérieur*, November 1924, p. 20. *Mobilier et Décoration*, July 1928, no. 8, p. 216. *Exhib*: Sd'A 1924, no. 351.

28 Armoire and bookcase (Armoire-bibliothèque), 1924. *Les Arts de la Maison*, Winter 1924, pl. I (gouache).

29 Armoire and bookcase (Armoire-bibliothèque), 1924-5. *Les Arts de la Maison*, Winter 1924, pl. VI.

30 Armoire, 1924-6. Palisander or rosewood. *Les Arts de la Maison*, Summer 1926, pl. XXXI. *Mobilier et Décoration*, no. 2, January 1927, p. 98; no. 8, July 1928, p. 225. Herbst, *Un Inventeur*, p. 79.

31 Standard lamp, known as "The Nun" ("La Religieuse"), 1923. Version with metal standard and shade made of triangular or trapezoidal panels of alabaster. Appeared in the sets of Marcel l'Herbier's film *L'Inhumaine*, 1925. C. Maria de Beyrie. *L'Amour de l'Art*, no. 4, April 1924, p. 116, 193. *Mobilier et Décoration d'Intérieur*, April-May 1924, p. 27. *Les Arts de la Maison*, Winter 1924, pl. II (gouache). *L'Art Vivant*, no. 32, April 1926, p. 305. Ed., R. Mallet-Stevens, p. 133. *Guide de la XIème Biennale...*, 1982, p. 115. *Exhib*: 15th S.A.D. Salon 1924, Ld'A 1981, no. 147. Metal version with fabric shade. Made for the Grand-Hôtel, Tours, 1928. *L'Art et les Artistes*, January 1928, no. 83, p. 131. *L'Amour de l'Art*, February 1928, no. 2, p. 61. *Mobilier et Décoration*, no. 2, January 1927, p. 99. *Encyclopédie des Métiers d'Art*, Vol. I, pl. 59. Version in Cuban mahogany and alabaster. *h.* 180. Made for the Grand-Hôtel, Tours, 1928. *Sale* original and reproduction: Cornette de Saint-Cyr, December 5, 1983, 52, 469,000 F.F.

32 Table lamp, known as "The Little Nun" ("La Petite Religieuse"), 1923-4. Sycamore or metal and shade in fabric or parchment. *L'Amour de l'Art*, no. 4, April 1924, p. 124. *Les Arts de la Maison*, Autumn 1925, pl. VI. *L'Art Vivant*, 1925, p. 27. *Exhib*: EIADIM 1925, in the lounge next to the French Embassy sports room.

33 Chandelier, 1923. Shade made of nine quarter-circle sheets of alabaster arranged in a corolla and set in a fixture of black-painted metal. *h.* 29.5, *w.* 45. *Sale*: Monaco, December 7, 1981, 265, 36,000 F.F.

34 Stacking chair in steel, 1937. *Acier*, no. 1, 1937, pp. 16, 17. Herbst, *Un Inventeur*, p. 94.

35 Stacking table in steel, 1937. *Acier*, no. 1, 1937, pp. 16, 17.

36 Armchair for the French Embassy desk, 1924-5. Gondola-shaped, arms curved inward and flared on the outside with exposed wood panels, supported by the extension of the quadrangular front legs with broad bases, the back legs saber-shaped; upholstered in leather and furnished with a loose cushion; differs from other armchairs of the same type by the shape of the front feet, which are not molded. *h.* 80, *w.* 72. Solid palisander and beech frame (the palisander has long been lacquered black). Designed for the French Embassy desk at EIADIM. Acquired from the artist in 1926 by the M.A.D. (N I: 25479). *L'Amour de l'Art*, no. 8, August 1925, p. 313. EIADIM, *Une Ambassade...*, 1925, pls. XXXVII, XXXVIII. *Art et Décoration*, July-December 1925, pl. 1. *Les Arts de la Maison*, Autumn 1925, pl. IV. *L'Art Vivant*, October 1925, p. 26. Herbst, *Un Inventeur*, pp. 54-57. Russell, Garner and Read, *A Century of Chair Design*, p. 104 (drawing). *Exhib*: EIADIM 1925, M.A.D. 1937, no. 689 and reproduction, Besançon 1963, no. 322, M.A.D. 1966, no. 578, Minneapolis 1971, no. 21, M.A.D. 1977, no. 316, M.A.D. 1983, not numbered.

37 Armchair, c. 1923. Cross- or lyre-shaped molded wood legs, exposed wooden arms, crossbars, and back uprights. Cf. MF 208, 217, 219. *h.* 80. Palisander. Made for numerous clients, this seat, whose back leg has served as the base for a vast family of descendants, was produced in quantity for the smoking bar of the Grand-Hôtel, Tours. Palisander or walnut, cushion covered with fabric by Hélène Henry. *h.* 83, *w.* 74, *d.* 95. C. Bernheim, Dalsace, Dreyfus, Fleg, L. R., Van Melle-Henry, Michel Souillac, *p.c. L'Art et les Artistes*, January 1928, no. 83, p. 131. *L'Amour de l'Art*, February 1928, no. 2, p. 61. *Les Arts de la Maison*, Winter 1926, pl. XXXIX. *Mobilier et Décoration*, no. 8, July 1928, pp. 217, 219, 224. *Art et Décoration*, January-June 1932, Vol. LIII, p. 35; 1932, Vol. LXI, pp. 134, 136. *Encyclopédie des Métiers d'Art*, Vol. I, pl. 59, *L'Art International d'Aujourd'hui*, no. 6, pl. 6. *Exhib*: M.A.D. 1984. *Sale*: Monaco, October 9, 1983, 237.

38 Young doctor's office suite. Desk and armchair, two armchairs, two small bookcases and stool, large bookcase, storage unit. Designed and executed for Dr. Dalsace in 1919. Cabinetwork in Macassar ebony, rust-colored leather, mirror. Desk: *h.* 79, *w.* 150, *d.* 48. A rectangular desktop supported by two rows each of four drawers with bronze pulls above two retractable surfaces concealed in the body of the piece; this rests on eight bun feet in chrome metal. Mahogany frame, cabinetwork in Macassar ebony. An extension, a four-legged table in blackened walnut and Macassar ebony cabinetwork, can be pulled out from the lower part of the desk. Desktop covered with rust-colored leather.
Doctor's chair: Macassar ebony, *h.* 110, *w.* 61, *d.* 46. Patients' chairs: Macassar ebony, *h.* 88, *w.* 60, *d.* 46. MP 117 Couch: Macassar ebony, *h.* 64, *w.* 205, *d.* 92. Armoire: Macassar ebony, *h.* 119, *w.* 192, *d.* 38. Small bookcases: Macassar ebony, *h.* 119, *w.* 48, *d.* 20. The vitrine, in Macassar ebony cabinetwork and plate glass on a metal frame, was designed when the suite was reinstalled in the Maison de Verre, 1932: *h.* 156, *w.* 275, *d.* 36. *L'Amour de l'Art*, no. 3, March 1923, p. 486. Moussinac, *Intérieurs I*, pls. 2, 3. Herbst, *Un Inventeur*, pp. 36, 40, 41.

39 Coat rack, c. 1932. Duralumin tubing untreated or painted black. *h.* 210, *w.* 90, *d.* 30. C. Dalsace, *p.c. Acier*, 1934, p. 65. Herbst, *Un Inventeur*, pp. 17, 45.

40 Chaise lounge, c. 1933. Duralumin tubing and woven cord. C. Dalsace. Whereabouts unknown. *L'Architecture d'Aujourd'hui*, November-December 1933, p. 4.

MA 112

MA 99

MB 9
MB 84
MA 69

MA 374, 420, 1092 (version with mirror)

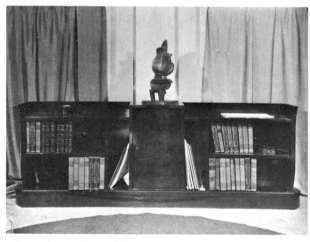

MA 788   MA 333, 334
MU 265   MD 234

MA 109
MD 236, 234

MA 205
MD 237

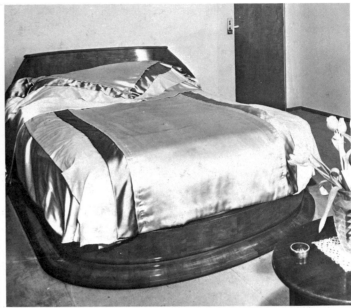

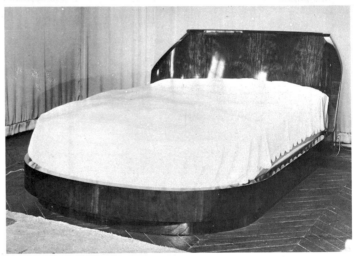

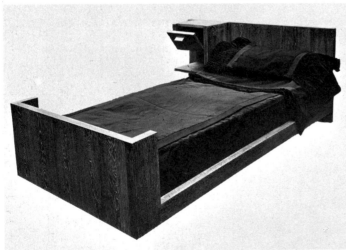

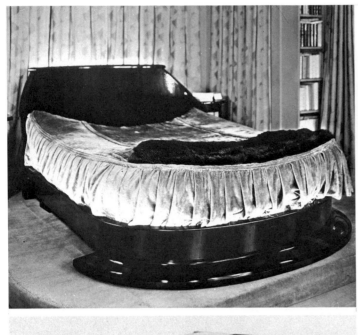

MP 389
MP 764

MP389
MP 901

EH 294
19

EH 52
MP 747

MP 215
MP 13

MP 174 *bis*
MF 313

MP 273
MP 526

MP 1029
MP 761

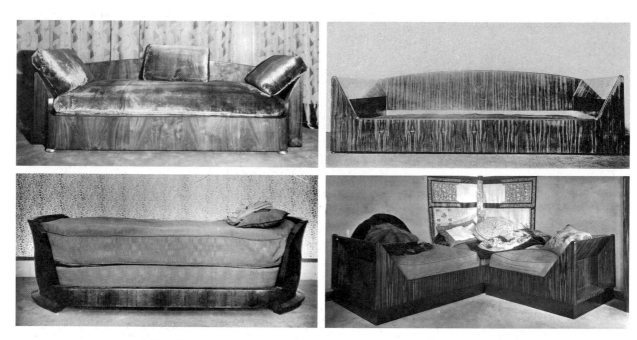

MP 287
MP 102

38
MP 230

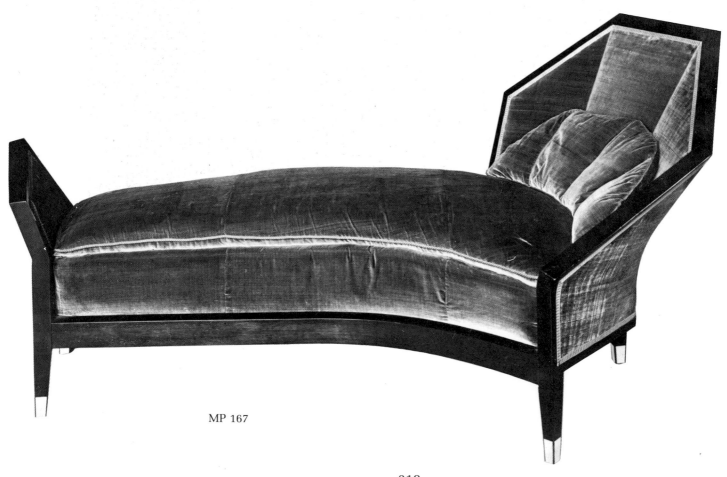

MP 167

MB 960
Unnumbered document.

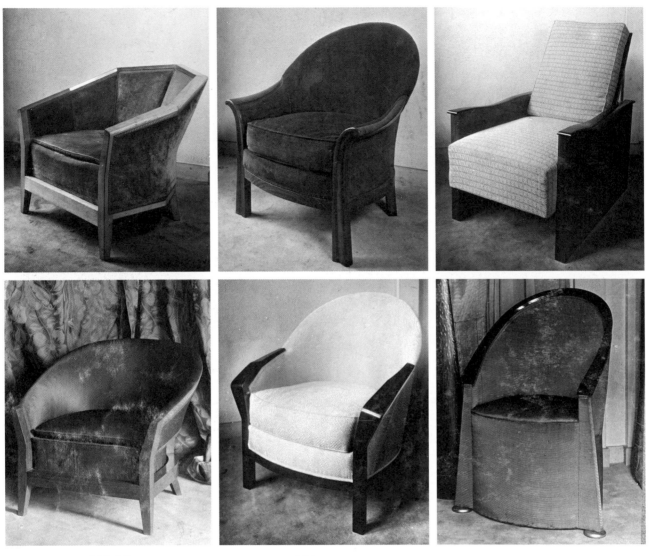

MF 172   MF 208, 217   MF 75
MF 15   MF 732   EH 176

MF 220
MF 19

MF 8
MF 310

MF 219
MF 18

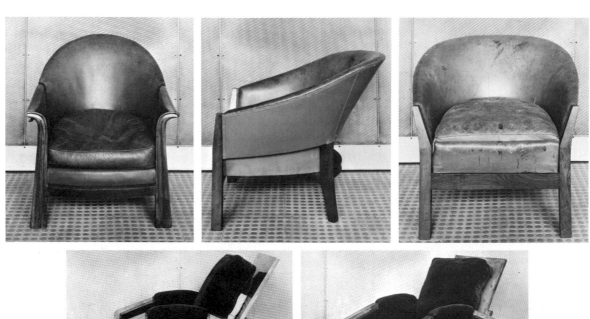

MF 208, 217   MF 15   MF 15
MF 220 (version with floor skirting)   MF 220
MF 1050, 1050 *bis*, 1050 *ter*, 1051
MF 11   MF168

34
MF 195
MF 158

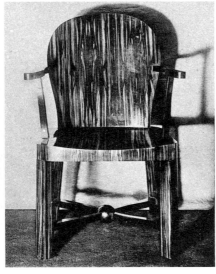

MF 275 D   38   MF 182
MF 276   38   MF 275

MC 767
MC 767 (variant)

MP 671
MC 763   MC 762

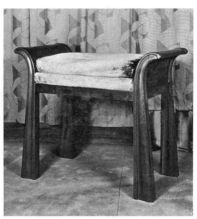

MT 1015   3   MT 286
MB 106 (flat-edged version)   13

Unnumbered, in the MB 388 range.
MT 876

MB 106
MB 410

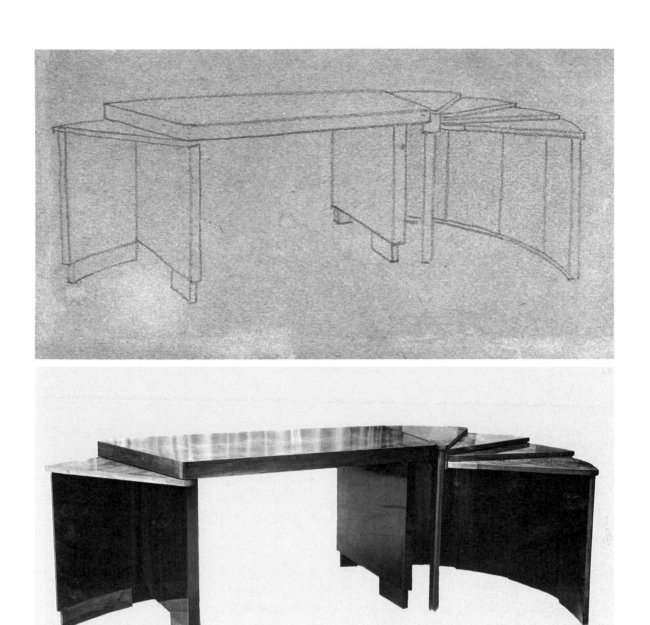

MB 771, 773, 774

38 (version with shell-shaped handles)
MS 1013

MB 113, MB 808, 810

MS 1009, *bis, ter* (closed)　　　　　　MB 277
MB 1049　　　　　　　　　　　　　　　MB 97

MB 2
MB 103

MB 1
MB 720

MS 14
MS 423

MB 820 (cf. MS 423)
MS 80 (cf. MS 423)

MS 417

MS 417 (variant)

MS 1009, *bis* (open)
MD 73

MS 418, 419, *bis, ter*

MB 170 and MB 770, MT 25, MB 110
MB 233, MB 413

MK 231   MK 751   MK 290
MK 677   MK 940   MK 678

LA 625
LA 625
ES 814

unnumbered
LA 317, LA 548, LA 415
LA 271, LA 272
LA 321

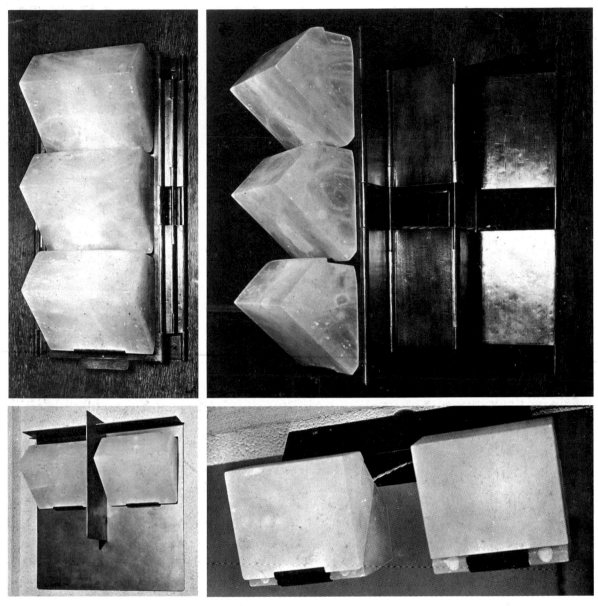

LA 250
LA 550, LA 551

LA 252, LA 254
LT 753

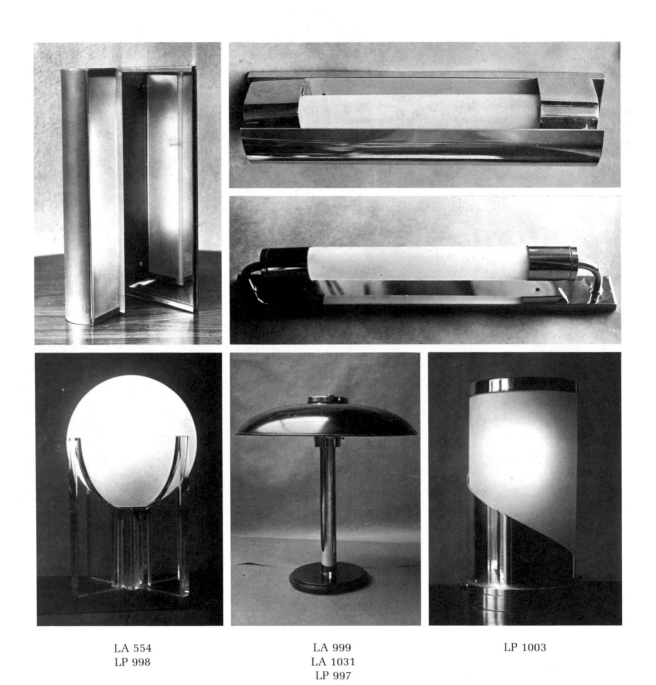

LA 554
LP 998

LA 999
LA 1031
LP 997

LP 1003

LP 270, LP 166
LA 550

LT 753, LT 314
LA 415

LA 555

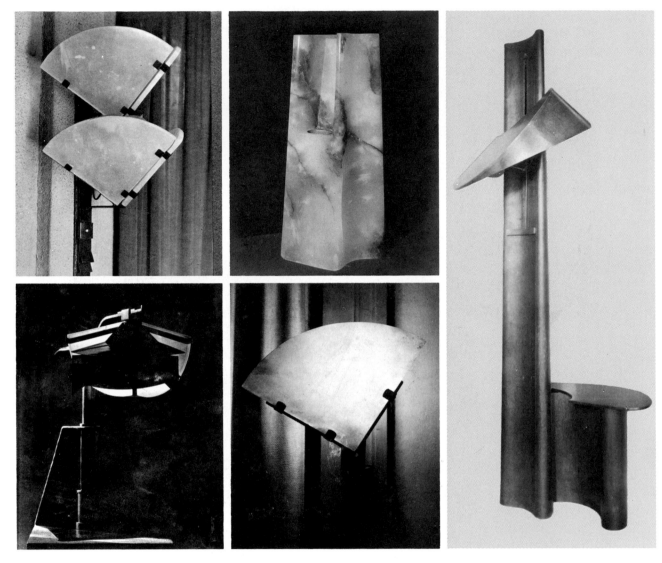

LA 188
LP 181

PF 213
LA 164

LP 133, LP 414

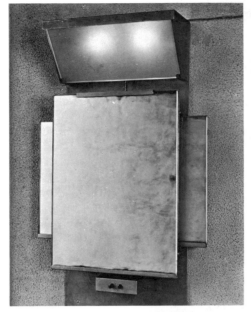

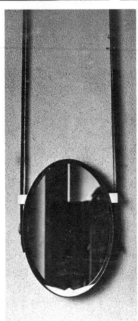

MG 820
MG 7

MG 821
MG 311, MG 312

PF 83, PD 698, PF 1007
unnumbered, PF 35

PD 1000, PE 209, OD 996
MB 864, PW 280

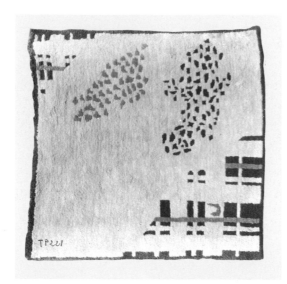

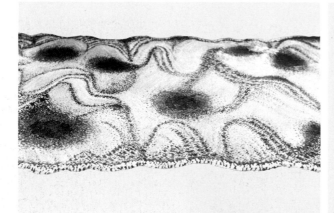

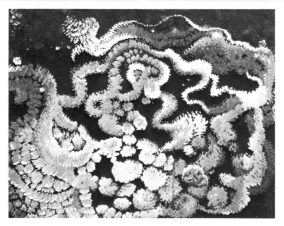

Carpets designed by various artists, produced by La Boutique, 1923–27.

TP 221
PT 867, PT 882
PT 869

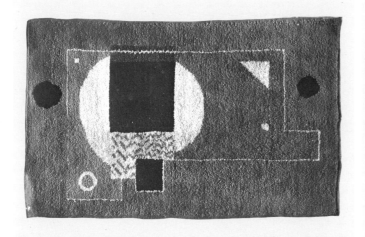

PT 803
PT 806

PT 807
PT 860

SELECT BIBLIOGRAPHY

The following list is not intended to be exhaustive. For further material, the reader should refer to the *Bibliographie 1925*, published by the Société des Amis de la Bibliothèque Forney in October 1976, for the exhibition "Cinquantenaire de l'Exposition de 1925" (Musée des Arts Décoratifs, Paris).

BOOKS

Amic, Yolande. *Les Assises du Siège Contemporain*. Paris, 1968.

Djo-Bourgeois, *Répertoire du Goût Moderne*, Paris, 1928.

Brunhammer, Yvonne. *Art Deco Style*. London and New York, 1984.

———. *1925*. Paris, 1976.

Camard, Florence. *Ruhlmann*. Paris, 1983.

Chareau, Pierre. *L'Art International d'Aujourd'hui, No. 7, Meubles*. Paris, n.d.

Deshairs, Léon. *L'Art Décoratif Français*. 2 vols. 1918–1925, 1925–1930, Paris, n.d.

Encyclopedie des metiers d'art, "Décoration moderne", Paris, n.d., Vols 1 and II.

Herbst, René (ed.). *Un Inventeur, l'Architecte Pierre Chareau*. Paris, 1954.

Jeanneau, Guillaume. *L'Art Décoratif Moderne, Formes Nouvelles et Programmes Nouveaux*. Paris, 1925.

———. *Le Meuble Léger en France*. Paris, 1952.

———. *Le Mobilier Français*. No. 26. Paris, n.d.

Johnson, J. Stewart. *Eileen Gray, Designer*. New York, 1979.

Kjellberg, Pierre. *Art Déco, les Maîtres du Mobilier*. Paris, 1981.

Moussinac, Léon. *Intérieurs I*. Paris, 1924.

———. *Le Meuble Français Moderne*. Paris, 1925.

Olmer, Pierre. *Le Mobilier Français Aujourd'hui (1910–1925)*. Paris, 1926.

Page, Marian. *Furniture Design by Architects*. London, 1983.

Sanchez, Leopold Diego. *Jean-Michel Frank*. Paris, 1980.

Russell, Frank, Philippe Garner, and John Read. *A Century of Chair Design*. London and New York, 1980.

Various editors. *R. Mallet-Stevens, Architect*. Brussels, 1980.

Wilk, Christopher. *Marcel Breuer, Furniture and Interiors*. New York, 1981.

GENERAL ARTICLES

ART ET DECORATION

January–June 1920, Vol. XXXVII
J. Laran. 'Notre enquête sur le mobilier moderne, J.-E. Ruhlmann,' pp. 1–13.
A. Fréchet. 'La laque,' pp. 41–48.
L. Deshairs. 'La Compagnie des Arts Français,' pp. 65–72.
G. Jeanneau. 'André Groult, Fernand Nathan,' pp. 186–192.

July–December 1920, Vol. XXXVIII
R. de Felice. 'Appareils d'éclairage,' pp. 46–55.
P. Lahalle. 'Notre enquête sur le mobilier moderne, Lucet, Lahalle et Levard,' pp. 118–124.

January–June 1922, Vol. XLI
R. Chavance. 'Notre enquête sur le mobilier moderne, Francis Jourdain,' pp. 49–56.

May 1925
G. Janneau. 'Introduction à l'Exposition des arts décoratifs; considérations sur l'esprit moderne,' p. 155.

January–June 1927, Vol. LI
G. Varenne. 'La technique moderne de l'ébénisterie,' pp. 129–139.

January–June 1928, Vol. LIII
A. H. Martinie. 'Djo-Bourgeois, architecte et décorateur,' pp. 65–79.
R. Chavance. 'Bureaux de dames,' pp. 97–108.
A. H. Martinie. 'E. Kohlmann,' pp. 130–136.

January–June 1929, Vol. LV
A. Salomon. 'L'éclairage moderne,' pp. 28–32.

January–June 1930, Vol. LVII
M. Terrier. 'Le mobilier métallique,' pp. 97–104.

July–December 1930, Vol. LVIII
A. Salomon. 'De l'éclairage,' pp. 97–103.

July–December 1931, Vol. LX
R. Cogniat. 'Techniques et esthétiques des tapis nouveaux,' pp. 105–116.

October 1932, Vol. LXI
R. Cogniat. 'Cheminées,' pp. 303–310.
R. Chavance. 'Applications et techniques nouvelles du verre,' pp. 311–330.

1933, Vol. LXII
R. Nalys. 'Le bureau bibliothèque et le cabinet de travail,' pp. 64–76.

January–June 1934, Vol. LIX
P. Laroche. 'Salles de bains,' pp. 97–108.

L'AMOUR DE L'ART

No. 1, January 1924
H. Clouzot. 'En marge de l'art appliqué moderne,' pp. 105–125.

No. 8, August 1925 (L'Exposition des arts Décoratifs et Industriels de 1925)
W. George. 'Les tendances générales,' pp. 283–291.
M. Dormoy. 'L'esprit de l'Exposition,' pp. 292–311.
———. 'Les intérieurs à l'Exposition internationale des arts décoratifs,' pp. 312–323.

No. 11, November 1929
E. Tisserand. 'Le meuble de métal et son avenir,' pp. 418–427.

No. 9, September 1928
A. Gain. 'Le cinéma et les arts décoratifs,' pp. 321–330.

No. 10, December 1932
R. Cogniat. 'L'Art Décoratif en 1932, Point de vue sur l'Art appliqué,' pp. 330–343.

No. 9, November 1935
B. Champigneulle. 'Enquête d'un style,' pp. 319–324.

1945
P. Verlet. 'Le meuble moderne et les leçons passés,' pp. 157–165.

LA RENAISSANCE DES ARTS FRANÇAIS ET DES INDUSTRIES DE LUXE

No. 1, January 1920
E. Sedeyn. 'Propos sur les meubles d'aujourd'hui, pp. 52–61.

No. 8, August 1925
H. Clouzot. 'Les ensembles mobiliers,' pp. 349–362.

LA REVUE DE L'ART ANCIEN ET MODERNE

January–May 1925, XLVII
Ch. Zervos. "Les tendances actuelles de l'art décoratif; le mobilier d'hier et d'aujourd'hui,' pp. 68–75.

L'ART VIVANT

No. 105, May 1, 1929
E. Tisserand. 'Chronique de l'art décoratif,' p. 372.

MAGAZINE ARTICLES ON PIERRE CHAREAU, WITH PHOTOGRAPHS OR OTHER REFERENCES TO HIS WORK

L'ARCHITECTURE D'AUJOURD'HUI

No. 9, November-December 1933
P. Vago. 'Un hôtel particulier à Paris,' pp. 4–8.
P. Nelson. 'La maison de la rue Saint-Guillaume,' pp. 9–11.
J. Lepage. 'Observations en visitant,' pp. 12–15.

No. 9, September 1935
P. Chareau. 'La création artistique et l'imitation commerciale,' pp. 68–69.

July 1950
'Maison d'été d'un peintre à Long Island,' pp. 50–51.

No. 31, 1950
Francis Jourdain. 'Pierre Chareau,' p. VIII.

ART ET DECORATION

July–December 1920, Vol. XXXVIII
G. Janneau. 'L'art décoratif,' pp. 141–160.

July–December 1921, Vol. XL
G. Varenne. 'Le mobilier et l'art décoratif,' pp. 175–192.

January–June 1923, Vol. XLIII
R. Chavance. 'L'art décoratif contemporain au pavillon de Marsan,' pp. 110–114.
G. Varenne. 'L'esprit moderne de Pierre Chareau,' pp. 129–138.
R. Chavance. 'Le XIVème Salon des Artistes Décorateurs,' pp. 161–192.

July–December 1923, Vol. XLIV
G. Varenne. 'L'art urbain et le mobilier au Salon d'Automne,' pp. 161–184.

January–June 1924, Vol. XLV
R. Chavance. 'L'art décoratif contemporain au pavillon de Marsan,' p. 117.

July–December 1926, Vol. L
R. Regamey. 'XVIème Salon des artistes Décorateurs,' pp. 1–32.
G. Varenne. 'Procédés et appareils modernes d'éclairage,' pp. 103–112.

January–June 1927, Vol. LI
L. Deshairs. 'Une étape vers les meubles métalliques,' pp. 104–110.

G. Varenne. 'La technique moderne de l'ébénisterie,' pp. 129–139.
L. Werth. 'Le XVIIème Salon des Artistes Décorateurs,' pp. 161–168.

July–December 1927, Vol. LII
R. Chavance. 'Chez un cinéaste,' pp. 43–48.

January–June 1928, Vol. LIII
Y. Rambosson. 'Un grand hôtel à Tours,' pp. 33–39.

July–December 1928, Vol. LIV
L. Deshairs. 'Une villa moderne à Hyères,' pp. 1–24.

July–December 1929, Vol. LVI
L. Deshairs. 'Le mobilier et les arts décoratifs au Salon d'Automne,' pp. 172–192.

January–June 1930, Vol. LVII
J. Gallotti. 'Goûts du Jour,' pp. 1–13.
M. Terrier. 'Meubles métalliques: les sièges,' pp. 33–48.
R. Chavance. 'Les bureaux de la Semaine à Paris,' pp. 153–155.

July–December 1930, Vol. LVIII
L. Werth. 'Le premier salon de l'Union des Artistes Modernes,' pp. 33–50.

January–June 1931, Vol. LIX
P. Laroche. 'Salles de bains,' pp. 97–108.

July–December 1931, Vol. LX
R. Cogniat. 'Deuxième exposition de l'Union des Artistes Modernes,' pp. 3–35.

January–June 1932, Vol. LXI
J. Gallotti. 'La troisième exposition de l'Union des Artistes Modernes,' pp. 97–101.
P. Migennes. 'Sur deux ensembles de Pierre Chareau,' pp. 129–140.

1933, Vol. LXII
R. Chavance. 'Bureaux industriels par Pierre Chareau,' pp. 123–128.
R. Brielle. 'IVème salon de l'Union de Artistes Modernes,' pp. 225–244.

February 1934, Vol. LXIII
R. Cogniat. 'La maison de verre de Pierre Chareau,' pp. 49–56.

1938, Vol. LXVII
L. Cheronnet. 'Cabinet de travail et salons de réception de l'administrateur du Collège de France,' pp. 113–120.

No. 19, 1950
B. Ch. 'Pierre Chareau,' p. 49.

No. 27, 1952
'Une maison française aux Etats-Unis,' pp. 24–25.

BEAUX-ARTS

No. 12, June 15, 1925
G. Janneau. 'La décoration intérieure, le mobilier,' pp. 181–196. L'Exposition Internationale des Arts Décoratifs et Industriels Modernes (EIADIM), Special number.

DOMUS

No. 443, October 1966
R. Rodgers. 'Parigi 1930, la casa di vetro di Pierre Chareau.'

FOREIGN TRADE

No. 12, Vol. 3, December 1928
Reproduction on p. 42.

GLACE ET VERRE

No. 178, October–November 1962
'Un inventeur, l'architecte Pierre Chareau,' pp. 18–20.

GLOBAL ARCHITECTURE

No. 46, 1977
P. Montes. 'La maison Dalsace.'

GOOD FURNITURE MAGAZINE

January 1927
H.S. Creswell. "The 1926 Autumn Salon,' p. 30.

HOUSE AND GARDEN

February 1983
'House of Glass, Walls of Light,' pp. 139–141.
M. Filler. 'A Beacon of Modernism,' pp. 143–147.
M. Vellay. 'An Insider's View,' pp. 148–152.

L'AMOUR DE L'ART

No. 3, March 1922
L. Vauxcelles. 'A propos du Salon des Artistes
    Décorateurs,' pp. 85–88.

No. 5, May 1923
G. Mourey. 'Le XIVème Salon des Artistes Décorateurs,'
    pp. 557–564.

No. 3, March 1923
W. George. 'Les intérieurs de Pierre Chareau,' pp. 483–488.

No. 11, November 1923
Y. Rambosson. 'Le Salon d'Automne, III les Arts
    Appliqués,' pp. 743–756.

No. 4, April 1924
H. Clouzot. 'En marge de l'art appliqué moderne,' pp. 105–
    125.

No. 6, June 1924
Y. Rambosson. 'Le Salon des Décorateurs,' pp. 190–194.

No. 11, November 1924
G. Varenne. 'Le Salon d'Automne, l'Art Décoratif et l'Art
    Urbain,' pp. 369–376.

No. 6, June 1926
G. Varenne. 'Le Salon des Artistes Décorateurs,' pp. 213–
    216.

No. 2, February 1928
G. Varenne. 'Un ensemble de Chareau au Grand-Hôtel de
    Tours,' pp. 59–62.

No. 7, July, 1928
G. Varenne. 'Les "Décorateurs" de 1928,' pp. 241–250.

No. 7, July 1929
G. Varenne. 'Les ensembles mobiliers au Salon des
    Décorateurs,' pp. 241–251.

No. 1, January 1930
G. Varenne. 'Les mouvements des arts appliqués,' pp. 65–
    68.

————. 'Les ensembles mobiliers au Salon d'Automne,'
    pp. 69–75.

No. 9, September 1930
G. Varenne. 'L'Union des Artistes Modernes,' pp. 367–373.

No. 7, July 1931
G. Varenne. 'Le Salon des Artistes Décorateurs et l'Union
    des Artistes Modernes,' pp. 310–312.

No. 10, December 1932
R. Cogniat. 'L'art décoratif en 1932; point de vue sur l'art
    appliqué,' pp. 330–354.

No. 9, November 1935
B. Champigneulle. 'Enquête d'un style,' pp. 319–325.

LA RENAISSANCE DE L'ART
FRANCAIS ET DES
INDUSTRIES DE LUXE

No. 1, January 1921
G. Janneau. 'Le mouvement moderne: le meuble au Salon
    d'Automne,' pp. 31–40.

No. 4, April 1923
G. Janneau. 'Le mouvement moderne: première exposition
    d'art décoratif contemporain,' pp. 203–208.

No. 7, July 1923
G. Janneau. 'Le mouvement moderne: le Salon des
    Décorateurs,' pp. 427–434.

No. 4, April 1924
H. Clouzot. 'Deuxième exposition d'art décoratif
    contemporain au pavillon de Marsan,' pp. 195–204.

No. 7, July 1924
H. Clouzot. 'Quinzième salon des Artistes Décorateurs,'
    pp. 386–400.

No. 1, January 1925
H. Clouzot. 'Les arts appliqués au Salon d'Automne,'
    pp. 5–16.

LA REVUE DE L'ART ANCIEN ET MODERNE

June–December 1925, Vol. XLVIII pp. 223–238.

L'ART ET LES ARTISTES

No. 38, June 1923
L.-Ch. Waterlin. 'Le Salon des Artistes Décorateurs,'
    pp. 356–360.

No. 46, April 1924
M. Gauthier. 'Art décoratif: M. Pierre Chareau,' pp. 281–
    286.

No. 66, April 1926
L.-Ch. Watelin. 'Le Salon des Artistes Décorateurs,'
    pp. 347–352.

No. 83, January 1928
E. Tisserand. 'Une oeuvre nouvelle de Pierre Chareau
    ensemblier,' pp. 130–134.

L'ART INTERNATIONAL D'AUJOURD'HUI

No. 6, Intérieurs
Introduction by Francis Jourdain

No. 7, Meubles
Introduction by Pierre Chareau

No. 10, Le métal
Introduction by Jean Prouve

L'ART VIVANT

January 1925
G. Remon. 'Les décors de la vie: l'habitation
d'aujourd'hui,' pp. 11–13.

No. 4, February 1925
G. Remon. 'L'habitation d'aujourd'hui, la salle à manger,'
pp. 14–17.

No. 20, October 1925
R. Rosenthal. 'L'Exposition des arts décoratifs et
industriels modernes: la cour des métiers et l'ambassade
française,' pp. 11–17.

No. 47, December 1926
E. Tisserand. 'L'art décoratif au Salon d'Automne,'
pp. 871–894.

LES ARTS DE LA MAISON

Winter 1924
E. Fleg. 'Nos décorateurs, Pierre Chareau,' pp. 17–24.

LES ECHOS DES INDUSTRIES D'ART

September 1927
R. Chavance. 'L'éclairage moderne,' pp. 22–32.

April 1928
'La salle à manger,' pp. 6–14.

September 1928
A. Diard. 'L'éclairage de la demeure moderne,' pp. 22–25.

October 1928
'Le cabinet de travail, bureaux et studios,' pp. 9–21.

LUX

April 1924
A. and R. Herbst. 'Salles à manger modernes,' p. 440.

MOBILIER ET DECORATION

April–May 1924
'Le mobilier au Salon d'Automne,' p. 22.
G. Henriot. 'Le XVème Salon de la Société des Artistes
Décorateurs,' p. 27.

No. 6, May 1926
G. Remon. 'Groupements et regroupements, exposition à la
Galerie Barbazanges,' pp. 143–148.

No. 2, January 1927
G. Remon. Les créations de Pierre Chareau,' pp. 97–106.

No. 5, April 1928
R. Chavance. Quelques exemples d'installations modernes,
rue Mallet-Stevens,' pp. 149–175.

No. 8, July 1928
R. Chavance. 'Les cinq,' pp. 43–51.
G. Henriot. 'Pierre Chareau,' pp. 215–230.

PARURES

No. 27, September 1928
'Les boules de verre,' pp. 32–34.

PERSPECTA

No. 12, n.d.
K. Frampton. 'Maison de verre,' pp. 77–126.

THE STUDIO YEARBOOK OF DECORATIVE ART, 1927

Reproduction on p. 81.

VOGUE

May 1, 1927
J. Gallot. 'Bureaux et cabinets de travail,' p. 41.

LIST OF EXHIBITIONS WITH WORKS BY PIERRE CHAREAU ON DISPLAY

This list excludes the Salon d'Automne and the Salon des Artistes Décorateurs where Chareau exhibited. Catalogues are available.

1923
1st Exposition d'Art Décoratif Contemporain, Musée des Arts Décoratifs, Paris.

1924
2nd Exposition d'Art Décoratif Contemporain, Musée des Arts Décoratifs, Paris.

1925
Exposition Internationale des Arts Décoratifs et Industriels Modernes.

1926
Exhibition at the Galerie Barbazanges, Paris.

1927
Exposition d'Art Décoratif Contemporain, Musée des Arts Décoratifs, Paris.

1928
Exposition des Cinq at the Galerie Barbazanges.

1930
1st exhibition of the Union des Artistes Modernes, Musée des Arts Décoratifs, Paris.

1931
2nd exhibition of the Union des Artistes Modernes, Musée des Arts Décoratifs, Paris.

1932
3rd exhibition of the Union des Artistes Modernes.

1933
4th Salon of the Union des Artistes Modernes, Galerie de la Renaissance, Paris.

1934
5th Salon of the Union des Artistes Modernes, Salon d'Automne.

1937
"Le décor de la vie 1900–1925," Musée des Arts Décoratifs, Paris.

1963
Besançon, France.

1966
"Les années 25," Musée des Arts Décoratifs, Paris, and Milan, Italy. Catalogue available.

1968
"Les assises du siège," Musée des Arts Décoratifs, Paris. Catalogue available.

1971
Minneapolis, U.S.A.

1975
Milan, Italy

1977
"Cinquantenaire de l'Exposition de 1925," Musée des Arts Décoratifs, Paris.

1978
"Paris-Berlin," Centre National d'Art et de Culture Georges Pompidou, Paris. Catalogue available.

1980
"Paris-Paris," Centre Nationale d'Art et de Culture Georges Pompidou, Paris. Catalogue available.

1981
"Quand le meuble devient sculpture," Louvre des Antiquaires, Paris.

1983
"L'Expo des Expos," Musée des Arts Décoratifs, Paris.

1984
"L'Empire du bureau 1900–2000," Musée des Arts Décoratifs, Paris.

INDEX

ACKNOWLEDGEMENTS

I am particularly indebted to Arlette Barré-Despond, without whom this book would not have seen the light of day: to Claude and Bernard Dalsace, Aline Vellay-Dalsace, Nathalie Dombre, André and Françoise Dalbet, who supplied me with a good deal of material for the book and their invaluable guidance.

I would like to thank Catherine Mathon for providing the book with a bibliography and being so kind as to check over it with Catherine Belfort's help, and Pierre and Marie-Noël de Gary whose encouragement, advice, and rereadings made the task of writing text and commentaries much easier.

My thanks also go to Elisabeth Loewenstein, Anne-Sophie Duval, Félix Marcilhac, the Association des Amis de la Maison de Verre, and the curators of the Musée des Arts Décoratifs, Paris, the Bibliothèque des Arts Décoratifs, Paris, and the Museum of Modern Art, New York, for having brought certain material to light, and made it available for me to examine.

And, finally, we must express our gratitude to CODIFA (Comité de Développement des Industries Françaises de l'Ameublement) for their sponsorship.

M.V.

PHOTO CREDITS

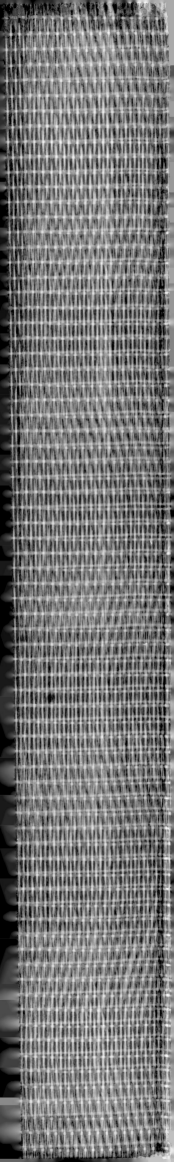